NOTHING LESS

Reforming Canada's Universities

Canada's public higher education system is in trouble. The economic and social benefits of the Canadian university system are widely seen as a public good, which raises a pressing question: Why should we aspire to anything less than a great system? For that to happen, everything about the way universities currently operate, from the boardroom to the classroom, must change – but this kind of operational and public policy transformation will not be easy.

Nothing Less than Great provides an expert analysis of the current state and challenges of Canada's university system, looking for positive change by reclaiming what a university is meant to offer for society and for citizens. Harvey P. Weingarten begins with the fundamental question that all students must ask about higher education: Is it worth going to university? From there, he stresses the need for transparency about what universities do and what they accomplish, addresses the importance of modernizing curriculum to emphasize skills over content, and provides recommendations for reform.

Exploring how universities might – and should – change to reclaim their central purpose for Canadians, *Nothing Less than Great* will be of interest to anyone who cares about the future of our country and the important role universities play in determining that future.

HARVEY P. WEINGARTEN is Principal of the School of Applied Health Sciences at the Michener Institute of Education at UHN and a senior fellow at the C.D. Howe Institute. He was formerly vice president (academic) and provost at McMaster University, president and vice chancellor at the University of Calgary, and president and CEO of the Higher Education Quality Council of Ontario.

UTP Insights is an innovative collection of brief books offering accessible introductions to the ideas that shape our world. Each volume in the series focuses on a contemporary issue, offering a fresh perspective anchored in scholarship. Spanning a broad range of disciplines in the social sciences and humanities, the books in the UTP Insights series contribute to public discourse and debate and provide a valuable resource for instructors and students.

For a list of the books published in this series, see page 217.

NOTHING LESS THAN GREAT

Reforming Canada's Universities

Harvey P. Weingarten

UNIVERSITY OF TORONTO PRESS
Toronto Buffalo London

© University of Toronto Press 2021
Toronto Buffalo London
utorontopress.com
Printed in the U.S.A.

ISBN 978-1-4875-0943-9 (cloth)   ISBN 978-1-4875-0946-0 (EPUB)
ISBN 978-1-4875-0944-6 (paper)   ISBN 978-1-4875-0945-3 (PDF)

___

Library and Archives Canada Cataloguing in Publication

Title: Nothing less than great : reforming Canada's universities / Harvey
   P. Weingarten.
Names: Weingarten, Harvey P., 1952– author.
Series: UTP insights.
Description: Series statement: UTP insights | Includes bibliographical
   references and index.
Identifiers: Canadiana (print) 20210158174 | Canadiana (ebook)
   20210158271 | ISBN 9781487509439 (cloth) | ISBN 9781487509446 (paper)
   | ISBN 9781487509460 (EPUB) | ISBN 9781487509453 (PDF)
Subjects: LCSH: Education, Higher – Canada. | LCSH: Universities
   and colleges – Canada. | LCSH: Educational change – Canada.
Classification: LCC LA417.5 .W386 2021 | DDC 378.71 – dc23

___

University of Toronto Press acknowledges the financial assistance to its
publishing program of the Canada Council for the Arts and the Ontario Arts
Council, an agency of the Government of Ontario.

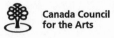

For my beloved Barbara, who makes all good things in my life possible,
and
Sarah and Laura, who fill my life with joy and pride

Woodrow Wilson was president of Princeton University from 1902 to 1910. During his tenure he engaged the faculty repeatedly, enthusiastically, and doggedly in an attempt to modernize and reform the curriculum. He had his successes. The current president of Princeton, Christopher Eisgruber, wrote in a recent article that Wilson "transformed the place from a sleepy college to a world-class research university."[1] But introduction of his reforms, innovations, and progressive ideas was difficult and often resisted, sometimes fiercely so, by other administrators, faculty, trustees, students, and alumni. When he resigned as president, it is reported that he was discouraged and emotionally bruised by his efforts. As his biographer notes, he eventually left Princeton for government service – as governor of New Jersey and eventually president of the United States – to get out of politics![2] Wilson summarized his frustrations about change in universities as follows:

"Changing a university curriculum is like moving a graveyard. You don't know how many friends the dead have until you try to move them."

This book examines the current state of the graveyard and how it might be moved.

Contents

Acknowledgments   xi

1 Introduction: Why This Book, by Me, Now?   3

2 Is Going to University Worth It?   15

3 Who Goes to University, and Do All Have an Equal Chance to
   Attend?   30

4 What Should Students Learn at University, and Are They
   Learning It?   44

5 The Relationship between University Education and Jobs   65

6 How Should a Government Manage Its Public University
   System?   83

7 Why Are Canadian Universities So Slow to Innovate?   103

8 Are Canadian Universities Sustainable?   120

9 Are Canadian Universities High Quality?   147

10 Canada's Public Universities in a Post-COVID World   161

11 Conclusion: A Recipe for Reform   169

Notes   177

Selected Bibliography: Books Cited in the Text   207

Index   211

Acknowledgments

I have been fortunate throughout my life to have known a host of individuals, teachers, and mentors who shaped my behaviour and thinking, influenced my life and career choices, supported me, and were instrumental in whatever successes I have enjoyed. I cannot acknowledge or thank them enough, but I will try.

Mr. Highland, my high school biology teacher, who was the first to expose me to the beauty of biological systems, a fascination that has stayed with me throughout my life.

Norman White, my undergraduate mentor at McGill University, who introduced me to the elegance of studying brain-behaviour relationships and who imparted many life lessons that stay with me to today.

Terry Powley, my PhD supervisor at Yale University, a rigorous, first-class scientist who drilled into his students the importance and significance of numbers, data, and evidence, and that good science meant pursuing solutions to problems regardless of where the problem took you.

It took me a long time to appreciate how fortunate I was to land my first academic job in the Psychology Department at McMaster University. The department provided a supportive and nurturant environment populated by outstanding behavioural scientists and wonderful colleagues – particularly Ron Racine, Shep Siegel, Jeff Galef, and the late Lorraine Allan – who also modelled how to be exemplary department and university citizens.

When I began my excursion into serious academic administration at McMaster University, I learned from a talented and dedicated group of colleagues, including Mamdouh Shoukri (later president of York University), Daniel Woolf (later president of Queen's University), the late Russell Joffe (later dean at Rutgers New Jersey Medical School), Alan Harrison (later provost and vice-president academic at Carleton University, University of Calgary, and Queen's University), Peter Sutherland (who later in a number of acting senior leadership roles shepherded McMaster through tough transitions), and Fred "music" Hall. They were thoughtful, reflective, devoted to the academy, committed to high-level scholarship, and a lot of fun, particularly at the annual 24 December "memo burning ceremony" (thanks to the fireplace in the provost's office).

At Calgary, three wise board chairs – the late Ted Newall, Brian MacNeill, and the late Jack Perraton – provided unwavering support and advice. They were a source of wise counsel about organizational change, the university, the city of Calgary, and Alberta, but only when asked. I hope I did not give them too much grief. My time at Calgary overlapped with Indira Samarasekera's presidency at the University of Alberta. Although we were heads of competing institutions, we worked collaboratively and colluded to overcome the traditional Calgary-Edmonton dynamic. She was a wonderful colleague and leader – smart, compassionate, and supportive. I also benefited tremendously from the counsel and humour of other presidential colleagues, especially David Naylor of the University of Toronto and Stephen Toope of the University of British Columbia. Roman Cooney, he of the gruff exterior but heart of gold, in his many years as vice-president (external) gave me a master class on communications and government relations. I was lucky to work once again with a provost, Alan Harrison, who knows more about running a university in Canada than anyone I know. Several giants in the Calgary community, especially Dick Haskayne and the late Jim Palmer, were exemplary community leaders and strong advocates for and supporters of higher education, who offered friendship, advice, support, and encouragement.

I was recruited to the Higher Education Quality Council of Ontario by its board chair, Frank Iacobucci, a wise man, and one of the finest examples in Canada of great accomplishment coupled with great humility. At HEQCO, I learned much from a continuing stream of terrific colleagues, especially Fiona Deller, Martin Hicks, and Sue Bloch-Nevitte. This book would have been impossible without the innumerable hallway conversations with them.

Of all of my teachers and supporters, though, the most influential have been those in my family.

My parents, who instilled in me a respect for education and a love of learning and books.

My in-laws, Molly and Shim Markman, especially Molly, a woman of great generosity and kindness, who exemplified how to look for the best in everyone.

My two daughters, Sarah and Laura, who raised me beautifully, who kept my professional life in appropriate perspective, and who are a constant source of pride, love, and joy. Their children, Molly and Jack, are two small but mighty sources of happiness and smiles.

And last, but in no way least, Barbara Markman, my life partner and soul mate, for all of the love, support, wise counsel (you have no idea how many bad decisions I and others avoided because of her), comfort and humour over all these years.

NOTHING LESS THAN GREAT

Reforming Canada's Universities

chapter one

Introduction: Why This Book, by Me, Now?

In 1910 my paternal grandfather, Harry Weingarten, immigrated to Montreal from Romania. My grandfather never learned to read or write. As my father says, "Until the day he died the best he could do was scrawl his name if someone showed him what end of the pencil to hold." Fortunately, he had apprenticed as a master tailor in the old country, so he could support himself and his family by practising this trade. My paternal grandmother also emigrated to Canada from Romania. She attended school for a couple of years and learned enough English to read Harlequin romances (which she quite enjoyed) and similar publications. She supported herself working as a wet nurse and child caretaker. My maternal grandmother was a Romanian peasant and remained so in attitude and behaviour for all the time she lived in Canada until she met an untimely death. My maternal grandfather, who died many years before I was born and of whom I know little, appears to have been a ne'er-do-well.

My paternal grandparents had five children. None was born in hospital. In fact, the youngest was born in the depths of a Montreal winter three months premature. My grandmother swaddled him in blankets and placed him in the oven with the pilot light on. (He survived and showed no ill effects of this inauspicious beginning.) When asked about his early life, my father describes that he was more interested in his friends on the street than anything to do with school. He flunked Grade 7, repeated the year, and scraped through into secondary school a year behind his age cohort. It was there that his life changed because of the influence of several teachers who, as he describes it, "taught me the love of learning and books." Nevertheless, his education continued to be spotty. After Grade 9, he left school and worked as a stock boy and general-purpose gofer in a pharmacy. One day the owner asked him whether this was the life he wanted and said that, if not, he needed to get an education. With the assistance of some private tutoring (which he paid for from his wages), he did well enough to be admitted to Grade 10 at Baron Byng High School, two years behind his age cohort. He completed high school and went to McGill to pursue a Bachelor of Science degree. He applied to McGill medical school, but these were the times of a quota on Jews. So, like many of his co-religionists with medical aspirations, he went instead to the Université de Montréal to obtain a pharmacy degree, doing the final year of BSc studies at McGill and the first year of pharmacy at the Université de Montréal at the same time.

My mother is an only child. She was an excellent student – winner of gold medals – but given the times, her path, as it was for so many talented women, was to end her education after she graduated from Montreal's Commercial High School, where she learned to be a book-keeper, a profession she worked at off and on as she raised our family.

My parents raised five children. We all attended university. Four of us are professionals. Collectively, we have a veritable alphabet soup of letters after our names from the various degrees and credentials we have obtained – BSc, BA, BSW, DVM, MSc, MSW, MD, MPhil, PhD, FRCP(C), RSW, CPsych. We have attended some of the best universities in the world, in Canada and in the United States. We have done so with the assistance of the Canadian public, who provided generous financial aid. I was supported for five years by provincial and federal grants to pursue graduate work at Yale University. My sibs and I are doing very well, as are our children. We are some of Canada's one-percenters, living prosperous fulfilling lives in our chosen professions.

In three short generations my family has gone from illiterate peasants to a privileged existence. How did this happen? I like to think that some of this success comes from hard work and talent, whether innate or acquired. But I am keenly aware that none of this great progress could have been achieved without access to and the benefits of a higher education system in Canada that taught us well and gave us the opportunity to pursue our life ambitions and to succeed in them. I am also keenly aware that the higher education we received was heavily subsidized and supported by public funds from people who did not know us and who themselves may not have had the opportunity to enjoy college or university. The higher education system in Canada is a great Canadian gift.

My family's story is not unique. It is the story of many families that started with little and through education and hard work carved out a better life. A high-quality public education was instrumental in our success.

The commitment of Canada to a public higher education system is an important Canadian value. It is a national attribute and an investment from which many have benefited. It distinguishes Canada from many other countries where access to higher education is more limited. The social contract between Canadians and its public higher education system is well understood. The country supports a high-quality higher education system and provides access to it for as many of its citizens as possible, particularly those who need it the most; the country in turn receives the benefits, economic and social, that result from an educated citizenry.

This book explores the current state of this social contract and asks whether the values, characteristics, and attributes that defined public higher education in Canada in the past are still in place. In a series of chapters, I examine some of the most fundamental questions one can ask about higher education. Things like: Is it still worth getting a higher education? Who goes to Canada's universities, and do all Canadians have an equal opportunity to attend? What should students learn at university, and is the education they receive there equipping them with the knowledge and skills that will allow them to succeed in the twenty-first century? Are universities changing with the times, and why do they have a reputation for being so slow to change and innovate? How should a government regulate its public higher education system? Are Canadian higher education institutions sustainable or are they teetering toward bankruptcy? Are Canadian higher education institutions getting better or worse? How do you measure their quality, and how do they compare to peer institutions internationally?

By examining the research, analyses, and data that answer these questions, the reader will get a good picture of the current state of the public higher education system in Canada – its challenges, triumphs, and tragedies. To anticipate what you will read later, not all is rosy. Canada's public higher education system is in trouble. In spite of all the understood benefits of higher education, curricula have not kept up with modern realities, the quality of education is declining, and institutions are not sustainable. Canada's system is behind those of other countries in its willingness or capacity to innovate, and it is managed by governments and internal practices in ways that resist change and may squelch innovation and reduce quality. The good news is that there are solutions, or at least strategies, to mitigate this decline, and these are offered as recommendations for reform.

The Canadian higher education system (also known as the post-secondary system) is composed of two main sectors – colleges and universities. Colleges offer two-, three-, or four-year diploma or certificate programs that have a primarily vocational orientation (some colleges now have limited degree-granting status). Universities offer a host of four-year baccalaureate and graduate programs (depending on the institution) that can range from the core arts and sciences to professional programs such as medicine and law. While I in no way undervalue the contribution of the college sector to higher education in Canada, this book focuses on universities. Universities are the institutions that dominate discourse and thinking about higher education. They receive the bulk of the policy considerations and attention in government. For many students they are still the preferred institutions from which to receive a higher education. Universities enrol about two-thirds of the postsecondary students in Canada; colleges teach the other one-third. Universities are the sector most researched and for which we have the most data. Universities are the institutions through which Canada competes with other countries in the international higher education space. It is also the sector I know best. There is a place and a need for someone to write a scholarly piece about the Canadian college system, its contributions, and its issues, but the college system is not my focus in this book.

Universities have a dual mandate – to educate and to conduct research. Both are important, and the analyses in this book will illuminate some of the issues and tensions as these two sides of the academy compete for a university's resources and attention. But the emphasis in this book is on the education Canadian universities provide. There is an understood need to revitalize and modernize university programs, and to rebalance the focus of universities more toward the undergraduate experience. As Donald Kennedy, former president of Stanford University, wrote in his book *Academic Duty*, "The commanding feature ... of redesigning the university will be reclamation of its central mission ... It works by the thoughtful, participatory transfer of knowledge and excitement from one generation to the next. Once that is done, the rest falls into place ... Placing students first is a simple design principle, but it has great power."[1]

This book focuses on the academic experience offered to current students and asks the following questions: How good is it? How well does it prepare students for future successes? Are current programs contemporary and relevant? What needs to change for the academic experience of students to improve?

The analyses, observations, and recommendations in this book are based on my more than forty years of involvement in higher education. After graduating from Yale (in, of all things, the biological controls of eating and obesity), and for reasons still unclear to me, I was hired as an assistant professor of psychology in 1979 at McMaster University in Hamilton, Ontario. For sixteen years I was a regular professor, more or less happy to be left alone to do my teaching and research. In 1995, I became the dean of science, the same year that Mike Harris got elected Premier of Ontario. Carrying through on the promise made in his party's Common Sense Revolution election platform, his government significantly cut operating grants to Ontario universities. Like many other university administrators, I spent the bulk of that year negotiating the early retirement of a large number of professors over the age of sixty and trying to figure out how to sustain the university's academic work in light of these significant departures. Apparently, the university leadership liked my style and one year later, in 1996, I was promoted to the position of provost and vice-president academic, the chief academic and operating officer of the university.

Provost and vice-president academic was the best job I ever had. You work with academics from all the disciplines and, if you are intellectually curious, delight in their different cultures, styles, traditions, and ways of pursuing their academic interests. You stay close enough to the scholarly side of the university so you can delude yourself into thinking that you are still an academic, even though your days are consumed with financial, labour, human resources, legal, and construction issues. It is often said that getting a PhD is getting to know more and more about less and less. Being a high-level university administrator is exactly the opposite. You get to know less and less about more and more.

In 2001, I left McMaster to be the president and vice-chancellor of the University of Calgary. Few who grow up in Montreal expect to live in Hamilton, let alone Calgary. I vividly recall the incredulity my wife and I both felt when we realized that Alberta was north of the state of Montana. But I was recruited by two very wise men, the outgoing and the incoming board chairs, who painted a compelling picture of the university, the city, the job, what they expected me to do, and the potential to accomplish it. A former university president once suggested that you need two things to be successful as a university president – grey hair to look distinguished and haemorrhoids to look concerned. There is surely more to the job than that. You serve multiple constituencies, many of which have diametrically opposed expectations of you and very different, often contrasting, opinions on what success in your job looks like. A university president serves as the chief executive officer inside the university and the primary face of the university to the outside world, the government, and the public. When people in the university complain that you are spending too much time outside, and people outside the university complain that you are spending too much time inside, then you probably have the balance right. The irony, of course, is that you know you are doing your job well when everybody is complaining about you. And they do, with great vigour. You interact a lot with government, and you often behave much more like a politician than an academic. You raise money, the more the better. As the quip goes, a university president is someone who lives in a big house and begs for money. Your education as a generalist continues. You become well-versed in government relations, labour relations, human resources, marketing and communications, construction, and fundraising, things you were never trained to do in graduate school or in your previous academic life. Clark Kerr, former president of the University of California system, described the job of university president as follows: "The mediator ... is always subject to some abuse. He [sic] wins few clear-cut victories, he must aim more at avoiding the worst than seizing the best. He must find satisfaction in being equally distasteful to each of his constituencies; he must reconcile himself to the harsh reality that successes are shrouded in silence while failures are spotlighted in notoriety."[2]

It is for others to judge how successful one was as a president. I choose to keep in my memory a short piece from the University of Calgary alumni magazine as they described my presidential legacy:

> He left the university a far better place than when he arrived nine years before. Under his leadership, the university increased access, invested in students, recruited world-class faculty and attracted record amounts of research revenue and philanthropic support. There were so many sod-turnings as a result of a billion-dollar capital growth plan he launched that he kept a shovel in his office. A relentless agent of change, he pushed for excellence across campus. Throughout it all, he never lost sight of the goal: do what's best for students.[3]

I lasted eight and a half years as the University of Calgary president, a little bit longer than the seven years I had expected to stay.

After thirty-one years in the academy, I had had enough. I had come to the conclusion that universities were unwilling, or did not have the capacity, to respond in the ways or at the speed required to accommodate changing societal and student needs and expectations. Although it pained me greatly (and still does), I found myself increasingly receptive to claims that the university was too self-centred, too self-absorbed, too slow to change, and insufficiently considerate of students. It was time to leave the academy, and I did.

But I am a lucky guy. Now living in Toronto, I received a call from Frank Iacobucci, board chair of an organization called the Higher Education Quality Council of Ontario (HEQCO), asking me if I was interested in being its president. HEQCO was created in 2005 by Dalton McGuinty's provincial Liberal government as a direct result of a recommendation made by former Ontario premier Bob Rae in a review of Ontario's postsecondary system. Rae's observation was that the province provides several billion dollars of public funding as operating grants to Ontario's forty-plus public colleges and universities but that the allocation of these funds was largely historical, or based on stories, perceptions, gut feelings, and anecdotes. His recommendation was that an agency be created that would do research on Ontario's public postsecondary system and provide policy and practical advice to the government to improve the system. He also suggested that this agency conduct regular assessments of the performance of Ontario's public postsecondary system and make those reports public. In short order, and with a wonderfully broad mandate, HEQCO was created to, as its legislation reads, "assist the Minister in improving all aspects of the post-secondary education sector, including improving the quality of education provided in the sector, access to post-secondary education and accountability of post-secondary educational institutions."[4]

For the next nine years, from 2010 to 2019, I had one job – to think deeply about, inquire into, and research postsecondary education in Canada; to compare it to best practices around the world; and to make smart and strategic recommendations to government to improve the higher education sector. I could not have written this book without that experience. I and a cohort of wonderfully talented and dedicated colleagues conducted research and provided evidence-based analyses on some of the most vexing and challenging issues facing higher education. Although Ontario was our prime focus and laboratory, the issues in Ontario are not materially different from those being faced by higher education in other provinces and internationally. The HEQCO experience exposed me to some of the best higher education thinkers, ideas, and organizations around the world. Although HEQCO was typically described as a research organization, we were not an ivory tower or abstract think tank. Rather, our mandate was to provide tangible and practical advice and solutions that could be woven into government policy and practice and used by institutions to improve quality, access, and accountability in higher education.

In contrast to the transactional perspective I had found myself adopting as a university administrator, at HEQCO I raised my thinking to consideration of the loftier values, issues, and challenges of postsecondary education institutions and systems. Debates about higher education in Canada are sometimes unduly influenced by what is going on in higher education in the United States. This tendency will only increase given the profile and radical solutions – such as free tuition – that were central to the competing platforms of contenders for the US presidency. While the two countries share some issues and challenges, there are some fundamental differences between the Canadian and American public higher education systems that caution against relying too heavily on the American experience or accepting too cavalierly proposed solutions to the challenges of the US system.

First, higher education in the United States is a mix between an array of state-supported public universities and colleges and many private ones. Discussions about higher education in the United States are dominated by ideas originating at a set of well-known prestigious universities (think Harvard, Yale, and Stanford). The dynamics of these high-prestige private institutions do not transfer well to even the vast majority of public US universities let alone the public ones in Canada. Higher education in Canada is essentially all public. There are a number of smaller private universities in Canada, many of them faith-based, but they represent a small fraction of degree-seeking students. In Canada, the future of higher education rests on the public system. There is no private system equivalent in scope or capacity to what exists in the States or other countries that we can rely on if Canada's public system fails or falters. If the public system in Canada fails to produce, we do not have other institutions to make the multiple contributions higher education is expected to make.

Second, higher education in Canada is a much smaller enterprise, with a considerably narrower quality range among institutions, than in the States. The United States has about 4,000 four-year degree-granting colleges and universities. Canada has about 100, though on a per-population basis we should have 400. The US higher education system houses some of the best and some of the worst universities in the world. Canadian universities vary in quality and reputation; a small number are among the world's best, but very few Canadian universities descend into the low-quality ranges of some American institutions.

Third, American higher education is now dominated by two significant considerations – the rapidly escalating tuition levels (and consequent rise in student debt) and the high percentage of Americans who start university but never finish. Canada is among world leaders in postsecondary attendance and has high graduation rates that American educators envy.

Finally, America has a much more expensive higher education system than Canada. Although Canadians complain about tuition levels, the reality is that tuition for Canadian university students is cheap relative to that in the States, even when compared to tuition in public US universities. Relative to the United States, Canada also has a more robust financial aid system, especially in some provinces, that helps to reduce the cost for students wishing to attend university.

There is much to be applauded and lauded in the Canadian university system. Yet it is a system at risk and under threat. Parents, students, governments, the public, and the media are questioning the value of a university education. Students are complaining that their programs seem increasingly irrelevant, out-of-date, and not able to prepare them for their future lives. Professors are complaining that too many students are ill-prepared for university and are not ready to put in the time or effort to learn as they (the professors) did when they were in university. Politicians are complaining that universities move too slowly, are out of touch, and are not adapting in ways society needs them to in order to address the complex social and economic challenges of modern times. Employers are complaining that graduates are not prepared for today's jobs and labour markets. In short, many stakeholders are increasingly vocal about their unhappiness with the current state of Canada's universities and their outputs. A recent survey of 10,000 people in eleven countries revealed that people in Western countries were generally sceptical or equivocal about the contributions and values of universities.[5] As a general rule, when so many different people are unhappy and complaining, it is reasonable to conclude that something is amiss. This book examines the reality of this general discomfort, its origins, and what can be done about it.

We should not ignore the consequences of this malaise. As a senior civil servant once told me, when you are sitting around the Treasury Board table and looking for savings, the easiest thing to cut is postsecondary education. This is not good for a country so reliant on its public university system and on what that system can, and must, offer to keep the country healthy and competitive. These trends are worrisome if you, like me, believe that investing in higher education is one of the most important funding decisions a government and public makes. Investing in education is an investment in Canada's future – our competitiveness as a country in an increasingly competitive global marketplace; our economic success in a knowledge-based economy; our capacity to sustain a country of aware, engaged citizens and a civil society that Canada aspires to achieve and share with all who live here.

This book is unabashedly about what should be a jewel in Canada's crown – a world-class public higher education system. Canada's university system should be nothing less than great. The stories, data, and analyses presented in the ensuing chapters describe and celebrate the past, illuminate the present and its challenges, and explore future solutions and remedies.

This book is not directed primarily to my former cherished university colleagues, although I think it is helpful and relevant to them. It is ironic that universities, a set of institutions that pride themselves on critical analysis and reflection, have subjected themselves to so little scholarly analysis. Rather, the book is intended to help the public understand the contributions and challenges of a

critical public sector in Canada, the public university system. My
desire, in the words of an astute colleague of mine, is for this book
to be more likely to be bought at an airport bookstore than a university one. If nothing else, I hope you will leave this read with a
better sense and appreciation of what the Canadian public university system does, how it operates, its challenges, and how it can be
reformed and revitalized, all to the goal of making Canada better.

Enjoy the read.

chapter two

Is Going to University Worth It?

The great promissory note of higher education is that a university degree is the ticket for a good life, a good job, and economic prosperity. Youth have been cautioned repeatedly about the dire consequences of not pursuing higher education or holding a university credential. These messages begin early in one's life. High school counsellors amplify this message by preferentially pushing a university education over one at a college or in the trades. The idea that higher education and hard work are requirements for and predictors of a better life is a fundamental tenet of the North American dream of upward mobility and a value and aspiration internalized by many immigrant groups.

Virtually every survey asking students why they have chosen to pursue postsecondary education indicates that the dominant, although not the exclusive, reason students go to university is to get the knowledge and credentials necessary to get a good job. Equally, the dominant reason Canadian governments now and in the past invest in a public higher education system is to educate a workforce that has the knowledge and skills to drive the economy – to fill the available jobs; to assure companies that the jurisdiction has the talented workforce that keeps companies in the region or that attracts new ones to it; and to sustain a wealthy, robust, globally competitive Canadian economy. We revel in the many rags-to-riches stories where a higher education was instrumental to a better life. The story of my family is but one example.

But recently something has changed. The ability of a university education to enhance the economic fortunes of the individual and society, a narrative that in the past was implicitly believed and internalized, is being seriously questioned. The *Economist* magazine has published a number of high-profile stories asking, "University education: Is it still worth it?"[1] When the *Economist* challenges the economic benefit of a university education, you have to know that many others are asking the same question. We now repeatedly hear stories of highly successful entrepreneurs and business people who never finished a university education. Think Bill Gates of Microsoft and Steve Jobs of Apple. The successful entrepreneur Peter Thiel offers a two-year $100,000 fellowship to students who wish to innovate and build new things; a requirement of the program is that students leave formal higher education.[2] Governments are also increasingly sceptical of the economic returns from investing in universities. Aside from the many statements from politicians deriding today's universities, typically unaccompanied by any evidence or data, politicians' diminishing opinion of universities is reflected by the steady decrease in public funds they are prepared to allocate to the university sector. There is much student grumbling, sometimes anecdotal and sometimes more formal, questioning the value they are getting from their university experience and the time, effort, and money they invest in it.

Few seem happy. Professors complain that their students can't write well enough and are not willing to put in the time or effort to work or read as much as the professors themselves did when they were undergraduates. Students complain that too many of their courses are irrelevant to their lives and aspirations and that it all costs too much. Employers complain that students have a skills gap and are unprepared for today's jobs. Governments complain that universities are too insulated, unresponsive, and insensitive to the needs of the province, students, or the public. Given this dynamic, it is probably reasonable to take a look at the facts about Canada's universities, particularly whether individuals who choose to go to them really do derive the financial and economic benefits universities claim they offer.

Higher Education and Lifetime Earnings

Multiple analyses conducted over many years show a strong positive correlation between level of education and lifetime earnings.
On average, individuals with university degrees earn more than
those with college credentials, who in turn earn more than those
with only a high school diploma. Those holding a graduate degree,
such as a master's or PhD, earn more than university graduates
with a bachelor's degree. Those who have not completed high
school are at the bottom of the economic ladder. This "earnings
(or economic) premium," the incremental earnings of university
graduates over non-degree holders, lasts over the lifetime and may
grow with years in the workforce.[3]

The earnings premium conferred by higher education can be
substantial. Thanks to the records maintained by Statistics Canada,
we can document the size of the earnings premium of university
graduates over others and the variables that influence the size of the
premium. In one study, Frenette examined earnings of a cohort born
in Canada between 1955 and 1957. He assessed the relative incomes
of university degree holders, college certificate holders, and high
school graduates with no postsecondary education from their mid-
thirties to their mid-fifties. The earnings premium of a university
bachelor's degree holder relative to those who graduated from
high school averaged $728,000 for men and $440, 000 for women.
The earnings premium of college certificate holders was lower –
averaging $248,000 for men and $180,000 for women.[4] Similarly,
Ostrovsky and Frenette found that the median cumulative earnings over twenty years for men who graduated from high school
was about $900,000 but for men with a bachelor's degree was about
$1,500,000 (the equivalent data for women were, for high school
graduates, $480,000, and for bachelor's degree holders, $980,000).[5]

A host of studies document the earnings premium enjoyed by
university graduates over their lifetimes as compared to those
with less education. For example, a StatsCan analysis of the 2016
census data and the 2018 National Graduate Survey comparing
earnings of Canadians in different parts of Canada continued to
confirm that those holding a university degree were the highest

wage earners in the country, although the degree of economic advantage, as always, can vary with gender, location, and the degree held. A 2014 report from the British Columbia government concluded that university graduates could earn between $500,000 to $2 million more over their lifetime than those with only a high school diploma.[6]

Other studies, including those from other countries, also show a substantial earnings premium from a university degree. The Georgetown University Center on Education and the Workforce estimates that university graduates may earn 80 per cent more than high school graduates over their lifetimes.[7] Universities Canada, the lobby group representing Canadian universities, estimates that university graduates will earn $1 million more than high school-only graduates during their working lives. The College Board has tracked the economic benefits of university education for many years. Their 2019 report shows that bachelor's degree holders earned on average $24,900 more per year than high school-only graduates. Degree holders were also more likely to be employed and to demonstrate enhanced health, social, and other non-economic advantages relative to those with lesser educational credentials.

The rigorous thinker will point out that it costs money to go to university. Aside from tuition fees and textbooks, the most significant cost of going to university is the foregone wages one could have earned if they were not pursuing a degree. This consideration leads one to ask whether the earnings boost associated with a degree is still apparent even once the costs of attending university are taken into account. Economists call these examinations analyses of "return on investment"; a positive return on investment demonstrates that the financial investment made in obtaining the degree still pays off in spite of the costs incurred to get that credential.

Studies from both Canada and the United States typically show a consistent positive rate of return on university education. Even in the United States, where the cost of attending university has increased considerably because of rapidly rising tuition levels, a 2018 survey of 1,461 public and private institutions by PayScale, a consulting firm specializing in compensation issues, demonstrated an impressive positive return on investment for a university education.[8]

Relationship of the Earnings Premium to Field of Study

The sophisticated thinker will point out that the data showing positive earnings premiums and rates of return are simply averages. This leads them to question whether all university degrees are equally valuable in terms of the expected earnings premium. This question underlies the considerable debate and angst about whether some degrees lead to more financial rewards and better jobs than others. The most pointed form of this argument recently is that governments should preferentially fund the STEM disciplines (science, technology, engineering, and mathematics) because, presumably, they offer good economic returns, and decrease or eliminate funding for disciplines in the humanities that presumably do not. A number of countries, including England and Japan, among others, have either instituted such a policy or are considering it. Students hear these messages and take them to heart, which accounts for the precipitous decline in humanities enrolments universities are now experiencing.[9]

There have been many studies looking at the variation in the economic premium from different degrees or fields of study. These analyses, very much like those determining the size of the economic premium, depend on when measurements are taken relative to time of graduation. Ideally, one would want studies looking over the long term – if not over an expected working lifetime then at least over ten years or more following graduation. These studies are notoriously difficult to do because, by definition, they take a long time to complete, and researchers (and their funders) are reluctant to wait so long to get the results. So, many of these studies look at the short-term (five years or less) impact of field of study on the size of the economic premium. Whether differences revealed in these studies persist in the long term is not clear, although it is generally believed that whatever differences in earning potential

may be apparent in different fields of study in the short term grad-
ually diminish or disappear the further out a graduate is in their
working career. For example, analysis of the earning power of the
much-maligned liberal arts graduates shows that while they may
start off earning less than students with other degrees, after ten
years or so they catch up and may in fact eventually out-earn university graduates from other disciplines.[10]

Studies reveal considerable variation in the economic advantage enjoyed by a university graduate depending on what they
studied in university and the degree they obtained. The most comprehensive and detailed data come from Anthony Carnevale at the
Center on Education and the Workforce at Georgetown University,
who for many years has been studying the relationship between
field of study and earnings and how this relationship changes
during times of recession or with changing labour markets. The
data suggest that a student's particular field of study may be the
most significant factor in determining job prospects and future
earnings. In the short term, degrees in engineering, mathematics,
the sciences, and business provide the best job prospects and the
greatest potential economic benefit in terms of the probability of
getting a good, well-paying job.[11]

Other studies reveal similar findings. The Institute for Fiscal
Studies took advantage of England's new Longitudinal Education
Outcomes dataset, which tracks students through their education
(elementary into secondary school into college or university) and
right into the labour market. They, like others, found that, by just
age twenty-nine, having a university degree increased subsequent
earnings substantially relative to a matched cohort of those who
did not attend university – 28 per cent for women and 8 per cent
for men. In addition, earnings after age twenty-nine increased
faster for degree-holding men, and probably also for women.
But all of these average effects were dependent on what students
studied in university and the degree they held. For both men and
women, degrees in medicine and economics conferred the greatest
economic advantage. Impressively, in a negative way, men holding degrees in the creative arts, English, or philosophy actually
earned less than those who held no university degree. Overall,

their analysis suggests that about 80 per cent of graduates gained financially from going to university but that 20 per cent earned less after graduation than those who had never attended university in the first place.[12]

In Canada, Frank, Frenette, and Morissette examined how salaries and employment patterns varied in the years 2005 to 2012 depending on field of study. As had been observed before, bachelor-degree holders earned more than college graduates who in turn earned more than high school-only graduates. The amount that wages grew (in real terms, i.e., adjusted for inflation) in that period varied with field of study. Male engineers saw a 10 per cent rise in real earnings; men with degrees in the social sciences, business, mathematics, and computer sciences saw no real rise. Women in education, health, and business jobs saw a 10 to 12 per cent wage increase; women graduating in the humanities saw none. A recent study looking at how the job outcomes of Ontario graduates were influenced by the 2009 recession showed also that earnings vary with discipline but that even those with the most modest return on their investment – males who graduated from the humanities – show a positive return on their postsecondary investment.[13]

Some of the most comprehensive data available in Canada relating earnings to field of study come from the Education Policy Research Initiative based at the University of Ottawa and led by Ross Finnie. One study tracked the level and growth of earnings of all the students who graduated between 2005 and 2012 in fourteen different institutions in four regions of the country. Earnings were obtained from the tax filings of graduates, providing a much more accurate measure of post-university earnings than the survey and questionnaire self-reports of many other investigations. They found that university graduates earn well and were less affected by the 2008 financial crisis than many pundits assumed. The highest earners immediately following graduation were graduates of engineering and health-related studies, followed by business, math, and computer science graduates. Mid-level earners were graduates of science, agriculture, social sciences, and the humanities. Graduates from the visual and performing arts were the lowest earners, although even they significantly out-earn the baristas (or presumably the counter employees at McDonalds) – those in jobs that some consider to be the sole fate of students in these disciplines.[14]

One can appreciate why questions about the relationship between fields of study and eventual jobs and earnings are so compelling. If the dominant reason students attend university is to get a well-paying job, then it stands to reason that they would want to know what disciplines or degrees give them that advantage. Similarly, parents who are contributing to the costs of university for their children, and who have aspirations for them to later get a good job, also want to know which fields and degrees pay off. Governments that support higher education because they want to make sure that students can fill and attract good jobs are also predisposed to fund those programs that produce this outcome. So, governments want data that measure the job outcome success of different programs in order that, as has been done in countries such as England, public funding can be allocated preferentially to disciplines, degrees, and programs that are associated with the best labour market outcomes and successes. The recent changes to how the performance of Ontario's universities will be monitored and how the universities will be funded have proposed precisely this measurement as a requirement for public funding. Other Canadian provinces, particularly Alberta, are likely to follow suit. All of this thinking presupposes, of course, a strong relationship between one's degree and field of study at university and the jobs one eventually obtains. Whether this assumption is valid is the central topic of chapter 5.

Some will argue that all of the data presented so far look backward in time and reflect what has been true in the past. It may be, some say, that the nature of work today – its more precarious and volatile nature, the gig economy – is a departure from historical trends, and so these generally positive effects of education on future earnings are smaller or no longer apparent. They may be right. As Yogi Berra said, "It's tough to make predictions, especially about the future." We will only know the validity of these arguments once we have the results of economic premium and return on investment analyses for those who are in university today. But, by definition, these analyses will take time, as the most informative of these analyses track graduates years into their careers. For the moment, it is probably best to recall the admonition that the safest and best predictor of the future is what has happened in the past: university graduates will find it easier to obtain employment, they will earn more in these jobs, and they will be more insulated in times of economic downturn and recession than those without a degree.

Universities and Intergenerational Mobility

The most likely scenario is that the economic and job advantages enjoyed by university graduates are likely to continue in the future, even if the magnitude of these advantages is modulated or influenced by the changing nature of work. The promissory note of higher education seems sound. But the promissory note is more than simply that people who hold degrees will be the best earners in the future. We know that students from richer families are far more likely to attend university than children from poorer families. So, it would be relatively uninteresting if the fact that university graduates become the highest earners simply reflects the fact that these kids were the rich ones in the first place. The most compelling stories of whether university is worth it are examples where a university education lifts the economic standing of a poor or disadvantaged student to a higher socioeconomic position. This is the primary objective of most student financial aid programs. They are targeted to economically disadvantaged youth in an attempt to get them to university so they will end up in a better financial situation than their parents.

To find out whether a university education increases the financial success of an individual beyond that expected on the basis of the family they came from, we conduct examinations of economic lift or intergenerational economic mobility. These studies are the most stringent test of the promissory note because they measure the degree to which higher education moves someone from an expected lower socioeconomic level to a higher one. These studies involve an assessment of the socioeconomic status of the family the student came from and the income the individual enjoys after they have completed their higher education and moved into the labour market. Data from these studies are typically reported as family incomes, measured as a distribution cut into five quintiles, going from the lowest quintile of family incomes to the highest quintile.

The Equality of Opportunity Project, headed by Raj Chetty and involving economists at Stanford, Harvard, and the US Census Bureau, is a large ongoing study that looks at the intergenerational mobility of 30 million Americans who attended college between 1999 and 2013. One of the variables they look at is the effect of education on upward mobility. It confirms that a higher education degree is a significant driver of intergenerational mobility, even though students from rich families are far more likely to attend university, especially a high-prestige university, than those from families with lower income levels.[15] The richness of their data also reveals which higher education institutions have the highest success rates in elevating the economic fortunes of students. Contrary to the expectation that these would be the high-prestige and high-reputation universities, such as Harvard, Yale, and Stanford, the universities most successful in moving students up the income ladder tend to be public, mid-tier universities that enrol larger numbers of low-income students, such as the City University of New York, University of Texas El Paso, and the Cal State system.[16]

The probability that a child born to parents in the bottom quintile of family income will reach the top quintile is about double in Canada what it is the United States.[17] Canada appears to be doing better at fulfilling the "American dream" than the Americans. We would expect, therefore, a more impressive intergenerational mobility impact of higher education in Canada relative to the States, particularly because a higher percentage of Canadians enrol in higher education than Americans.

Frenette tracked the earnings of students in 2015 who had graduated from an Ontario college or university in 2010 and compared them to a matched cohort that did not enrol in postsecondary education. The analysis revealed, once again, that students with a university bachelor's degree earn more than students with a college diploma, who in turn earn more than those with no postsecondary education. This trend was evident in students coming from every quintile of parental income. A significant, large, and positive earnings premium for postsecondary credential holders is once again revealed. Most importantly for the current analysis, the premium for youth coming from the bottom quintile of family incomes was considerably larger than for those from the upper quintile (a 165 per cent premium for bottom-quintile students versus an 86 per cent premium for top-quintile students). A university bachelor's degree is associated with an additional 236 per cent higher median annual income for families from the bottom quintile compared to only 54 per cent for students coming from the top quintile of family incomes. Given what we know about the relationship between earnings and the fields of study students choose, the research also revealed that the economic premium advantage of lower-quintile students did not result from their choosing to study disciplines or pursue degrees different from those of students coming from higher-income families.[18]

A similar study examined the postsecondary impact on mobility of students who come from families where neither parent had attended postsecondary education. Like students from low-income families, these "first-generation students" attend postsecondary education in smaller numbers than those from richer families. Yet, in spite of the fact that they attended in smaller numbers, those first-generation students who went on to university were more likely to complete their programs and, once they were in the labour market, did as well as students coming from families where the parents had postsecondary credentials, in terms of their earnings, positions, and likelihood of having a job with pensions and bonuses and job permanence.[19]

This chapter so far has stressed the *economic* benefits of a university education because this appears to be the largest concern of students, parents, and policy makers. But there is another literature, less exhaustive and definitive, on the *social* benefits of higher education. In general, individuals with a higher education credential are more socially engaged, more involved in their community, more likely to volunteer and vote, more philanthropic, and less likely to be incarcerated than those without postsecondary credentials. Degree holders are also healthier than others, to the point where some have recommended that the best way to reduce Canada's rising health care costs is to increase the education level of Canadians.[20] Many, perhaps all, of these positive social outcomes reflect simply that university graduates are wealthier and more prosperous. We would like to think, though, that attending university also opens one's mind – exposes students to new ideas, cultures, ways of thinking, and social issues that lead them to be more socially aware and engaged in their later lives. Although we do not fully understand how university education leads to these positive social outcomes, it is comforting and important that the personal and societal benefits of such an education are more than just financial.

We are always making choices about investments we should make now that will pay off in the future. Should we buy or rent a house? What car should I buy? Is it worth buying that extended warranty? The results of multiple studies in many countries tell us that one of the best investments we can make is to pursue higher education. Yes, it costs money and time to go to university. But the overwhelming conclusion is that this is money and time well spent. Yes, the amount of return you will see from your investment depends upon which institution you attend, the subject you study, the credential you hold, your gender, and the state of the economy. But rates of return vary for different people for all types of investments. And the overwhelming conclusion is that the return will be positive. Best of all, the investment works best for those who need it the most. A university education still appears to be not only the great economic leveller but also the great economic uplifter.

We still have much to learn about the economic benefits of university attendance to graduates. Analyses of the type reported in this chapter represent a glimpse into the candy shop of research questions and projects that will over time reveal more details about how a university education produces its benefits and how these are influenced by a host of personal and societal variables. Perhaps the most fundamental unanswered question is why there is such a clear and consistent relationship between higher education and earnings. Two fundamentally different opinions are offered. For some this is all about what students learn in university. Specifically, their university studies give them the knowledge, skills, and capabilities they need to get the most demanding, high-skill jobs, and it is these jobs that pay the most. For others it has little, or nothing, to do with what students learn at university. Rather, having a degree represents a signal to future employers that this is a knowledgeable, highly skilled, and capable individual, regardless of how or where that knowledge and those skills come from. This perspective argues that the role of universities is to act as a filter to create or identify the possible best future employees. Later chapters examining what students actually learn in university and how this relates to their future jobs will provide some evidence from which to assess the validity of these two positions.

For the moment, however, two conclusions are clear. The first, supported by reams of data, is that going to university is worth it, both financially and socially, and is likely to remain so in the future. Not only do university graduates earn more, they are also less likely to be unemployed and are more buffered in times of recession and economic downturns than those without a university credential. Even during the COVID pandemic, when North America experienced one of the largest and most dramatic periods of job loss, the unemployment rate of university graduates was considerably lower than that of workers with no university degree.[21] The second conclusion is implicit but no less obvious. One can only receive the significant social and economic benefits from higher education if you actually go. This forces us to address the question of who is actually going to our universities, the central question of the next chapter.

Recommendation for reform: Public disclosure of information showing the relationship between institution, field of study, and future earnings

It is not clear or necessarily advisable that students pick what to study at university based upon what they hope to eventually earn. Surely there are other variables that should weigh heavily in that decision. That said, the desire to get a good job is a dominant reason why students go to university. It is a primary consideration for parents and the public in supporting their studies, and it is the most significant motivation for governments to continue to invest in public education. It seems reasonable, therefore, that all of these constituencies should have access to as much information as possible about the relationship between universities, fields of study, jobs, and earnings. In the United States, these data are readily available to the public. When President Obama's administration provided stimulus funds to colleges and universities after the 2008 recession, a requirement was that higher education institutions obtaining these funds make available a public scorecard of key facts and figures about the institution providing information about such things as the cost of going to state universities, the debt load of students who had graduated, and the percentage of students employed post-graduation. Currently, these College Scorecards have been refined to the point where they provide, for more than 4,500 postsecondary institutions in the United States, customized and accessible data on potential debt and earnings based on fields of study and graduation rates. These data are offered in interactive websites allowing interested individuals to customize the comparisons they want to make about the performance of individual institutions, programs within these institutions, and the various credentials one could acquire. Based on these scorecards, Anthony Carnevale's Center on Education and the Workforce has provided a ranking of the return on investment of more than 4,500 American colleges and universities. These scorecards can also reveal which institutions or programs graduate students into jobs where their expected earnings are not sufficient to pay off their student debt.[22]

Some data relating university education to jobs and earnings are available in Canada, but they are hard to find and are reasonably inaccessible except to the higher education researcher or aficionado. The general trend for increased transparency in public funding and public institutions should lead Canada to make this information more readily available. The brochures and propaganda material distributed by the universities themselves simply do not suffice. If universities wish to publicize information about their outputs and impact that go beyond financial and job considerations, they can easily incorporate the data into these public scorecards.

Some will see this is an exercise in accountability. More than that, though, it is an attempt to provide the public, stakeholders, and potential students with information that is top of mind for them. Universities should not be hesitant to provide this information. The good news is that the data we have reinforce the significance and contribution of universities to the economic good fortune and health of the individual and society. As will be discussed in chapter 6, governments are moving anyway to require this disclosure; it is better for the universities to shape these public-disclosure reports than to have them dictated by government. The technology for handling and analysing the proposed data is currently available, and it would not take long for a public-disclosure regime to provide helpful answers to the kinds of questions students, parents, the public, and governments are asking about the worth and value of universities and their programs. This public disclosure would go a long way to dispelling some of the myths and unsubstantiated and ideological arguments some now put forward. We have the means and capacity to inform the public. All we need is the will to do so.

chapter three

Who Goes to University, and Do All Have an Equal Chance to Attend?

A dominant and long-standing policy goal in virtually all Canadian provinces has been to ensure that our public university system is widely accessible to all Canadians who are qualified and who wish to pursue a university education. This is the policy goal of *access*.

Access policies and practices have been driven by two different but interrelated questions. The first is whether Canadian universities have the capacity to accept all the qualified students who seek a university education. This is a question of the number of spots available, and it inevitably relates to the growth of our university system. The second is whether all Canadians have an equal opportunity to be admitted to university and to get a university education. This is a question of who actually occupies these university spots, and it speaks to the equity of access to Canada's universities.[1]

Growth of the University System

The growth of the university sector in Canada has been remarkable. In 2000, there were approximately 847,000 students enrolled in Canada's universities. In 2018, there were about 1.34 million, an increase of about 58 per cent. By 2019, there were 1.4 million students at Canada's universities. Some of these university students study full time, others part time. When the full- and part-time numbers are combined to get a count of full-time equivalent (FTE) students, Usher suggests a 69 per cent enrolment increase from 2000 to 2016.[2]

The postsecondary participation rate (i.e., the percentage of students in a defined age group who attend college or university) is monitored routinely by Statistics Canada. In their latest analysis, they report that 44 per cent of Canadians aged eighteen to twenty-four (the traditional age of entering postsecondary studies in Canada) were enrolled in Canada's colleges and universities in 2018. This represents a 29 per cent increase in the postsecondary participation rate since 2000. This increase is due almost totally to an increase in university attendance; the rate of participation in college programs during this period was largely unchanged. The increased participation in higher education varied by province, with Quebec and Ontario showing the largest increases and the Maritime provinces showing non-significant increases.[3]

Some believe that university enrolments are a simple function of demographics and that we can expect enrolments to decrease in the middle of this decade because the declining birth rate has resulted in a smaller eighteen- to twenty-four-year-old demographic, the cohort that represents the bulk of university entrants. There is little to support this belief or prediction. A university education is increasingly understood to be a ticket for success in the knowledge-based economy, so that more and more students, even those who might not otherwise be inclined to go to university, are pursuing university studies. It seems that whenever an enrolment decline is predicted for demographic reasons something else intervenes that results in ever-increasing student numbers. When fewer men were attending university, there was a sharp and sustained increase in female participation. Women now constitute the majority of students in Canada's universities, and the more serious gender concern in some university circles is how to recruit more men and increase their success.[4] (One wonders whether there was analogous thinking about women when females were underrepresented.) Canada's immigration policies, which preferentially recruit immigrants with higher skill and education levels, are also driving university enrolments, as the children of immigrants are more likely to go to university than the general population. When the economy sours, as in times of recession, university enrolments actually increase because students cannot find jobs or look to increase their competitive edge by more education. Several Canadian universities are already reporting enrolment increases during the COVID pandemic, in spite of student concerns over an on-line university experience.[5] The growth of Canada's universities has been the rule regardless of any contra-indicators in the demographic, economic, and social spheres. There is every reason to believe that the trend for increasing enrolments, growth, and a demand for more spots in Canada's public university system will continue.

Enrolment growth is not surprising given the ways that Canadian provinces fund their universities. In virtually all provinces, the amount of money a university receives from government depends on its enrolments. The larger the enrolment, the larger the grant. The greater the growth, the greater the incremental funding to the university from the public purse. A stellar example of this dynamic between government funding policies and enrolment increases was provided in Ontario when the former McGuinty government set out on a ten-year *Reaching Higher* program to expand Ontario's postsecondary system. It provided funding designed to create an additional 100,000 new spaces in the province's colleges and universities. Ten years later the system had indeed reached higher, having added 170,000 new students – well beyond the intended target. The growth of the university system has been uneven, however. The growth of university, as opposed to college, enrolments in Alberta and British Columbia was exaggerated by the conversion in both of those provinces of a host of colleges to university status, though overall enrolments still grew. University enrolments in the Maritime provinces have not increased at the same high rate as in other provinces, and in New Brunswick are actually declining, as the universities are reliant on the migration of students from other parts of Canada or international students to maintain their student numbers.[6]

At this point, Canada is a world leader in access to and participation in higher education. Every year the Organisation for Economic Co-operation and Development (OECD) provides a detailed report, *Education at a Glance,* outlining key education statistics for its thirty-six member countries. The 2019 report shows that Canada ranks third among OECD countries and first among

G7 nations in the percentage of the population between twenty-five and thirty-five years old that has a tertiary (college or university) education, behind only Korea and the Russian Federation in first and second place. Only 8 per cent of Canadians have less than a high school education. These are impressive statistics, data that many politicians cite, boasting that this shows Canada to be among the most highly educated nations in the world. The reality is somewhat more nuanced. Canada's high ranking reflects that it exceeds all other OECD countries in the percentage of higher education students enrolled in college, and this is due mainly to the CEGEP system in Quebec. Specifically, about 26 per cent of twenty-five- to sixty-four-year-olds in Canada completed college (short-cycle tertiary education in OECD parlance); the OECD average is 7 per cent. In contrast, Canada is in the middle of the OECD pack in the number of students pursuing a university baccalaureate education – 32 per cent of twenty-five- to sixty-four-year-old Canadians have attained a bachelor's degree, the same number as the average of the other OECD countries. The university attainment rate varies among the provinces, with Ontario demonstrating the highest number of inhabitants with a university credential at 35 per cent and Nunavut the lowest at 15 per cent. In terms of students who are studying at the graduate level for master's or PhD degrees, Canada falls below other OECD countries.[7]

The Canadian public university system has shown the capacity for great growth and elasticity of enrolments. The system is as accessible as any in the world. This benefit, though, has come at some cost. Other resources needed to support this growth – physical and human – have not kept up with enrolment increases; as a result, as will be discussed in greater detail in later chapters, the academic environment available to students – the quality of the student experience – has suffered. We are at a point where something like 60 to 70 per cent of high school graduates pursue post-secondary studies either immediately or at some point soon after high school graduation. Two-thirds of those enrolments will be in Canada's universities, the other third in its colleges. Far from wondering whether we have enough spaces for university students, the more frequently asked question now is whether universities are admitting too many students! Whatever the theoretical answer to this question, the pragmatic reality is that universities will continue to accommodate greater numbers because of the revenue students bring into the institution through government grants, tuition, and fees and because assuring access – a spot for every qualified student – is the highest priority for students and their parents and consequently the most pressing political imperative.

Equity of Access: Financial Considerations

An implicit assumption underlying policies and programs to expand access was that growth of the university system, if coupled with sufficient student financial aid, would result in achieving greater equity of access; specifically, that the gap between the number of disadvantaged students, who previously had been under-represented in universities, and the number of more advantaged students, who were going at higher rates, would decrease.

Canada is noteworthy for the attention and funds it provides to financial assistance programs to help students go to university. Alex Usher provides a particularly useful summary of student financial aid programs in Canada in his annual *State of Postsecondary Education in Canada* reports.[8] Yet, because each province administers its own program that it ties to the Canada Student Loan Program administered by the federal government in its own way, the rules of navigating the financial assistance system are complex, even Byzantine. And, yes, more financial assistance could always be provided. But, although the details vary from province to province, Canada has some very advantageous and generous financial aid programs, certainly more so than the much-heralded Pell Grant program[9] in the United States. The sad reality, though, is that the promise of greater access equity with enrolment expansion and more financial aid has not necessarily been achieved.

Perhaps the most striking example of the failure to influence equity of access through more generous student financial aid is provided by the results of the "free tuition" experiment in Ontario. In the 2016 budget, the Liberal government under Premier Kathleen

Wynne announced bold and dramatic changes to Ontario's Student Assistance Program (OSAP) targeted specifically to increase the probability that low-income students would go to university in greater numbers. The revised OSAP program was designed so that students coming from families with incomes of less than $50,000 per year would receive all of their student aid in the form of non-repayable grants (as opposed to loans that needed to be repaid) and that more than 50 per cent of students with family incomes of $83,000 per year or less would receive non-repayable grants that exceeded their university tuition. Hence, the designation of this new policy as "free tuition." These changes to OSAP were made in 2017. It is difficult to imagine a more generous and attractive financial incentive for low-income students to attend university. A review of the impact of this program by Ontario's auditor general in 2018 was disappointing. The auditor's finding that was most widely discussed was that these changes led to unexpected, and likely unaffordable, increases in OSAP costs, resulting in an overall program cost of $2 billion by the year 2020, a 50 per cent increase relative to 2016. More importantly with respect to equity of access, however, was that a 24 per cent increase in the number of university students receiving non-repayable grants as opposed to loans produced only a trivial 1 per cent increase in the number of students going to university and no evidence that poorer students were any more likely to attend university than they had been before.[10] In short, more free money was ending up in the pockets of students who were already going to university, but the program was not enticing more low-income students to attend. It might have been that continuing the program would have better achieved the intended results, but we will never know, as many key elements of this program were reversed by the Progressive Conservative government of Premier Ford.

There are some significant groups in Canada that are still under-represented in Canada's universities. These include students from families with low income, first-generation students, Indigenous students, and students with disabilities.

Marc Frenette of Statistics Canada analysed changes in the relationship between family income and postsecondary (college and

university) participation rates from 2001 to 2014. As had been
known, and was confirmed by this analysis, family income was
significantly related to the probability that a student at age nineteen would be pursuing a postsecondary (college or university)
education; the higher the family income the more likely that the
student would be studying at a college or university. The good
news is that the participation gap between students coming from
low-income families relative to students from higher-income families diminished slightly over this period. Specifically, from 2001 to
2014, the percentage of nineteen-year-old students coming from
the lowest quintile of family incomes enrolled in postsecondary
studies rose by 9.4 percentage points, and for those students from
the highest family income by just 6.1 percentage points. The bad
news is that students coming from low-income families were still
far less likely to be attending higher education than students from
higher-income families. Only 47 per cent of nineteen-year-olds
from low-income families were enrolled in postsecondary education compared to a whopping 79 per cent of students from families
with higher incomes.[11]

Frenette's earlier work provides insights into the variables other
than money and tuition costs that influence the lower participation of students from low-income families in university. Compared
to students from low-income families, youth from well-to-do
families performed better in high school in reading, math, and science tests; were more likely to have parents who were university
educated or who expected their children to attend university; and
attended secondary schools that were more oriented to graduating university-bound students. In fact, these variables explained
84 per cent of the access gap between students from the highest-
and lowest-quintile family incomes. Only 12 per cent of the access
gap was related to financial concerns or financial constraints.[12]

Another comprehensive review of the impact of financial aid
policies across Canada on the university participation of students
revealed that only those changes that had been introduced in
Ontario had any effect, albeit a small one, on the university participation of students, and this was evident in youth coming from
all income levels. There is more to the access gap than just money.[13]

Equity of Access: Non-financial Considerations

The contribution of factors other than financial ones to the under-representation of certain groups in universities can be considerable. Parental modelling and expectations may play a particularly significant role. It has been known for some time that first-generation students – youth from families where neither parent has attended university – enrol in universities in lower numbers than students from families where at least one parent has a postsecondary education. Ross Finnie's Education Policy Research Initiative team at the University of Ottawa scoured the Youth in Transition Survey (YITS) longitudinal database and found that among the myriad of variables that influenced university participation, having parents who did not attend university was the most significant contributor to the under-representation in universities of children from these families.[14] A similar finding of the significance of parental education over and above financial issues was found using data from the Survey of Labour and Income Dynamics (SLID) database.[15] The most recent analysis, in 2019, of the relationship between being a first-generation student and the probability of going to university reinforces and extends understanding of this dynamic. Chatoor and colleagues linked data in an elegant way from the Longitudinal and International Study of Adults (LISA) database with tax files. They showed that students from families where neither parent had attended postsecondary education were still less likely to proceed to higher education than their non-first-generation counterparts – 56 per cent versus 89 per cent, respectively – and that this gap appears to have changed little over time in spite of the availability of more generous financial aid to first-generation students. Perhaps the greatest contributor to this gap was the observation that first-generation students were twice as likely as non-first-generation students to drop out of high school. The most telling and optimistic finding was that those first-generation students who actually did enrol in postsecondary studies were more likely to complete their programs than non-first-generation students and that they eventually had jobs, incomes, and job permanence equivalent to those of students coming from non-first-generation families.[16]

One of the largest higher education policy challenges in Canada today is the under-representation of Indigenous youth in higher education. Indigenous youth represent the fastest-growing cohort that will enter Canada's labour markets. Indigenous populations recognize the importance of and aspire to postsecondary education to the same degree as non-Indigenous cohorts.[17] Yet Indigenous youth access higher education in far lower proportions than non-Indigenous youth. Based on the data from the 2011 National Household Survey, 48 per cent of Indigenous Canadians between the ages of twenty-five and sixty-four held a postsecondary credential. The proportion of non-Indigenous persons with a postsecondary credential was significantly higher at 65 per cent. Indigenous and non-Indigenous Canadians also differed in terms of the postsecondary credentials they held. These two groups held trade, college, and university certificate or diploma credentials in similar proportions. However, non-Indigenous persons were almost three times as likely to be university graduates. A comparison of the growth in postsecondary participation between this survey and the 2006 census shows that whatever gains Indigenous youth made between these two periods reflects increased enrolments in the trades, colleges, and universities. In contrast, the increased participation of non-Indigenous youth in postsecondary education over these five years reflects predominantly an increase in university attendance. A 2018 report underscores the observation that the access gap between Indigenous and non-Indigenous populations is predominantly a difference in university attendance.[18] As with all other students, the level of education matters in terms of future success in the labour market, with Indigenous students holding a postsecondary credential doing better than those without. Matthew Calver from the Centre for the Study of Living Standards estimates that, aside from the economic benefit that would accrue to the individuals themselves, closing the educational attainment gap between Indigenous and non-Indigenous students could result in an economic benefit to Canada of as much as $261 billion.[19] As with other groups of first-generation youth, financial considerations may not represent the most important variable limiting Indigenous participation in higher education. Rather, a set of academic and sociocultural factors play a significant role.[20]

Interventions to Close the Access Equity Gap

There are groups within Canada that historically have been significantly under-represented in our public universities and that continue to be so today. Ironically, these under-represented groups are the ones that would likely derive the greatest benefit from higher education. Research over the last several decades has provided important findings about this access equity gap and about the types of programs and interventions that might work best to close or at least diminish it.

First, although it may not be the most important determinant of whether a student will choose to go to university, money matters: it always matters. We cannot expect students to decide to pursue higher education if they believe they will end up with a crushing debt that will require a lifetime to repay. The evidence suggests, also, that students from low-income families are more sensitive to the price of university education than those from richer families. They also tend to exaggerate the debt they will incur as a result of university, and they minimize the benefits they will derive from a university credential.[21] First-generation and Indigenous students show similar tendencies. So, the structure of financial aid packages also matters. Financial aid programs that pay off debt after graduation through loan elimination or tax credits are not likely to be as effective as providing the financial aid at the front end, when students are considering or are just starting their programs. Non-repayable grants are always better than loans, even if the loans are ultimately reducible or forgivable. Targeting the maximal financial aid to students who need it the most as early as possible is an effective strategy.

The annual reports from Statistics Canada of university tuition levels and the pickup of these data by student groups and media distort the financial argument for going to university and, regrettably, may well discourage students from low-income families from considering university. As shown in the previous chapter, going to university may be one of the best financial investments anyone makes in their lifetime. Relative to the public system in the United States, and certainly the private university system in that country, tuitions in Canada are far from exorbitant. (University tuition levels are also often lower than the tuition charged by many private secondary schools.) Regrettably, what typically gets reported by Statistics Canada and others is the sticker price of tuition – the advertised tuition rates. What does not get reported is the net or real tuitions students pay after scholarships, grants, bursaries, and other forms of financial assistance are factored in. The difference between the sticker price and net tuition can be considerable. In 2016–17, the advertised sticker tuition price for an undergraduate in the arts and sciences at the University of Toronto, one of the top twenty or so universities in the world, was $7,143. When financial aid and scholarships offered to these students was factored in, however, the average arts and science undergraduate was paying just 41 per cent of this amount, or $2,928. Over the entire university, typically students were paying just 47 per cent of the sticker price of tuition out of their own pockets.[22] No one cares what the auto dealers advertise as the sticker price for a new car. After all the discounts and haggling are factored in, what really matters is the net cost – what a consumer actually pays. When we think about the possible constraining influence of money in the decision to attend university, we are well advised to have that conversation tempered and contextualized by what students actually pay, the net tuition.

Second, there are variables other than finances that influence the decision whether to attend university, and these non-monetary factors can be as powerful an influence as monetary ones. These non-financial influences include factors such as parental expectations of the ultimate educational achievements of their children, or parental modelling of university participation by the fact that they have gone to higher education. There can be differences in the level of academic preparedness of students that influence the decision to attend university. We know that differences in academic achievement between those who will eventually go to university and those who will not can appear as early as primary school.[23] We also know that students who have been streamed into academic programs and courses in secondary school that limit or block their path to university entrance are also less likely to attend postsecondary education. This is the argument used by People for

Education, which advocates successfully for the benefits of ending streaming in high school.[24]

Third, and flowing from the arguments above, it is clear that the pathway to a university education and the decision whether even to consider university are determined well before the end of high school. While our efforts to close the access equity gap have been dominated by infusions of financial aid to students at the time that they are graduating from high school, the evidence indicates that this strategy has not been particularly effective in closing the access equity gap. The first order of business to help close the university equity gap is to ensure that as many students as possible from currently under-represented groups actually graduate from high school. This is a prerequisite for getting into university; once enrolled, even students from disadvantaged groups appear to do as well and be as successful as anyone else. The second, but no less important, order of business is to attend to the many other academic, social, and cultural variables that powerfully influence whether a secondary school student will make a successful transition to university.

The success stories and best practices of programs that make access to university more equitable have incorporated these key findings. One of the best recent examples is Pathways to Education. The program was started in 2001 by Carolyn Acker, then the executive director of Regent Park's Community Health Centre. Regent Park was an area in Toronto with significant social challenges for youth and a high school dropout rate of 56 per cent. Pathways to Education offered a community-based suite of academic, social, financial, and one-on-one supports for students throughout their high school years. Now, 71 per cent of program participants complete high school and transition to higher education.[25] The Pathways to Education program has now been expanded to more than twenty low-income communities across Canada, and multiple independent evaluations of program success show positive results, with implementation of the programs resulting in substantial increases in high school graduation rates and a much higher percentage of students who proceed to postsecondary studies.[26]

Fiona Deller, one of Canada's leading experts on access equity, in her review of programs that have improved the participation of under-represented groups in university, suggests that successful programs incorporate a spectrum of financial aid and academic supports, including mentoring, tutoring, counselling, and often parental and community involvement.[27] Are these programs expensive and resource intensive in both financial and human terms? Undoubtedly. As currently structured, can they impact the large numbers of students who are currently under-represented in Canada's universities? Likely not. Is it possible that only some elements of these comprehensive programs are instrumental to the success of the program? Surely, yes, but we do not know which ones, and the experiments that would be required to figure out the essential elements would be difficult, expensive, and time consuming. Knowing the benefits that a university credential confers, perhaps the more sensible conclusion is to just invest in these programs to give low-income and other disadvantaged students a better and more equitable chance to go to university. With everything we know about the private and public benefits and returns of a university credential, this investment would be worth it, for both the individual and the country. To paraphrase a popular maxim, "If you think education is expensive, try ignorance."

This discussion of equity of access in Canada cannot end without a reminder that the Canadian university system and Canadian universities are far more egalitarian in their admission policies and student bodies than those in other countries, most notably the United States. In the States, the high-prestige private and public universities preferentially enrol students from high-income families. Despite attempts to diversify, a host of US universities enrol more students from the top 1 per cent of family income than from the bottom 60 per cent.[28] In contrast, in 2017–18, 46 per cent of the freshman cohort entering the University of Toronto, Canada's top-ranked university, came from families with incomes of $50,000 or less. As Carnevale and his colleagues point out in their recent book, *The Merit Myth: How Our Colleges Favor the Rich and Divide America*, the American higher education system has a deeply inequitable admission system, exacerbates economic and social inequalities in the country, favours the rich, and offers little social mobility.[29] Overall, this is not true in Canada. Although equity of access to Canada's universities should and can be improved, in general Canadians of greatly varying circumstances and needs have access to a suite of high-quality higher education institutions spread across the country.

Recommendation for reform: To close the equity of access gap, preferential allocation of funds to programs for elementary and secondary school students who are currently under-represented in colleges and universities to influence them to consider, and prepare them to succeed at, higher education

Canada should be rightfully proud of the access the public university system grants to its citizens. A spot for all qualified students is a value the Canadian university system has held for years, and it is more successful in achieving this important goal now than it has ever been. Canada can, and should, declare victory on the growth of the university system and revel in this significant achievement. The more important imperative now is to design policies and practices to ensure that all Canadians have an equitable opportunity to participate and succeed in the country's universities. This means preferential allocation of the funds that now go to enhance financial assistance to students entering university to community-based programs targeted to elementary and secondary school students who are at present less likely to consider or attend university. Most students at the end of high school have already decided if they are going to pursue higher education. Financial issues influence but are not likely to be the dominant factor. The strategy should be to influence students unlikely to consider university at an earlier age to understand and appreciate the benefits of a university education and to prepare them adequately for admission and success.

chapter four

What Should Students Learn at University, and Are They Learning It?

The quintessential obligation of a university is to provide its students with a high-quality education that instils the knowledge, capabilities, and skills graduates need to live fruitful, productive, and fulfilling lives, both personally and professionally. In loftier discussions of this issue, particularly in academic scholarly publications, this fundamental responsibility is often encapsulated as the question "What are the 'purposes' of the university?"

There are as many descriptions of the purposes of a university as there are commentators. According to a former president of Yale university, A. Bartlett Giammati, the university's "purpose is to teach those who wish to learn, to learn from those it teaches, to foster research and original thought, and, through its students and faculty, to disseminate knowledge and to transmit values of responsible civic and intellectual behavior."[1] A former Harvard president, Derek Bok, in his book *Our Underachieving Colleges*, reminds us that "Any useful discussion of undergraduate education must begin by making clear what it is that colleges are trying to achieve" – that is, its purposes. His book then provides a more detailed and focused review of what, in his view and that of many others, an undergraduate education should achieve – things like the ability to communicate, a capacity for critical thinking and moral reasoning, preparation for citizenship, a capacity for global thinking, and so on.[2] Stanley Fish suggests that the purposes of the university are but twofold: "1) to introduce students to bodies of knowledge and traditions of inquiry ...; and,

2) [to] equip ... students with the analytical skills – of argument, statistical modelling, laboratory procedure – that will enable them to move confidently within those traditions and to engage in independent research after a course is over."[3] Some others describe the purposes of a university education in far more instrumental terms; recent calls for universities to focus on preparing students for jobs and the workplace are prime examples.

While there is consensus that the fundamental responsibility of universities is to educate, this has not stopped innumerable discussions, debates, controversies, and sometimes fisticuffs throughout the history of universities about what knowledge, skills, and capacities a university graduate should have and how all of this is best taught.

What Should a Student Learn at University?

The contemporary manifestation of these ongoing debates about what universities should teach and what their students should learn is captured in the concept of "learning outcomes." Learning outcomes are defined by the Lumina Foundation, a leading education think tank in the United States, as "what students should know and be able to do when they graduate." The question, which distils so elegantly and simply a fundamental question about higher education, is another way of asking what kind of education a modern university in the twenty-first century should offer its students.[4]

In some areas of university study, such as teaching, nursing, medicine, engineering, and social work, there is a long tradition of a third-party regulatory body establishing the necessary learning outcomes required for entrance into the profession. In these so-called "regulated professions," it is firmly understood that the program needs to teach to these requirements and graduates need to demonstrate competence in relation to these learning outcomes. But in the majority of undergraduate programs and disciplines, particularly those constituting the core arts and sciences disciplines in which most students are getting degrees, curriculum was never so formalized or cohesive. Rather, the purpose or intended learning of a course in these areas has been left to the discretion and authority of the individual instructor; the idea that some outside body should dictate to individual faculty members, especially tenured faculty, what they should teach or how they should teach it is seen as an infringement of a professor's authority and academic freedom. Instructors design courses and decide on their content based upon their professional opinion of what is important in their area. In many cases, especially in research-intensive universities, these decisions are highly influenced by the instructor's research interests. As a result, the breadth and depth of exposure a student gets to the knowledge and ideas in their chosen field may vary widely from student to student – they may be taught the same content in several different courses or they may never be introduced to some concepts or ideas if no specific professor they have encountered has deemed this knowledge important for their particular course. This approach to curriculum design can often inhibit interdisciplinary ideas or collaboration among different departments.

It is rare to see curricula or programs designed in a collaborative or cohesive way to ensure that a student who completes a particular program or degree has been exposed to the full range of knowledge and ideas a group of experts has decided someone in that field should have. I have been involved in two such comprehensive curriculum design exercises, one at McMaster and one at Calgary, both leading to a bachelor of health sciences undergraduate degree. In these cases, the curriculum design process began with the question of what a person involved in and perhaps even leading in health care should know – from an understanding of basic human physiology, to health administration, to health economics. Courses were then designed to ensure that each one contributed to the comprehensive knowledge and skill base a graduate of the program should have, regardless of whether their eventual career was to be as a physician, a physiotherapist, a health policy analyst, or a minister of health in the federal government. Both of these programs are extremely popular among students and have been enormous successes.

A learning outcomes perspective forces this kind of organized, cohesive, and comprehensive approach to curriculum design. It requires an institution to define the purposes and expected out-comes of their courses and programs and measure whether these outcomes have been achieved. A learning outcomes perspective requires professors to be articulate and precise about the knowl-edge, capacities, and skills a student should acquire as a result of taking a course and program and about how student achievement will be measured to determine whether this knowledge and these capacities and skills have in fact been acquired.

For many instructors, the requirements of a learning outcomes framework are novel, challenging, and often resisted. Neverthe-less, the idea that one should actually define what one should learn at university was so naturally compelling and so delightfully attractive to those questioning the value of a university education and demanding accountability from universities that the demand for a learning outcomes perspective became a movement. This in turn spawned a veritable cottage industry of academics, professors, policy makers, and pundits who generated innumerable learning outcomes frameworks. Some of these frameworks were focused at the level of individual courses. Others listed the learning out-comes of fields of study, programs, or disciplines – as, for example, what a historian or chemist should know and be able to do. Other frameworks were directed at even more macro levels, to capture what students in groupings of allied disciplines – such as those graduating from programs in the social sciences, physical sciences, fine arts, or with a bachelor of arts or bachelor of science degree – should know and be able to do. At the grandest level, there were learning outcome frameworks delineating what every graduate of a particular institution, regardless of their field of study or disci-pline, would be expected to know and be able to do. Some learning outcomes plans focused exclusively on undergraduate programs, others on graduate programs.[5]

The smorgasbord of learning outcomes frameworks is almost always associated with a catchy acronym and colourful and com-plicated charts. Some of the most ambitious are from the Organ-isation for Economic Co-operation and Development (OECD) Directorate of Education and Skills, which, as is their mandate, attempted to define learning outcomes that would be valid across cultures, languages, and the diversity of institutional settings and missions. This multi-year exercise, termed AHELO (Assessment of Higher Education Learning Outcomes), examined desired learning outcomes in three areas – civil engineering, economics, and generic learning. Canada (or, more precisely, Ontario) participated in the civil engineering component. The results of this work were mixed. If nothing else, however, the exercise revealed how difficult it was to get agreement about learning outcomes and how they could be assessed, particularly given the goal of achieving agreement across cultures and countries.[6]

The Bologna Accord of 1999, consistent with the concept of a European Union, was a significant European initiative that attempted to harmonize the structure and curricula of higher education across European countries and was a major stimulus for the learning outcomes movement. That accord spawned a host of "tuning" studies that attempted to define, for individual disciplines and fields of study, what a student should know and be able to do upon completion of their program. These exercises were regarded as essential to ensure unfettered mobility of students and equivalent application of quality standards, allowing students to move easily and seamlessly among institutions of higher education in European countries.

There have been many tuning studies in a host of countries. The Higher Education Quality Council of Ontario (HEQCO) led a multi-year project to define specific and general learning outcomes in three types of disciplines – health sciences, physical sciences, and social sciences. The project, like many other tuning studies, led to some important conclusions. First, even those academics uninitiated in or initially resistant to the concept of learning outcomes came to appreciate the utility and power of using a learning outcomes lens in their teaching. As one initially resistant faculty member commented, participating in this exercise fundamentally changed the way he thinks about what should be taught, how a course should be designed, and how learning should be evaluated. Second, these projects also revealed that in spite of the different nature of the disciplines and the vocabulary they use, there was considerable and remarkable consensus on a set of general or generic learning outcomes that students should acquire, such as critical thinking and communication skills, regardless of the specific field of study they were in. Finally, it became clear that it was a relatively easy task to define a slate of desired learning outcomes; the hard part was in figuring out how to assess or evaluate whether students had in fact acquired the desired learning.[7] The difficult challenge of assessing learning outcomes persists and will be discussed in more detail later.

A learning outcomes perspective is now integral to how educators, governments, and students think about what university graduates should know and be able to do and how programs are assessed. Based on their learning outcomes work, the Lumina Foundation has generated a Degrees Qualification Framework that identifies the learning outcomes for students graduating from two-year college programs, four-year degree programs, and graduate level (master's level) programs. Similarly, the Province of Ontario has adopted an Ontario Qualifications Framework that identifies the specific competencies it expects graduates (whether of college certificate or doctoral degree programs) to possess, including those competencies deemed essential for success in the workplace. Universities are required to map their courses and curricula onto these learning expectations, demonstrating which courses contribute to which learning outcomes. Similarly, the quality assurance processes in the province that are prerequisite to the funding of any new university programs are increasingly guided by the expected learning outcomes.

Implications of a Learning Outcomes Perspective

The adoption of a learning outcomes perspective is a significant advance in the design and delivery of university curricula. It forces instructors and curriculum designers to be articulate about the purpose of their courses and what students should learn as a result of taking the course or degree program. It also requires evidence that the desired learning outcomes are being achieved. Yet, in spite of the plethora of these frameworks, and the clarity and common-sense approach of a learning outcomes framework, it is not clear how much impact this philosophy has had on the development and design of university curricula. Many university professors still resist the notion of learning outcomes. The modus operandi of much curriculum design and programming in universities is still very much that a professor is assigned a course to teach and has absolute control over what to teach, how to teach it, and how students should be evaluated.

Academics should control the curriculum and what is taught. But the learning outcomes perspective requires that professors be very explicit with students about what they will learn, how this learning will be evaluated, and how the knowledge and skill set of the student will be advanced or fostered as a result of taking a particular course. This perspective also expects professors to be able to show that whatever they intend students to learn is in fact being learned – the days of simply asserting without evidence that students know or are able to do something are over. These are expectations that many university-level professors are not yet required to meet, although an increasing number of people now teaching in the academy operate in this way as a result of having internalized the perspective of learning outcomes.

What Should a University Graduate Know and Be Able to Do? Classes of Learning Outcomes

Once one gets beyond the jargon, acronyms, and colourful graphics of the learning outcomes frameworks, it turns out that they largely converge on a widely accepted view of what a university education should teach and what graduates should know. Virtually all serious learning outcomes analyses suggest that there are four classes of learning outcomes a university graduate should have achieved.[8]

First, graduates should have acquired disciplinary knowledge – the important information and content of their discipline. The best programs also teach students why this content is important in the field, and how the understanding of this content has evolved over time. So, for example, engineers must understand fluid dynamics and principles of mechanics. Economists must understand what

inflation means, principles of monetary policy, and how to calculate net present value. Chemists should know the laws of thermo-
dynamics, the structure of the periodic table, and which chemicals
can be mixed without exploding. Business graduates should know
principles of marketing and management.

Second, graduates should have achieved a certain level of basic
cognitive skills such as literacy and numeracy. After all, these are
graduates of institutions that represent the highest rung of the
education hierarchy, and logically we would expect these graduates to be among the most literate and numerate in the population.

Third, graduates should also have achieved a certain level of
higher-order cognitive skills, particularly critical thinking, problem solving, and communication skills. There is not a university
president alive who has not at some point in their tenure said
that graduates of their institution will be better and deeper critical thinkers and problem solvers upon graduation than when they
first entered their university. A 2010–11 survey of college and university faculty by the Higher Education Research Institute reported
that almost all, 99.5 per cent, of faculty surveyed said that it was an
"essential" or "very important" goal of a university education to
get students to think critically and to be able to evaluate the quality
and reliability of information.[9]

Finally, we expect graduates to have acquired and demonstrate
a set of personality or behavioural attributes – often termed "transferable skills," "soft skills," "human skills," or "people skills" –
such as persistence, creativity, grit, adaptability, and the ability to
work in a team. These skills are seen as increasingly important for
success at work, but they are also relevant and necessary for navigating the decisions and complexities an individual will encounter in their personal lives. Included in this category are qualities
related to character – such as citizenship, ethical understanding,
and appreciation of diversity or multiculturalism.

This taxonomy of skills that university graduates are expected
to have illuminates a number of issues about what students should
learn in university.

First, the term "skills" can mean different things to different
people, and can be used in many different ways. This seriously

confounds current debates about the possibility of a "skills gap" in today's university graduates. Sometimes the term "skills" is used to refer to the core expected disciplinary knowledge or content of a field. Others use the term to refer to cognitive capacities such as critical thinking or adaptability. Other use the term to refer to very specific capacities in disciplines – such as the ability of a physicist to perform certain mathematical calculations or a philosopher to read in the original Greek. It is difficult to have a sensible or meaningful conversation about the place of "skills" in a university curriculum or the existence of a skills gap when people are using the term to mean so many different things. The ongoing debates and controversies about the goals and value of a university education would be greatly assisted if there was some consensus about how we will use the term "skills." There have been some modest attempts to establish a common nomenclature, but these efforts have led to no agreement or consensus. So, we continue to have fervent arguments about whether students are learning the right skills, especially those that may be related to success in the workplace – arguments that cannot be satisfactorily resolved when we are referring to fundamentally different skills and knowledge.

Second, there is an important distinction between disciplinary knowledge and the other three categories of skills. Disciplinary knowledge is the information and content of a discipline. Disciplinary knowledge is what most professors teach, what they evaluate, and therefore what the universities credential. It is not that professors or universities think that the other categories of skills, such as problem solving or communication, are unimportant. On the contrary, they regard them as just as important as the acquisition of disciplinary knowledge. As Alan Harrison, a former chief academic officer at Carleton University, University of Calgary, and Queen's University, puts it, content is actually the vehicle for skill development.[10] The implicit assumption for years, however, has been that through the teaching of content and disciplinary knowledge the other cognitive and behavioural skills will also be fostered and acquired

Third, different levels of the public education system stress different categories of skills. Pre-school educators and programs focus on the development of personality and behavioural traits, since they are regarded as important for school readiness, and much time, effort, and money are spent on figuring out how best to foster these skills, especially for students who are seen as disadvantaged. In every province in Canada, elementary and secondary schools spend a lot of time, effort, and resources on measuring skills such as literacy and numeracy, using a variety of provincial and international tests. The publicly disclosed results of these tests attract considerable media attention, fanfare, angst (when results look bad or are moving in the wrong direction), and/or celebration (when results looks good). Except in rare and exceptional circumstances, however, universities do not measure literacy and numeracy. When there have been attempts to do so, sometimes at the insistence of future employers, the efforts are often abandoned, especially if the results of such testing do not reflect well on the institution or the students it accepts. Critical thinking, too, is rarely measured, at least not directly. Rather, the development of this essential skill is assumed or inferred. Similarly, there is no attempt to measure the development of behavioural traits. Simply put, the development and acquisition of these skills is assumed on the basis of handwaving and untested assertions, with little evidence to support any statements institutions and programs make.

Fourth, it once again becomes clear that the hard part of the learning outcomes perspective is not making the list of desired learning outcomes but rather assessing whether those outcomes are achieved. This became patently clear in the project run by HEQCO that brought together professors from the social sciences, physical sciences, and life and health sciences to design learning outcomes and to recommend how they should be measured. The groups spent hours debating the list of learning outcomes – which of them were unique to specific disciplines and which were generic across all university programs – and fought over every word, comma, and semicolon. Yet, regardless of how hard they were pressed, they were reluctant to clarify – or even enter into much discussion about – how the skills and capacities they eventually agreed upon should be measured. Their reluctance did not stem from a failure to recognize the importance of assessment. In fact, there was general recognition that their learning outcomes frameworks were relatively useless without a meaningful way of assessing whether they were being achieved. Rather, the difficulty was a lack of agreement on how a university could even approach the problem of learning outcomes assessment.[11]

Are University Graduates Really Learning What Universities Say They Are Learning?

It is one thing to articulate a slate of desired learning outcomes. It is quite another matter to know whether students have actually learned these skills or at least acquired an adequate level of mastery of these skills.

There appears to be little concern over the amount of content or disciplinary knowledge university students acquire. Universities have become quite expert at drilling large amounts of information into students' heads and, as noted before, content is largely what professors teach, what they evaluate, and what the universities credential.

There is considerable controversy, however, over whether students, in the right numbers and to the right extent, are acquiring the cognitive and behavioural skills we expect graduates to possess. University sceptics are now all from Missouri – show me! The problem is that we have few data to show or make the case that universities are doing the job students and society expect in these other domains of learning outcomes. Why? Because for years it was simply assumed that, as students learned disciplinary knowledge, they were also becoming more literate, more numerate, better problem solvers, better critical thinkers, and better communicators. This assumption has underpinned the assertions of university educators for years. As Max Blough, former president of Wilfrid Laurier University, said in an opinion piece in the *Globe and Mail*, "When a university graduate is recruited, the employer has in their new hire an experienced communicator, an adept researcher, a problem solver and a critical thinker – skills that have long been valued."[12] Nicely put, but as acknowledged in the same piece, there are others who disagree. As Derek Bok, former president of Harvard University, pointed out in *Our Underachieving Colleges*, a book devoted to describing the weaknesses and failures of current undergraduate education,

> Requirements are adopted in the belief that hearing professors discuss great books and reading masterpieces of literature will develop caring, ethically discerning students or that taking a variety of courses – any courses – in several different fields of knowledge will be enough to produce broadly educated, intellectually curious adults ... Rarely is any attempt made to approach these assumptions with anything like the care with which professors confront propositions in their own scholarly work. As a result, much of what emerges ... can be better thought of as a set of well-intentioned aspirations, possibly valid but often not, and rarely resting on a convincing body of evidence.[13]

Tony Randall of the sitcom *The Odd Couple* put it in a less eloquent but equally poignant way: "When you ASSUME, you make an ASS of U and ME." Most academics would not like to be regarded as an ass. The assumption that skills develop naturally in parallel with the teaching of content needs to be validated by evidence. Regrettably, the emerging research data are beginning to underscore the prescience of Tony Randall's comment.

Students, parents, governments, employers, and the public are now increasingly demanding proof that university students graduate with the full range of skills today's complex societies and workplaces demand. There are severe disagreements among academics about how to assess learning outcomes other than content. There are those who insist that measurements of skills like critical thinking or literacy must be done within the context of the discipline; specifically, that how one would measure critical thinking would be different for a political scientist and a chemist. Others insist that some desired learning outcomes, critical thinking being the prime example, are context independent and can be measured in a similar way regardless of the field of study of the student. Proponents of this view often gravitate to the use of standardized tests. To many in university circles, the concept of using standardized tests to measure university-level skills is anathema if not abhorrent, even though their use is commonplace in secondary schools. The use of standardized testing, even for admission decisions (something that has been ubiquitous in the States but is not so widespread in Canada), is made less likely following a recent decision by the University of California system to phase out the popular SAT and ACT standardized tests over the next five-year period.[14] To soften the objections to standardized testing, others have moved to the use of rubrics, consistent scoring guides to evaluate the work students produce; these require the professor to assess and grade not only the level of content mastery but also the degree to which the student's responses have shown creativity, evidence of critical thought, and effective communication of ideas. Whatever instrument or test is used to assess skills, all agree that the testing instrument must meet the basic psychometric requirements of reliability (the degree to which the testing instrument produces stable and consistent results) and validity (the degree to which the test instrument accurately measures what it is one wants to measure). The reality is that we simply do not have reliable and valid tests to measure some of the key skills, especially the softer transferable skills. However, we do have tests that reliably and validly measure attributes such as literacy and numeracy. As well, Roger Benjamin has led an organization, the Council for Aid to Education, that developed a frequently used, context-free test for critical thinking, the Collegiate Learning Assessment. This test has been subjected to rigorous psychometric evaluations to demonstrate its reliability, validity, and utility in higher education circles.[15] (Ironically, similar concerns about reliability and validity exist around many procedures university professors currently use to test content and disciplinary knowledge, although university professors are typically prepared to ignore these considerations for this class of skills.) If there are attributes that are important learning outcomes of a university education, and we do not have psychometrically rigorous tests to measure them, then it behoves a system that makes claims about these outcomes to develop these tests, thus providing the evidence needed to demonstrate the validity of its claims.

The immature state of learning outcome assessment is taken by some opposed to the concept of better measurement of learning outcomes as evidence that the whole enterprise should be abandoned. It is not uncommon to hear expressions like, "What we do at university cannot be measured." But this argument will not win the day. As the management guru Peter Drucker reminds us, what gets measured gets done. The question of whether university students are really learning the things we expect a university graduate to know and be able to do is so central, significant, and compelling that a concerted effort should be made to overcome the challenges of measuring whether graduates have acquired the expected range of skills. If no reliable and valid tests now exist to measure these skills, then we will need to develop them.

Efforts to measure learning outcomes other than disciplinary content are more developed in other countries than in Canada. The United States can claim organizations such as the National Institute for Learning Outcomes Assessment (NILOA), a multi-state initiative dedicated to figuring out how best to measure and teach the range of skills we expect university graduates to have;[16] the Council for Aid to Education, which focuses on the development and use of psychometrically rigorous tests for measuring critical thinking;[17] the Association of American Colleges and Universities, which develops rubrics to assess learning outcomes in a host of disciplines;[18] and the Wabash College Centre of Inquiry in the Liberal Arts, which works with more than forty-nine institutions encompassing over 170,000 students to track the development of skills acquisition in liberal arts disciplines.[19] The work of these organizations has been going on for decades. The Office for Students in England invested more than £4 million to fund an extensive set of research projects, involving more than seventy higher education institutions, to measure not only the knowledge, skills, work readiness, and personal development of students but particularly how these skills and traits develop during a student's time in higher education.[20] Regrettably, there are no equivalent groups in Canada (or foundations or organizations, except for HEQCO) dedicated to supporting work on learning outcomes, nor does the Canadian higher education system appear to be as attuned to the whole issue of measuring learning outcomes as are the Americans and British.[21]

The imperative to gain a better understanding of universities' success in fostering the range of skills expected in their graduates by directly measuring these skills in university students is underscored and should be motivated by the few but influential studies that paint a discouraging picture of the skills some university graduates possess.

In a demonstration trial involving several thousand students, HEQCO worked with more than twenty colleges and universities in Canada to measure literacy and numeracy levels in first- and final-year students. The trial, called the Essential Adult Skills Initiative (EASI), was one of the first attempts to quantify the literacy and numeracy skills of postsecondary students in Canada. The measurement instrument used was an online version of an OECD-based internationally accepted test for measuring literacy and numeracy that had already been validated for use in Canada. As in all OECD tests, student performance is categorized in terms of five levels of achievement, with Level 3 generally considered to be adequate for navigating today's world (the reasons for this are presented in greater detail in a later chapter that looks at the relationship between university education and labour markets). In the trial, 45 per cent of students scored at Level 3. About 30 per cent of students scored at higher levels 4 and 5. But the remaining 25 per cent – that is, one in four of the students tested – scored below Level 3. There was little difference in these percentages between the scores of first-year and final-year students.[22]

The greatest data-driven arguments about how well universities teach and students learn revolve around the development of critical thinking skills. In 2011, in a study that received considerable media attention, Arum and Roksa concluded that in about 45 per cent of students tested there was little meaningful increase in critical thinking ability in their first two years of study. Their conclusion was based on an assessment of the performance of about 2,300 students at twenty-four higher education institutions as measured by a test, the Collegiate Learning Assessment (CLA) tool, considered by some to be the gold standard for discipline-free assessment of critical thinking.[23] Ironically, the creator of that test, Roger Benjamin, concluded based on his analyses of the thousands of students who have taken the CLA over the years, that critical thinking as measured by that test increases over the course of university but that some universities do significantly better than others in promoting this learning.[24] Similarly, using a different test to measure critical thinking skills and in a very limited number of institutions, Finnie and colleagues found small improvements in critical thinking skills in university students but not college students over the course of their programs.[25]

If we know little about basic and higher-order cognitive skills in university graduates, we know even less about their behavioural, soft, or transferable skills. The fundamental reason for this is simple. We do not measure these skills, traits, or attributes. In part, this is because we lack reliable and valid measurement tools. In most cases, it reflects the willingness of universities to assert, as they do with cognitive skills, that these capacities are fostered as part of university studies – but without data to substantiate this assumption. For example, recently in Canada a great deal of attention has been paid to the need to graduate students who have entrepreneurial skills. This has led to a blossoming of innumerable "entrepreneurship" programs. Yet few of these programs actually assess whether their graduates demonstrate more entrepreneurial skills than students who do not take these courses or programs.[26] Similarly, a considerable amount of funding is being directed to co-operative education or work-integrated learning programs – so-called experiential learning – in the belief that such learning experiences will allow students to develop the soft skills employers desire and that presumably one cannot teach or learn in a traditional classroom. As intuitive as this belief might be, it would be comforting if some of the considerable funding being allocated to these programs were used to evaluate whether experiential learning really does foster the desired employability-related skills. The dominant complaint of employers is that university graduates lack job-related soft skills.[27] The traditional university transcript, which lists the courses a student has taken and the grades earned, is seen as largely irrelevant as an evaluation of a student's soft skills. That is why some employers argue that a student's grade-point average should be ignored in making hiring decisions and why major companies like Google, Penguin Random House, Apple, IBM, and Bank of America are not even interested in seeing an applicant's transcript or whether they have a university degree.[28]

Universities are in a bind. They cannot, and should not, let up on teaching disciplinary knowledge. But an increasing area of concern is whether university curricula are doing an adequate job of teaching the range of other cognitive and behavioural skills that were always included in the list of capacities and skills we expected a university graduate to have and that universities advertised they did have. Increasingly, research is corroborating what university professors and employers have been saying for some time – that these skills are inadequate in some percentage of university graduates. Some will argue that it should not be the job of the university to ensure adequate literacy, numeracy, and soft skills, and that surely this is the job of elementary and secondary schooling. Whether or not one agrees, the fact remains that universities appear to be admitting some students with substandard skills and that, when they do, they have a responsibility to ensure that these skill deficits are ameliorated by the time these students graduate. There is a strong argument to be made that no student should graduate from a Canadian university with less than Level 3 literacy and numeracy, yet a non-trivial percentage appear to be doing so. Others will point out that university enrolments have soared and that students with inadequate skills are those who would not have been admitted to university some time ago. Although that may be true, once again the fact that universities are accepting these students means that they have an obligation to ensure that their skills are at reasonable levels when they graduate.

A necessary (though possibly not sufficient) step toward ensuring that students graduate from university with the right level and range of skills is to begin measuring these skills. Assertions or assumptions about the skill levels of graduates that are unsupported by evidence are simply not enough any longer, particularly with the increasingly loud complaints from employers, students, parents, the public, and governments about a "skills gap" among university graduates. This means adjusting what and how we teach, what we think is important for students to learn, how we assess what students have learned, and how we credential this learning. It requires nothing less than a serious rethinking of university curricula as we make the inevitable move from the dominant emphasis on content to at least an equal, if not a greater, emphasis on enduring skills and capacities.

There are encouraging signs. There is far more attention now being paid in university circles to the idea of learning outcomes, skills, and competencies than there was in the past.[29] A decade ago, conferences and workshops devoted to these topics attracted only a handful of teaching and learning aficionados; they now attract hundreds. A focus on learning outcomes other than content is occurring not only at the undergraduate level. Based on the fact that only about a half of students who obtain a PhD end up working in academe, a recent survey looked at the skills and competencies of more than 1,200 doctoral graduates across a broad range of disciplines. That analysis showed that, aside from their specific disciplinary knowledge and technical skills, PhD holders across disciplines showed a variety of core competencies – such as analytical and in-depth thinking, and communication, behavioural, and transferable skills like perseverance and time management skills – that aligned reasonably well with the attributes employers had identified as requirements for success in labour markets.[30]

The reasons for focusing on skills goes well beyond consideration of the job prospects of graduates. We often lament that the electorate does not pay sufficient attention to or do an adequate job of assessing the platforms of different political parties at election time. To do so, though, requires a certain capacity for critical thinking – for example, the ability to critically assess the claims made in a party's platform or an op-ed piece. The data we have so far suggest that the critical thinking capacity of some degree holders may be insufficient to perform these assessments. In its 2018 budget, the federal Liberal government – with the aim of preserving democracy and thwarting the attempts of foreign governments to influence the Canadian electorate – allocated $7 million to assist individuals to think more critically about the claims they hear during political campaigns.

It is unclear how these funds were to be spent to accomplish this goal. A good place to start might be to ensure that all graduates of Canadian higher education institutions have acquired the critical thinking skills to make such critical assessments. The data to date suggest that a considerable number have not.

Recommendation for reform: Rebalancing of university programs and curricula from a dominant focus on information and content to an increased emphasis on the teaching, evaluation, and credentialing of cognitive and behavioural skills

The world of higher education is making the transition from a predominant emphasis on content and information to a focus on enduring skills. This is a sensible transition. In today's world, facts and figures change quickly. The content of a discipline may change rapidly; what we learn today might be considered irrelevant or obsolete in a decade or less. Regardless of how information may change over time, however, what endures is the capacity to think critically about this information, to solve problems using this information, to communicate ideas and solutions to others, and to work with others in productive ways that accommodate the volatile nature of jobs and the complexities of modern society. These have always been the dominant purposes and goals of a university education.

Universities have always been interested in these enduring cognitive and behavioural skills, and there is every reason to believe that the majority of university graduates possess these skills to a reasonable, if not high, degree. But the data are equally clear that some percentage of graduates do not have adequate skills, even though they may hold a university degree. It would be a good outcome if more university graduates left with superior skills.

Albert Einstein once said, "Not everything that counts can be measured and not everything that gets measured counts." He was undoubtedly right, up to a point. The good news, though, is that the types of skills students, the public, and the university want to see in their graduates can be measured. Some point out that we do not have reliable and valid tests to measure all of the skills that we hope a university graduate would possess. But we do have some, more than people think. Decades ago, the Canadian government identified a set of generic skills they deemed essential for job seek-ers to have to be successful in labour markets – things like literacy, numeracy, thinking skills, communication skills, and the ability to work with others.[31] These are the same competencies and skills that students and employers are demanding, and their short sup-ply is what contributes to claims of a skills gap. In 2019, the Social Research and Demonstration Corporation reviewed the long list of tests currently available to measure some of these skills. It also identified testing gaps; where such gaps exist, psychometrically rigorous tests should be developed to measure those skills that are deemed essential.[32]

It is time to incorporate skills measurement into the fabric of university curricula. There are already some good examples of experiments in Canadian universities that demonstrate how skills can be assessed in a rigorous way. An increased emphasis on skills, as opposed to content, has implications for how we design courses, how we evaluate students, and how universities credential what they have learned.

Canada, in particular, should have no fear about direct measure-ment of the skills of its university graduates. The country already participates in large-scale international skills assessment exercises such as the PISA (Program for International Student Assessment) and PIAAC (Program for the International Assessment of Adult Competencies) managed by the OECD. The performance of Cana-dian high school students on these instruments is excellent, if not world leading, relative to other countries, although our ranking may be slipping.[33] There is every reason to believe that, overall, an assessment of the skill levels of Canadian university students would be equally impressive in an international context. The value of measuring skills is that it would provide the stimulus for us to do even better – and, in particular, to work to enhance the skill levels of those students who are demonstrating substandard skills. Given the global competition for talent, clear demonstrations of the high skill levels of Canadian university graduates can only serve the country, and its students, well.

Focusing on skills over content means nothing less than a seri-ous rethinking, if not transformation, of undergraduate curricula.

This will not be easy. Curriculum reform is not easy. I recall the comment of Woodrow Wilson: "Changing a curriculum is like trying to move a graveyard. You never know how many friends the dead have until you try to move them."

It is time to move the graveyard. It starts with reliable and valid measurements of relevant skills, such as critical thinking and communication, in undergraduate programs and appropriate credentialing of those skills.

chapter five

The Relationship between University Education and Jobs

The dominant reason students attend universities is to obtain the credentials necessary to get a good job. The dominant reason the public, through the government purse, continues to fund universities is to ensure a steady and reliable supply of the educated and talented individuals needed to fill the jobs of today and to meet the labour market needs of the future. There are lots of boutique programs governments introduce to meet labour needs. The reality, though, is that the funds provided by federal and provincial governments to public education represent, by orders of magnitude, the largest investment the country makes in job training. It is critical to ensure that this investment is geared and leveraged appropriately to fulfil the labour market aspirations of individuals and the country. That's why there is so much attention devoted to understanding, and optimizing, the alignment between higher education and labour markets and jobs.

What Do We Know about the Relationship between University Education and Jobs?

Scores of studies have been done and millions of dollars have been spent on finding answers to two fundamental questions. First, can we predict which jobs will be available in the future and whether we are educating enough people to fill these expected jobs? Second, which fields of study (disciplines or programs) lead to which jobs? The good news is that we have clear and definitive answers to both of these questions. The bad news is that the answers are not what we expected.

The answers are these. First, aside from suggesting broad directions of future labour markets (e.g., digital skills will be important in the future), we cannot predict with any degree of accuracy what jobs will be available in the future, in what numbers, and at what times. Second, there is no strong correlation between the postsecondary programs that students pursue, the credentials they acquire, and the jobs they will eventually occupy, even in the regulated professions.

Here are some recent examples that illustrate these conclusions. Information obtained from the National Household Survey (the 2011 voluntary survey that replaced the mandatory long-form census form abolished by Stephen Harper's government) revealed, as had other research, that students who studied a specific discipline occupied a wide range of jobs and, conversely, students working in a specific type of job came from a wide variety of disciplines.[1] Simply put, one cannot reliably or with any confidence predict what job a person will have based simply upon what they studied at university.

One would think that there would be a greater, if not very tight, linkage between field of study and jobs in the regulated professions, because students enrol in these university programs precisely because they seek careers in those regulated jobs. Yet there are many engineers who no longer practise as engineers – many have highly infiltrated management and business jobs. Many of those with a law degree are not practising law some time after graduation; they may represent the largest bloc among our political class. A study in Ontario found that between 2006 and 2011 Ontario graduated an estimated 26,000 more qualified teachers than there were available teaching jobs.[2] These education graduates are not living in boxes on the street, at least not in these large numbers. Presumably, many of them, although not teaching, have found reasonable employment in some other profession.

The absence of a strong relationship between field of study and jobs is also evident in STEM (science, technology, engineering, and mathematics) disciplines, areas of study that now receive intense public discussion and policy debate. An Expert Panel report, *STEM Skills for the Future,* prepared for the Council of Canadian Academies, revealed that a majority of STEM graduates end up working in non-STEM jobs, and even in STEM-intensive occupations a proportion of workers do not possess a STEM credential, a non-trivial percentage in some cases.[3]

The inability to predict the job market and the absence of a strong correlation between disciplines and jobs befuddle and frustrate politicians who believe that government should fund university spots in specific programs to match the specific number of presumed jobs out there for these graduates. The absence of an evidentiary basis to support such a policy (because having studied a specific field of study, discipline, or degree program does not predict the job one will get) has led some to suggest that labour market planning is futile and that all talk of universities' role in meeting labour demands should be abandoned. This sentiment is especially held by some academics who disagree that it is the role of universities to prepare students for jobs. Others, accepting the importance of understanding the relationship between university education, jobs, and the economy, are not willing to give up the fight. Rather, they have suggested that high correlations between what someone studies at university and the job they get would be found if analyses became more granular – with fields of study dissected into smaller categories (e.g., chemical engineers versus engineers in general) and regions broken down into smaller areas (e.g., job needs in Toronto versus across Ontario). Some of the work of Canada's newly created Labour Market Information Council adopts this strategy.

A more reasonable conclusion, given the ubiquity and consistency of the research findings to date, is to accept the finding that university fields of study do not correlate well with eventual jobs and start asking different, and more relevant, questions about the relationship between a university education and jobs.

This is easier than it sounds. Even when confronted by consistent findings to the contrary, there appears to be a natural human tendency to do the same thing over and over again, albeit with some twists. Governments, in particular, are notorious for this tendency. Following on from Einstein's admonition that doing the same thing over and over again and expecting different results is the definition of insanity, the renowned economist John Maynard Keynes captured this behavioural flaw well in the introduction to his *General Theory of Employment, Interest, and Money*, as follows: "The difficulty lies not in new ideas, but in escaping from the old ones which ramify ... into every corner of our minds."[4]

Given the data we have on the relationship between universities and jobs, we might consider asking the following question: What should a university education look like in a world where the workplaces of the future are likely to be increasingly precarious and volatile; where we do not know what jobs a student will have; where, whatever their first job, they are likely to change careers five to seven times during their working lives; and, most critically, depending on which pundit you believe, where a substantial percentage of the jobs that will be available to students tomorrow have not been created yet?

This question leads the educator to contemplate a university education that fosters the high-level development of a set of skills that will serve students well regardless of the profession or workplace to which they initially aspire or which they will encounter throughout their working lives. Big business has come to understand that preparation for work depends more on developing a suite of necessary employment-related skills than on mastering specific fields of study or acquiring specific degrees. In the words of Jamie Dimon, chairman and CEO of JPMorgan Chase and Company, "The new world of work is about skills, not necessarily degrees."[5] It is also the reason the Royal Bank of Canada has embarked on a $500 million ten-year program that focuses on skill development to prepare youth for the future of work.[6]

So, what do we know about university-level education, skills, and jobs?

What Skills Do Employers Want and Are They Seeing Them in New Graduates?

A starting place to answer this question would be to ask employers what skills they deem critical for success in jobs. There is no lack of studies and surveys providing this information.[7]

Employers, of course, want disciplinary knowledge; a graduate. must have acquired the information and content that allows them to know and do the things a job requires. But lack of content or disciplinary knowledge is not the dominant complaint of employers.

The source of greatest concern among employers is their sense that graduates' cognitive and behavioural skills are the most critical for success in today's workplace, and the ones where they perceive the biggest gaps in future hires. For example, the Canadian Council of Chief Executives and the Royal Bank reported that the qualifications employers most look for in entry-level hires are cognitive and behavioural skills such as problem solving, communication, and relationship building rather than disciplinary knowledge. Unfortunately, Conference Board of Canada and other surveys reveal that this is where the largest skills deficits among graduates are found.[8] This list of skills identified by employers as most important in the future is not unique to Canada. The World Economic Forum suggests that the top attributes students need in order to thrive are complex problem solving, critical thinking, and people management skills and creativity. In addition to these, the World Economic Forum emphasizes the importance of literacy, numeracy, and communication skills.[9]

At first glance, there appears to be an impressive convergence between the skills a university graduate should have, as identified in the previous chapter, and the skills employers say they look for in future hires. Universities say they are graduating literate and numerate students. Employers want literate and numerate students. Universities say that their programs foster and develop critical thinking and problem solving skills. Employers say they want employees who can think critically and who can solve problems. Universities say they graduate students who are good communicators. Employers want employees who can communicate well. So, why is there still so much chatter and angst about a skills gap and employers' difficulty in finding individuals with the skills they need? The answer to this dilemma appears to be that there is a significant difference of opinion between university educators and employers about whether graduates really have acquired the skills universities say they have and that employers desire.

McKinsey and Company examined the relationship between postsecondary education, skills, and jobs in nine countries (Brazil, Germany, India, Mexico, Morocco, Turkey, Saudi Arabia, the United Kingdom, and the United States). When asked if graduates were adequately prepared for the job market, 72 per cent of university administrators claimed they were ready, but only 42 per cent of employers and 45 per cent of graduates agreed.[10]

A 2014 Gallup survey found that over 90 per cent of chief academic officers at American universities claimed that they were doing a very effective or somewhat effective job of preparing students for the world of work. Yet, Gallup surveys at the same time found that just 14 per cent of Americans and only 11 per cent of business leaders agreed that graduates had the skills and competencies needed to succeed in the workplace. A similar Gallup survey in 2020 revealed that again 96 per cent of chief academic officers in US universities believe that their institution does a "very" or "somewhat" effective job of preparing their graduates for jobs. The judgments of business leaders and employers are significantly less positive. The good news, if one can consider this good news, is that the percentage of chief academic officers who think their programs are "very effective" in preparing students for work dropped from 56 per cent in 2014 to 41 per cent in 2020, thus revealing an increasing concern and disquiet among university academic leaders about how well they are preparing students for work.[11]

A survey of more than 1,500 employers conducted by the Institute of Competitiveness revealed that 70 per cent of them believed that their employees' critical thinking and problem-solving skills were insufficient.[12]

The situation appears not to have improved in spite of attention to the need to close the skills gap. A 2019 survey reports that only 22 per cent of Americans say that higher education prepares workers for future jobs.[13] A Harris poll conducted in 2019 surveyed the opinions of more than 11,000 people in nineteen countries around the world asking them for their opinion of whether their higher education prepared them for their careers. The resulting Global Learning Survey reported that 42 per cent of Canadians, 44 per cent of Americans, 42 per cent of Australians, 51 per cent of those in the United Kingdom, and 45 per cent of Europeans said that their higher education did not prepare them for their careers.[14]

Even university students are expressing concern about how work prepared they are. In the McKinsey study referred to above, fewer than half of the youth surveyed said that their postsecondary education prepared them adequately for employment opportunities. A recent survey of more than 6,000 Ontario postsecondary students revealed that respondents perceived a gap between the skills they acquired during their higher education and what they needed in their future careers.[15] More alarmingly, a survey of more than 2,200 students at York University, Western University, University of Waterloo, and University of Toronto (Scarborough and Mississauga campuses) found that only about 44 per cent of students felt they had the skills needed to do well in their academic studies let alone in any future job they might get. Forty-one percent of respondents could be deemed to be at risk of failing to complete their higher education because of their limited skill levels.[16]

The previous chapter reported the results of the Essential Adult Skills Initiative (EASI), which measured the literacy and numeracy of Canadian postsecondary students. The test used in the EASI trial, an online version of the OECD's PIAAC test, does not primarily measure students' reading level or their ability to perform certain arithmetic manipulations. Rather, it asks whether students can apply information provided in prose form and writing (literacy) or numerical and graphical form (numeracy) to answer questions and solve given problems. EASI is as much an evaluation of problem solving and critical thinking skills as it is of literacy and numeracy. The results of that research demonstrated that perhaps as many as one in four postsecondary graduates failed to achieve Level 3 literacy and numeracy. The types and complexity of problems one can expect someone operating at Level 3 literacy and numeracy provide insight into why employers are complaining about the skills of some of their potential hires who are not performing reliably at that level.

The shift from Level 2 to Level 3 marks the transition from concrete to abstract reasoning. It reflects the difference between those who can extract content and information from written or numerical information – Level 2 – to those who can draw inferences, generate conclusions, and apply that information to solve problems – Level 3 and above. So, for example, a Level 2 thinker can read an employee newsletter and extract the two reasons given in it for an increase in sales. But it takes Level 3 numeracy to be able to look at a monthly bill from a utility company and figure out whether the company accepts the same payment if given online or via mail. Similarly, it is Level 3 literacy to be able to search several Web pages of a national health organization for evidence supporting the claim that exercise can lead to greater work productivity. Level 4/5 literacy demands greater ability to search and analyse information – for example, the ability to determine which claims in a newspaper article about the benefits of sleep are supported by information in two long research articles.[17]

Level 2 numeracy allows one to calculate the price of a shirt that will be discounted by 25 per cent. Level 3 numeracy allows one to determine the amount of concentrated lemonade flavouring and water needed to make a large container of lemonade that is in the same ratio of flavouring to water as a smaller amount of lemonade. Level 4/5 numeracy allows one to calculate profit from a table containing lists of income and expenses or to determine how much medicine to give to a child when the dosage is based on the child's body weight.

These exemplars tell us that someone operating below Level 3 thinking might have difficulty running a lemonade stand, and, if they were so employed, determining whether they were making a profit or going bankrupt. Someone below Level 3 would have difficulty mounting a marketing campaign extolling the value of their product over others or evaluating the claims of other lemonade stand owners.

Workplaces today demand the capacity to absorb information, to think, and to problem solve. Repetitive, rote tasks are likely to be performed in the future by robots and other automated machinery. The job of the proverbial truck driver does not match the stereotypes of yesterday. The logistics of warehousing and transportation and the complexity of truck cabs require a sophisticated operator with skills beyond Level 2. As Joseph Aoun, the president of Northeastern University, said in his book *Robot-Proof: Higher Education in the Age of Artificial Intelligence*, "When the economy changes, so must education ... To ensure that graduates are 'robot-proof' in the workplace, institutions of higher learning will have to rebalance their curricula."[18]

The dependence of jobs on those with Level 3 skills was shown impressively by Lane and Murray, who found, based on data provided by Employment and Social Development Canada (ESDC), that most new jobs being created in Canada require skills at Level 3 or beyond and that 97 per cent of all jobs that have been created in Canada over the last twenty years have required that level of cognitive functioning.[19] A 2019 study by HEQCO investigating the predictive power of credentials and skills for labour market outcomes showed that while both predict earnings and employment status (full- versus part-time or unemployed), skill levels may be better predictors of job success than credentials held, and in particular, higher numeracy skills are more predictive of good labour market outcomes than literacy skills.[20] Given these findings, there is reason to worry that the one in four postsecondary graduates who fail to achieve adequate skill levels may be just as disadvantaged in terms of getting a job and succeeding at it than those who have failed to obtain a higher education credential.

In sum, there is a widening gap between the views of employers about the skills of recent graduates and the skills required to be successful in today's labour markets. This is true even for entry-level jobs where there is a sense of a gap between the skill set of recent university graduates and the requirements of these positions. This observation underlies the rationale for the creation of specific programming within university programs, or for focused short programs designed specifically to bridge the skills gap between graduation and first job.

The economic impact of this skills gap and the number of Canadians with inadequate skills for today's jobs may be substantial. Based on OECD data, Schwerdt and Wiederhold calculated that a mere 1 per cent increase in a country's literacy level can lead over time to a 5 per cent rise in productivity and a 3 per cent rise in GDP.[21] Given Canada's low productivity relative to other countries, particularly the United States, and the increasing challenges to the robustness and competitiveness of Canada's economy, these are economic benefits the country cannot afford to forgo.

How Can Universities Better Teach the Skills Students and Employers Want?

Both employers and universities have responded to the increased emphasis on employment-related skills, concern over the skills gap, and the recognition that skills represent the sweet spot in the necessary alignment between higher education and jobs.

Employers are becoming far more articulate in identifying the skills that are needed for jobs, including detailed analyses of which jobs require which skills.[22] Similarly, universities are increasingly willing to trumpet their role as job preparers and to implement curriculum changes that presumably foster skills needed in workplaces. (For historians of public relations efforts in higher education in Canada there is an incredible irony that the current emphasis in the marketing and messaging of the university sector is how well they prepare students for work and how much better they are at it than other education sectors, including the colleges; twenty years ago, their messaging was that universities' role was not job preparation. In contrast, it is now the colleges in Canada, which for years promoted themselves as vocational institutions specifically designed to prepare students for work, that increasingly emphasize how good they are at teaching the transferable and soft skills that are necessary for job success.)

For universities, the emphasis on skills prompts a critical question: How do we teach skills like critical thinking, problem solving, communication, adaptability, and resilience? This question goes a long way to explaining the current emphasis in universities on experiential learning (learning by doing), co-operative education, and – more generally – work-integrated learning. The belief is that these pedagogical techniques will foster precisely those work-related skills their graduates appear to lack and that presumably are not easily taught or learned in lectures or traditional classroom settings. Governments at both the federal and provincial levels are investing millions of dollars to create more experiential learning opportunities. Some governments, like Ontario, suggest that they will link some of their funding for public higher education institutions to the extent to which their students are able to engage in work-integrated learning. Businesses and universities are working collaboratively in ways they have not done before, through such organizations as the Business–Higher Education Roundtable, to create thousands of new experiential learning opportunities.[23] Governments are investing heavily in research to understand better the skills gap and how to address it. The investment by the federal Liberals of more than $250 million to create Future Skills Canada and a Future Skills Centre is one example, among several.[24]

It may well be that the expansion of experiential learning elements into university programs will alleviate some of the skills gap. This is certainly the intent. But we will only know if this strategy is effective, and whether the dollars being invested in experiential learning are worth it, if we measure the outcomes of these programs to see whether graduates have actually acquired the identified skills. Regrettably, it appears that the primary focus will be on funding and introducing these experiential learning programs and not on assessing whether the desired outcomes have been achieved. This problem would be easily remedied if some small portion – even as little as 5 per cent – of the funds allocated to implement the programs were reserved for a mandated review of outcomes.

Some will argue that it is not the job of universities to provide the specific skills training some employers seek. Rather, this is the job of employers themselves, and those holding this view will observe, accurately, that the investment of Canada's companies in job training has been declining. Others will argue that the college system provides such training and will point to the increasing number of university graduates who return to college to get the preparation they presume they need to actually get a job. Notwithstanding the inefficiency of a postsecondary system that asks students graduating from a four-year baccalaureate program to take up to three years more to get the education they need for a job, there is little evidence that this route – of a college program following university – actually improves a candidate's job prospects. In the absence of rapid action by universities to address the skills gaps, private sector entities such as coding camps, "last-mile providers," or companies like LinkedIn that offer skills-training modules through Lynda.com will take on the task of (and secure the profits from) providing training programs to give job applicants the skill sets they need for employment.[25]

Analysis of the relationship between a university education and jobs almost invariably migrates to consideration of the role of the liberal arts and humanities. Enrolment in these programs, particularly the humanities, has declined precipitously, presumably because students have internalized the message that these fields of study do not lead to jobs, or at least good ones. There are few data to support this conclusion. Furthermore, it is precisely the liberal arts and humanities that should do an admirable, if not the best, job of preparing students for the volatile and unpredictable world of work they are entering. Fareed Zakaria, in his book *In Defence of a Liberal Education*, describes a report from Yale University as early as 1828 asserting that "the essence of a liberal education was 'not to teach that which is peculiar to any one of the professions; but to lay the foundation which is common to them all.'"[26] The hallmark of a liberal education was to train the mind to think critically, enquire, and appraise, and to give students the ability to communicate their thoughts and ideas purposefully and effectively, both in writing and orally.[27] These attributes of a good liberal arts education are precisely what employers are asking for. It is unfortunate that somehow the role and purpose of liberal arts and humanities programs have been diminished as result of the emphasis on jobs, workplaces, and the economy.[28] If anything, given their essential elements and structure, these are exactly the programs that might do the best job of preparing students. It does not help that some faculty in the humanities and liberal arts have responded to today's dynamic by adopting a siege mentality, lamenting the lack of respect and resource allocation they are accorded in the academy. Their energies would be better spent in documenting the skill levels that students acquire as a result of education in these fields. There is every reason to predict that such empirical studies would demonstrate the capacity, and the superior ability, of the liberal arts and humanities to prepare students for the professional and personal challenges they will encounter in the twenty-first century.

Competency-Based Education (CBE)

An encouraging outcome of the angst over higher education, skills, and jobs is the expansion of a transformative model for higher education called competency-based education (CBE). The traditional university course looks something like this: an instructor is assigned to teach the course and decides what will be taught (typically, the course is heavier on content and information than on skills development); classes are delivered to all students at the same time, according to the university's timetable; the instructor creates evaluation tools that, because of the nature of the material taught, emphasize information and content and not assessment of skills and competencies; and students get a grade for the course that reflects how well they have mastered the material.

CBE works on a fundamentally different philosophy. First, it privileges the teaching and learning of skills and competencies over content. Second, it suggests that all students should master material deemed to be important, appreciating that it will take some students longer to master the material than others.

In the traditional model, students are given a fixed amount of time to learn the material – the so-called seat-time model (e.g., a course is delivered in three fifty-minute classes per week for thirteen weeks) – but the amount of material mastered by individual students is variable. In contrast, in the CBE model, students have a variable amount of time to learn the material, but the amount of material to be mastered by individual students is fixed, and it is all the stuff the instructor deemed important enough to include in the course.

In a complete CBE program, (1) competencies are clearly articulated as outcomes of the program; (2) competencies are assessed using proper psychometric instruments, and students' progress to the next stage only after mastery has been demonstrated; (3) programs are designed after an initial assessment of students' prior learning and current competencies; (4) students are permitted to learn at their own pace and may demonstrate mastery of the material at different rates; (5) graduates receive a credential describing the competencies the graduate has mastered.[29]

The Western Governors University is a prime example of an innovative university that has adopted the CBE model. Founded in 1997 by a group of state governors in the United States (specifically, in Indiana, Missouri, Nevada, Tennessee, Texas, Washington, and North Carolina), it provides online, customized programming targeted to areas of labour market shortages such as health, education, business, and information technology. The targeted students are those with some postsecondary education and working experience who are currently working and are looking to upgrade their skills. The model works as follows: A student seeking to upgrade their credentials in order to get a better job (e.g., by completing a bachelor's degree) contacts Western Governors and describes their career aspirations. A mentor assesses the student's prior learning, skills, and competencies and determines the gap between the student's current skills and competencies and those required by the job they seek. The university designs a program of study using existing online courses and programs that have been customized to address the learning needs of the student. The university assesses skills and competencies when the student says they have mastered them. At the completion of the program, the student is awarded the appropriate credential, which is often identical to that granted by traditional universities in the jurisdiction, and receives a transcript that lists the competencies a student has achieved. The program of study is overseen and monitored by a personal mentor assigned to the student. The student is charged approximately US$3,000 per semester, less than most students in Canada pay per year for their undergraduate programs. Because of the assessment of prior learning and the customized online programming, many students can fast-track their degrees; the average student completes a bachelor's degree in 2.5 years. The satisfaction levels of students are significantly higher than national averages. Most importantly, the labour market outcomes – whether graduates get jobs and the quality of the jobs they get – are as good as, if not better than, those for graduates of traditional university programs.[30]

Other highly rated universities in the United States – including Michigan, Purdue, and Wisconsin – have incorporated CBE elements into parts of their curricula. The poster child for CBE may be Southern New Hampshire University, which, after the introduction of a CBE-based curriculum, was transformed from an institution in financial trouble to one enrolling more than 90,000 students. While other American university leaders have expressed considerable enthusiasm for CBE programs (at present there are about 600 US colleges and universities offering a CBE-based program), it is clear that there is an appetite for more. It is seen as a compelling model that decreases student debt loads, because students finish their programs faster, and successfully addresses the concerns of employers about inadequate skill levels of university graduates.[31]

Canada is moving more slowly than the States to adopt CBE, although some in Canada, such as the University of British Columbia (UBC) and the Royal College of Physicians and Surgeons (which licences medical residency programs), have signalled an intention to move that way in the future. Simon Fraser University and the University of Ontario Institute of Technology (Ontario Tech University) have both introduced short courses to enable students to develop work-related skills and competencies. The acquisition of these skills will be certified by a verifiable micro-credential the student receives upon completion of the short course.[32] There may be less incentive for the use of CBE programs in Canada than in the United States because two major drivers of CBE education in the States – mounting student debt and low completion rates – are less prevalent in Canada. It is also possible that there is less appetite for innovation in the Canadian university system than in the States (more on this in chapter 7). Finally, it is noteworthy that much of the impetus for competency-based education in the States has been financially supported by grants from two independent foundations – the Lumina Foundation and the Gates Foundation; it is likely that there would be fewer CBE initiatives without this financial backing. The US federal government has also enabled CBE initiatives by relaxing certain regulatory financial aid rules to motivate experimentation with and implementation of CBE (although this financial support has recently been discontinued).[33] No such foundation or government supports exist in Canada.

Credentialing Skills

The increased emphasis on skills will demand that universities develop new ways of awarding credentials for what students have learned. The current transcript, which lists the courses a student has taken and the grades earned, is simply insufficient to document the skills and competencies a student possesses. This is why some employers who say they value skills over degrees, including Google, Apple, Ernst & Young, and Penguin Random House, no longer wish to see an applicant's transcript or even require a degree for some of their top jobs.[34] It used to be the case that the institution granting the transcript contained much, if not all, of the signal value employers needed to attest to the worth of a future employee; a graduate from Harvard, Yale, or University of Toronto was seen as, by definition, highly skilled. In fact, some employers would restrict their hiring to a limited number of high-reputation and high-prestige universities. But the signal value of the degree-granting institution itself, no matter how prestigious, has broken down. A recent survey indicated that a substantial percentage of Americans believe that an internship at Google would lead to better career success than a Harvard degree.[35] Increasingly, employers consider skills of greater importance than degrees in the hiring decision.[36] A recent survey of more than 500 hiring managers in the United States indicates that the great majority, 74 per cent, perceive a skills gap in current workforces and that a majority, 59 per cent, say that it is becoming more difficult to hire employees with the skill sets modern jobs require. As a result, 67 per cent of respondents expect to incorporate formal skills assessment in their hiring decision. A US poll of 1,139 people involved in hiring decisions conducted by the Strada Educational Network and Gallup revealed that 77 per cent of them would hire someone without the advertised degree desired or required, and many have already done so, showing a willingness to privilege other skills and competencies over the degree credential that has already been evident in Canadian hiring decisions.[37]

Universities can leave skills assessment to employers and the private sector. There are already private companies entering this space to provide the skills assessment information future employers seek. But if universities really believe they are fostering employment-related skills, and skills development is going to be an increasing focus of university education (as was suggested in the previous chapter), then it behoves universities to actually validate and credential the skills their students possess. This will require a credential for graduates that goes beyond the traditional transcript.

Many institutions, including prestigious ones such as Stanford, are attempting to provide a more complete record of the skills and competencies a graduate has acquired. Others are partnering with industry to provide industry-specific certification of the knowledge, skills, and competencies that a student has acquired either as part of a degree program or as a terminal credential.[38] There is little doubt that these efforts, which have led to documents such as co-curricular transcripts, electronic portfolios, and comprehensive student records, will become more prevalent as universities become more attuned and responsive to calls to document what they teach and clarify how they credential this learning. As Alan Harrison summarized in his review of skills, competencies, and credentials, "Universities should accept that it is their responsibility to prepare their students for the workplace ... Having helped the student to develop the skills, the universities also need to ensure that there is good evidence to support the claim that this skill development has occurred."[39]

Recommendation for reform: The granting of university graduation credentials that complement the current traditional transcript and that document the skills and competencies a student has acquired

Throughout his impressive career, Robert Reich has been one of the world's leading commentators on the future economy, the changing nature of jobs, and the skills that will be required for individuals to succeed in the new, knowledge-based economy.[40] As he states in his book *I'll Be Short*, "The thing about the twenty-first-century economy that distinguishes it most sharply from the economy that preceded it is the central importance of people's minds, and skills. 'Human capital' is the asset that matters most."[41] The previous chapter recommended that universities modify their curricula to emphasize the acquisition of skills and get on with the task of measuring and assessing skills, including those that have been demonstrated to be in high demand for employment success. For this recommendation to be helpful, those institutions that purport to offer an education that fosters these skills will need to validate and credential them. Universities, institutions that increasingly advertise how well they prepare graduates for future jobs, should take on the responsibility of credentialing these skills and competencies. It is something students, employers, governments, and the public will expect them to do.

It is also something they should be comfortable doing. Universities are in the credentialing business. Right now, the credentials they offer are traditional transcripts that list the courses a student has taken, the grades earned, and the degree obtained. The limitation with these traditional transcripts is that they say little in a meaningful or useful way about the skills a student possesses. The signal value of the traditional transcript with respect to skills is incomplete and inadequate, as many employers and students have already concluded. The traditional transcript must now be accompanied by documents that capture the institution's assessment of a student's skills and competencies. Handwaving and indirect inferences will no longer suffice. The good news is that institutions insist on enormous integrity around the credentials and transcripts they provide. A move to providing more comprehensive and relevant documents to accompany the traditional transcript will drive universities to attend to the rigour and validity of the instruments they use to assess skills. This, in turn, will motivate increased research to develop reliable and credible skill measurement instruments – a highly desirable outcome.

chapter six

How Should a Government Manage Its Public University System?

By definition, the government, because it is the allocator and steward of public funds, has a role to play in the management and regulation of a public university system. Aside from determining the amount of the public grant to universities, government also controls the other major source of university revenue – tuition – because it establishes a tuition policy that regulates the tuition and fees universities can charge students for their programs. Governments also indirectly, or in some cases directly, control the major expenditure of universities – wages and compensation – by including universities as part of the broader public sector when a provincial government decides to cap or constrain public sector compensation. Governments have also not been hesitant to insist that universities create or modify some of their internal policies and practices on matters such as sexual harassment, mental health services, experiential learning, or freedom of speech. Contrary to the belief of many that Canada's universities are autonomous institutions, the reality is that higher education in this country is a highly regulated industry. Those who object to government regulation of the higher education sector and who defend or advocate for more university autonomy should consider that it is difficult to claim autonomy when universities continue to receive a significant portion of their revenue from government, a revenue source no university appears ready to give up.

The increasing tendency for governments to hold public institutions like universities to account is only going to increase.

Governments are less willing to grant universities the hands-off autonomy they once enjoyed and that universities continue to demand. Aside from exercising their legitimate role to ensure appropriate use and stewardship of public funds, governments themselves are being held to greater account by citizens, opposition parties, the media, and auditors. It is only to be expected that governments in turn will impose greater accountability on those institutions that receive public funds.

Another quintessential role for any government is to ensure that publicly funded institutions are of high quality and that they use the funds they receive to deliver the public goals and outcomes promoted by the political party in power as part of their campaign platform. The elected government sets public goals, and presumably a plurality if not a majority of the electorate supports these goals. One should expect a government to worry, then, about whether the funds it allocates to its public institutions are being used to achieve the government's stated goals. In fact, the electorate is entitled to become angry if governments fail to deliver on their promises.

In Canada, governments are fully engaged and obligatory partners in the public university system. In Canada, in contrast to the United States and other countries, few significant higher education institutions have attempted to liberate themselves from government by going private. In Canada, no matter how bold or courageous a university, its president, or its administration might be, the university's capacity to change or innovate requires engagement with politicians and government. The essential question, then, is not whether governments are or should be involved in the public university system but what role a government should play in the management of public universities – what relationship governments should have with universities.

In his book *How to Run a Government So That Citizens Benefit and Taxpayers Don't Go Crazy*, Michael Barber, the father of "deliverology," offers a playbook that has been adopted by Canadian federal and provincial governments and foreign governments, including in the United Kingdom and United States, to optimize the achievement of public goals desired by governments and the public that elected them.[1] The lessons are directly applicable to understanding what a harmonious and productive relationship between a government and its public universities might look like. A good relationship starts with the reality that the elected government sets the public goals desired in a jurisdiction but that these can only be achieved by working with the institutions that are directly responsible for accomplishing these goals and objectives. The government is then advised to establish targets for these goals and to create metrics that measure the current state of affairs and progress toward the desired goals. This is the only way of determining whether the policies and practices introduced by the government or used in the institutions are effective in achieving the desired goals. If targets are being met, then success can be claimed. If they are not, then policies and practices should be amended to move more effectively toward the public goals.

There is nothing particularly revolutionary or mysterious about "deliverology." Rather, it is simply an attempt to get government to operate in ways that internalize the basic elements of proper and sound performance management. If done well, it enables governments to use public resources effectively and work with public institutions purposefully and harmoniously to achieve what is desired – in the case of universities, a set of higher education institutions that are of high quality and that deliver to individuals and the public a set of beneficial outcomes commensurate with the level of investment made in them.

Chapter 9 will explore in more detail how one can measure the quality of Canada's universities. For the moment, the question is how governments should relate to and engage with public universities to ensure that public goals are being achieved.

A performance management system can be designed well or poorly. If done well, it creates an environment in which governments and universities work together and spend resources wisely to achieve desired goals effectively and efficiently. If done poorly, it creates an environment characterized by frustration and cynicism. As is often said, the devil is in the details. And designing a good relationship between governments and universities requires the government to get right the details of the system by which it regulates and manages its universities. Getting the details right requires reflection on a number of fundamental questions that are critical to the design of any good performance management system. Questions like: What are reasonable public goals for a public university system and how should they be set? How does one select metrics that accurately, effectively, and usefully measure progress toward public goals? What design features of a performance management system by government optimally link the pursuit of public goals with the behaviour and practices of universities?

Setting Public Goals for the University System

It is the job of governments to set public goals. That is why the party in power, not some other political party, was elected to form the government. Some of these goals will be shared by other political parties and some will not.

Goals are not the same as strategies. Goals are things a government is trying to achieve, the outcomes they are trying to achieve on behalf of the public. Strategies are processes and actions that are employed to achieve these desired outcomes.[2] Political parties may well differ on their goals, and may be even more sharply divided on the strategies they use to achieve these goals. All of this influences how a government relates to the universities in its jurisdiction and the policies it introduces to manage and regulate them.

We would like to think that a government's goals and the strategies used to achieve them reflect deep analysis and decisions based on evidence and data. This is not typically the case. Rather, most governments develop university agendas and policies based on stories, anecdotes, gut feelings, and personal reminisces. This is especially true when new policies are put forward in the heat of a political campaign.[3] In the United States there are many foundations and privately funded think tanks that dissect and analyse education-related issues in detail. It is noteworthy that only one Canadian province, Ontario, has an independent, evidence-driven research shop dedicated to providing government with objective, evidence-based advice on higher education. Governments could supplement their lack of expertise on universities and higher education if they consulted earlier and more extensively with experts, many of whom sit in the universities themselves. Alas, today there is a dearth of trust between governments and universities, and as a result, appropriate consultation before policy development is not necessarily a hallmark of Canada's current higher education world.

An essential first step for governments in managing their relationship with universities is to be clear about the goals or purposes they have for the higher education system. As noted above, many goals are possible, and at some point many have been identified by government as priorities. These may include increasing enrolment, graduating engaged citizens, creating and driving societal change, enhancing the quality of the student experience, lowering the cost of a university education, driving the economy, assuring greater sustainability of universities, optimizing the physical and mental health of the citizenry, creating jobs and serving as a magnet for talent from around the world to come to Canada, and promoting new and entrepreneurial companies that will create jobs.

Michael Barber suggests that the greatest number of goals a government can effectively pursue is three. One of the things that frustrates universities that legitimately wish to work with government is that governments typically have a much longer shopping list of goals than three and the priority assigned to these goals changes regularly depending on the latest political imperative, university controversy, or media report. Nevertheless, historically, through all of this chatter and confusion, two goals appear to be top of mind for governments over time and throughout Canada: (1) increasing enrolment to ensure the widest possible access to higher education, and (2) improving the quality of institutions to ensure that the province and students receive the maximal benefit from their private and public investment in university education.[4] In Canada, these two priorities appear to be the things that matter most to government. How governments define whether they have successfully achieved these goals depends on their interpretation of what success looks like and how progress toward these desired goals is measured. These priorities are the basis on which governments design a performance monitoring and management system – in particular, the measures and metrics by which achievement of the goals will be evaluated.

Setting Measures and Metrics

There are three types of measures governments can use to monitor, evaluate, and regulate the performance of universities: inputs, outputs, and outcomes.[5]

Inputs are the resources that go into universities, including dollars, books, faculty and staff, students, and the physical plant. Outputs are the things that universities produce, such as graduates and research publications. Outcomes are the benefits that result from the activities of universities, such as economic growth, good jobs for graduates, a healthier population, and a more civil society.

Inputs are the easiest things to measure. It is easy to count the number of students a university has, the number of faculty and staff they employ, the number of books in the library, and the square footage of their buildings. Indeed, much of the reporting of universities to governments describes these input variables in robust and exhaustive detail. But inputs convey little information about the things about universities that matter most to governments, students, and the public. Having more faculty or fewer students or a bigger library does not tell you much about how well a university is performing, the quality of the education it is providing, or the benefits students and society derive from its activities.

Measuring outputs is more meaningful. Knowing how many students are enrolled at a university – an input measure – is not as important as how many graduate – an output. It is not especially illuminating to know how many faculty are employed by a university – an input measure. It is more important to know whether they are conducting and disseminating research by counting the number of publications they produce – an output measure. So, measuring outputs is better than focusing on inputs; many outputs are also relatively easy to measure.

The most important and meaningful measures of university performance, though, are outcomes – the consequences of the university's work and efforts. Outcomes map most directly to the goals that are of greatest concern to government and others. If the motivation for an individual to pursue a university education and for the province to fund universities is to increase the probability of getting a good job, then the relevant outcome is how many graduates get jobs and, as one measure of how good the jobs are, how much they earn. If the desired goal of a public university is economic benefit to the province through research, measuring how many faculty members are conducting research – an input measure – is not as meaningful as the number of publications they produce – an output measure – which in turn is not as meaningful as the number of jobs created as a result of these activities and the increase in the wealth of the population or the size of GDP – all outcome measures of economic impact.

Outcomes are harder to measure because it may be difficult to draw a clear causal link between the activity of the university and a particular outcome. Outcome measures are influenced by other factors that are not in the control of the university. For example, universities may be engaging in activities that prepare students for good jobs, that create jobs, and that contribute to economic growth, but a recession or a pandemic will have a large impact on the number of jobs available and their quality. There may be some statistical manoeuvres that try to parse out the impact of universities on desired outcomes measures but these are open to interpretation. Recently, governments at both the federal and the provincial level have begun to exploit the large databases they possess to more closely link the work of universities to outcomes. A good example is the federal Education and Labour Market Longitudinal Linkage Platform created by the federal government in 2018 and supported by a $27 million investment in that year's budget. That platform and linkages with other databases in the provinces allow us to follow the trajectory of individual students through university and link them via their tax files to the jobs they eventually get and how much they earn in them. The richness of these data-linkage opportunities allows us to address questions such as which universities provide graduates with the best job possibilities and the highest-paying jobs and how factors such as gender and field of study influence these outcomes.[6] Many claims are made by universities about the impact and goals of a university education; it is sensible, then, no matter how messy the interpretation may be, to look at the outcomes of university performance, especially those that relate to goals the government and the university have identified for themselves (and that, therefore, may make universities worthy of greater investment and funding).

In the past, governments focused on measuring inputs, everything from the number of students, to staff counts, to tuition revenue, to the number of international students, and the amount of electricity consumed. Enrolment numbers (counted in different ways and according to different definitions) received special attention because of the emphasis of governments on access. More recently, governments have shifted their focus to outputs and outcomes. The two major outputs measured are the graduation rate (how many of the students who started university actually graduated) on the education side, and research publications, faculty awards, publication citation counts, patents, and start-up companies created on the research side. Many provinces within Canada have now shifted their focus to outcomes. Ontario was the first to move in this direction, followed by Alberta, New Brunswick, and Manitoba.[7] It is inevitable that more provinces will bias their measurement of university performance to outcomes since these are the things that relate directly to public goals and so really matter to governments.

Ontario introduced outcomes measurement of their universities soon after the election of a Progressive Conservative government in June 2018.[8] They identified a slate of ten performance measures in areas such as skills and job outcomes; community and economic impact; and productivity, accountability, and transparency. Some of the proposed metrics were sensible and understandable given the economic and social climate. To determine whether universities were really graduating students who could succeed in labour markets, the salaries of graduates would be measured at some point after they left university. To know whether graduates had acquired employment-related skills, the government would require universities to actually measure employment-related skills such as literacy and numeracy and critical thinking. This is a revolutionary step that addresses a glaring omission in past evaluations of university performance. What students learn and how well they are learning it should be a fundamental concern. Yet, in spite of all the facts and data universities were required to report to government, there was no requirement for direct evidence about what students were learning. The current attempt by the government to get its universities to document the skill levels of its graduates not only focuses the institutions' attention on the importance of skills but also requires them to document the level of skill acquisition. There are many different ways to measure skill acquisition and what students learn – as well as controversies about how to do so – but the incorporation of these measurements is a significant step in any contemporary performance monitoring scheme.[9] Equally revolutionary was the requirement that universities publicly disclose the workloads of faculty. Some proposed metrics were less sensible. Given the evidence that the program a student pursues at university may bear little relation to the job they eventually get, it is unclear why the proposed metric of institutional focus – what percentage of students are enrolled in programs of priority to the university – has much meaning. Similarly, while Ontario wishes to assess the economic impact of universities, it is unclear why the proposed metric – the percentage of university graduates who work in the same region as the university – means much. The performance measurement plans being adopted by other provinces resemble Ontario's. Even so, despite a clear shift away from using inputs as the sole indicators of universities' effectiveness, it will take some time and effort to identify the best metrics and indicators to measure how well outputs and outcomes reflect public and governmental goals.

The metrics and indicators being selected by Canada differ from those dominating this discussion in the United States. Low participation and graduation rates in the States have led state governments to focus on metrics that emphasize how many students get in, the percentage of those students that come from minority or disadvantaged groups, whether students proceed through their programs in a timely way (retention rate), and the percentage of entering students who eventually graduate (graduation rate). Canada performs very well in these domains – Canada can boast participation, retention, and graduation rates that the Americans envy. This offers the opportunity for Canada's governments to concentrate on second-generation performance metrics, such as whether the university education leads to jobs, whether students acquire the skills they will need in the future, the economic impact of universities' contributions, and the quality of education a university offers. If the American university system ever succeeds in achieving the enrolment and graduation rates to which they aspire, the performance measurement regimes their governments impose will gravitate more to the outcome measures being considered in Canada.

The selection of appropriate metrics to measure progress toward or achievement of desired goals is a critical step for a government's evaluation of the worth and contribution of the university system. When a government articulates the metrics and indicators it will use to regulate and manage its universities, the institutions will respond to optimize their performance on those metrics. That is the whole rationale underlying performance management. But in any such system one should be cautious about unintended consequences – outcomes that are not intended or foreseen. For universities, the most frequently expressed concerns about the unintended consequences of applying graduation-rate performance measures are that (1) more stringent admission standards will be applied to screen out average or less qualified applicants and admit only students with very high secondary school averages who seem most likely to graduate; and that (2) the standards and rigour of courses and programs will be lowered to enable most students to succeed and complete their degrees, thus optimizing the graduation rate.

One should always be cautious about unintended consequences in any measurement exercise. The argument that a focus on graduation rates will lead universities to bias their admissions to the very best students is particularly ironic, since that is exactly what has been going on in Canada for decades. In Canada, universities compete with one another and are not shy to boast about their high admission standards. It is not uncommon for universities to advertise the quality or value of a program by referring to the fact that it takes a 90 per cent average to get in. Universities are seen to overtake their competitors when their entering average requirements exceed those of other institutions. Notwithstanding a host of arguments that question the real meaning and validity of claims based on the entering average, the fact remains that Canadian universities already work assiduously to admit only the best students with the highest averages, so concern over this unintended consequence may be just too precious. Equally, there is little evidence that a metric that advantages a higher graduation rate will lead instructors to water down the rigour of their courses or their evaluations of students. This would require an institution-wide conspiracy, with all faculty agreeing to lower standards simply to promote their institution's standing with government. It is hard to get faculty to agree on anything (viz. the maxim "running a university is like trying to herd cats"), and academics would rightly interpret a directive to lower standards to let more students graduate as an invasion of their academic freedom and the right to teach and evaluate according to their professional judgment. As Henry Rosovsky, former dean of arts and sciences at Harvard University, pointed out, "professors have ... the freedom of artists," and as professors they "recognize no master save peer pressure, no threat except, perhaps, an unlikely charge of moral turpitude. No [other] profession guarantees its practitioners such ... independence."[10] In any case, if one is concerned about the unintended consequence of lowered standards, one can check for this by actually monitoring the rigour of the academic work professors demand of their students.

Given their current obsession with ensuring transparency and accountability in the public institutions they fund, governments are increasingly using performance management measures to monitor, manage, and regulate their universities. Some see this strategy as an attempt by government to impose more control and accountability on recipients of public funds. Nevertheless, the use of performance management systems can also be seen as a legitimate attempt by governments to exercise their role as stewards of public funds. More loftily, if we get the goals and metrics right, performance management can also be the foundation for continuous improvement of the university system. Do we now have them right? Not yet. The performance management systems governments are now designing have too many goals, confuse goals with strategies, have some indicators that are not supported by evidence and data, and, because most governments do not really understand how universities work, are too open to being gamed by clever university administrators. Despite such flaws, performance management and greater intrusion of governments into the operations of universities are not going away. They will continue. Rather than argue about whether governments should be engaged in this exercise, it would be more productive for governments and universities to figure out how to work together to design effective performance-management systems that will enable them to generate the data needed to improve the university system.

Designing an Effective System

Once a government decides on its public goals and creates a slate of indicators that effectively measure progress toward those goals, it remains to figure out how to engage the universities to work toward those goals.

Governments have two mechanisms at their disposal to influence the behaviour of universities. The first is to insist on public disclosure of information that is meaningful to students and the public. Universities work hard to increase their profile and improve their reputation. Public disclosure of information about how universities are performing influences the decisions they make. That is why universities in Canada are so attentive to the annual *Maclean's* rankings of universities and why various universities have changed practices and policies to propel them higher in those rankings. It appears that disclosure of information that gives the public, the government, and potential students information about the structure, state, and accomplishments of universities influences them to change. For better or worse, universities are eager to enhance their prestige and profile. This is why public disclosure can so powerfully influence what universities do and how they operate, and why those who would like to see changes in the university system endorse government demands for more public disclosure of data and information.

The other powerful, and time-honoured, mechanism available to governments to influence universities' performance is to link government funding to the achievement of desired goals. This is known as performance-based funding.

There is nothing mysterious about performance-based funding. Parents operate on this principle when they say to their children, "I will give you an allowance of $10 per week, but for that you have to make your bed every day and keep your room clean." When we ask a plumber to fix a leaky faucet, we do not pay them when they show up at the house – an input measure akin to paying universities for enrolling a student. Rather, we pay them only when they achieve the desired outcome – a faucet that no longer leaks. In spite of all of the angst, controversy, and resistance in university circles about performance-based funding, it is a simple and sensible mechanism that we regularly use to incentivize desired behaviours.

The United States has a longer history with performance-based funding than does Canada. At present, somewhere between thirty and forty-six states are considering, transitioning to or implementing some form of performance-based funding for their public universities. As I have noted earlier, many of the systems that have been introduced are targeted particularly to increase participation, retention, and graduation rates at universities and, especially, to increase the participation of minority groups or students enrolled in presumed job-related disciplines such as the STEM disciplines.[11]

One of the earliest and most sophisticated performance-based systems was introduced in Tennessee in 1979 and amended in 2010 in an attempt to address some appallingly low graduation rates in public colleges and universities. In one year, after clear direction from government that it was moving boldly to performance-based funding, and intense negotiations between the Tennessee Higher Education Council and the state's public institutions, the state switched its funding from about a 98 per cent input-based model to a 98 per cent performance-based model. Tennessee is now seeing some of the participation, retention, and graduation rate improvements it had sought and is beginning to consider applying its performance-based funding model to promote achievement of outcomes such as job success.[12]

The research on the success of performance-based funding in the United States has delivered mixed results.[13] Research findings can be difficult to interpret because of the wide range of program designs that have been included as performance-based funding models and the diversity of institutions at which these models have been applied. Performance-based funding has not yet led to some of the participation and graduation rate improvements that were hoped for. There is evidence, however, that it has led to changes in institutional behaviour, such as a greater focus on student advising, mentoring, services, and counselling – changes that may eventually lead to improved graduation rates. Some have taken these mixed results to indicate that performance-based funding is inappropriate or cannot be applied to universities. This is a specious argument. The reality is that performance management always works if done well and if the principles of behaviour change are appropriately understood and applied.[14] But there are many ways to get a performance management scheme wrong. In an undergraduate course I took in laboratory methods in experimental psychology, students were required to teach a rat to navigate a simple maze. About half of the class succeeded in getting their rodent charges to learn the task; the other half did not. The difference was that the successful behaviour managers appropriately applied the conditions and processes that change behaviour, and the others did not. Those cases where the introduction of a performance-based funding system has not been as successful as hoped provide important lessons about essential design elements that promote greater success.

What are the principles a government should attend to in designing an effective performance-based system? First, you need a motivated organism to see behaviour change. In universities, motivation is induced by dire financial circumstances or the promise of a big reward. Some will argue that the financial situation of Canada's universities is not sufficiently perilous to make them consider serious change, particularly, as noted earlier, since governments are reluctant to let any of their universities fail or go bankrupt. Alternatively, the promise of a sufficiently large reward might motivate the adoption of a successful performance-based system. A 1, 2, or 5 per cent funding incentive may be insufficient. Tennessee's movement to a 98 per cent performance-based funding model got the university's attention. Ontario has promised to increase its performance-based funding for universities from its current level of about 2 per cent to 60 per cent in four years. For performance-based funding to be effective, it must involve a significant portion of the funding a university expects to receive from government.

Second, performance-based funding fails if the wrong indicators are selected. It is relatively easy to select good metrics to measure inputs like student numbers, but it gets more complicated when outputs and outcomes are being measured. That is why appropriate consultation with university experts who know how these institutions actually work is always helpful when designing a performance-based funding system that is also structured to avoid negative unintended consequences.

Third, even after appropriate metrics have been selected, details of the design of the performance system are critical. The devil is indeed in the details. It is important to consider whether institutions are competing against themselves or other institutions for a fixed pot of funding. It is important to know what happens to the funds that universities lose as a result of poor performance. It is important to set the right targets for institutions. One can design a 100 per cent performance-based funding regime that is totally toothless and ineffective if unambitious targets are set, a design flaw that Michael Barber cautions against.

Fourth, as is true for any system that aspires to influence behaviour, it is important to select the right reward. For a hungry rat learning to negotiate a maze, the reward is food. It is assumed, rightly, that the dominant reinforcer for universities is money, especially for the administrators who have the responsibility of keeping the university afloat and the lights on. But money is not the most effective reinforcer if you want to influence the performance of individual faculty. For most faculty, the currency of the realm is colleagues; the promise that more professors will be hired in their area of expertise will motivate more action and change than any promise of greater overall funding for their institution. The simple principle is to select a reinforcer that is aligned with the interests and designed to influence the behaviour of those who have to perform in particular ways to achieve the hoped-for goals.

Finally, performance regimes are effective in influencing performance only if they are rigorously and consistently applied. This can be hard to achieve, since governments often change their minds about their priorities, or undermine their own policies by periodically granting funds or favours to satisfy some political objective, or cave to opposition when the political heat becomes too intense.

Such caveats aside, performance-based funding is an effective tool governments can use to steer and influence universities to achieve publicly desired goals. Evidence to support this assertion may be found in the many examples when Canadian universities jumped, and jumped high, and when government was clear about the outcomes it wanted and put money – even in ten-cent or fifty-cent dollars – toward the achievement of those goals. For several decades, governments have used funding to encourage universities to admit more students. What happened? Universities responded with significant enrolment increases that often exceeded the targets the government had set and the universities' own capacity. When the Ontario government wanted more graduate students, the system responded by going over the targets. When the government provided capital funds to stimulate construction as part of Harper's economic-stimulus program, universities responded with a lot of new building and construction even though the infrastructure funds typically did not cover the full cost of the construction. When Nortel rang the alarm bell about the dearth of information technology graduates in the late 1990s and governments allocated funds for new programs and buildings in these areas, universities responded massively to the call. When the Harris government funded the Access to Opportunities Fund – a philanthropy-based matching program to raise funds for scholarships and student financial aid – universities pivoted their activities towards this goal and raised funds that exceeded any expectation of government.

At a meeting of university presidents, I once asked whether in this time of greater incursions into university autonomy there was anything the government could ask them to do that they would refuse to do. There was a pregnant pause followed by the skill-testing question: "Is there money tied to it?" This mindset now pervades the thinking of resource-starved universities and ensures that well-designed performance-based funding models will succeed.

Institutional Differentiation

Universities are not homogeneous organizations. They differ from one another in many important ways. Some are small, others are large. Some are intensely involved in research, some less so. Some have student bodies that are largely or exclusively made up of undergraduate students pursing a bachelor's degree. Others have a wider mix of students that includes many pursuing advanced graduate master's and PhD degrees. Some have curricula restricted to traditional core disciplines within the arts and sciences. Others have a large range of programs, including multiple graduate and professional programs such as medicine and law.

Universities acknowledge their differences by saying that they are "differentiated." Classification schemes have been developed to place universities into different categories based on the scope and nature of their activities, their size, and their missions or mandates. Perhaps the best known and longest-standing differentiation scheme is the Carnegie Classification of Institutions of Higher Education, which since 1970 has distinguished US universities according to a number of variables, including the scope and size of their graduate programs, their degree of research intensity, their educational focus, and the balance between undergraduates and graduate students.[15] The United States also has a long tradition of identifying the special category of "liberal arts colleges" – universities such as Amherst College, Swarthmore, Pomona College, and Williams College – a category used by the much-read US News & World Report ranking of American colleges and universities to identify institutions that provide an undergraduate education in the liberal arts and sciences.[16]

The most well-known differentiation scheme in Canada was developed by *Maclean's* magazine, which, as part of its annual ranking of universities, classifies universities as Medical/Doctoral, Comprehensive, or Primarily Undergraduate.[17] Analogous to the R1 research universities in the Carnegie Classification, the most intensive research universities in Canada have self-identified themselves as the U-15.[18] Similarly, four Canadian universities – Bishop`s, Acadia, Mount Allison, and St. Francis Xavier – have banded together as a "Maple League" to work collaboratively to promote premier liberal arts undergraduate education and the institutions that provide this programming.[19]

Differentiation is a powerful policy that allows individual institutions to do more of what they do best and, as a result, optimizes the performance, quality, and contribution of a university system. California's Master Plan for Higher Education, one of the most celebrated and successful designs for a public university system ever, made California the first US state to guarantee universal access to higher education and led to the development of a host of some of the best research-intensive universities in the world.[20] In general, pursuit of a policy of differentiation creates the opportunity to improve the quality of a public university system, improve the sustainability of the universities in the system, and offer clarity of institutional choice to students.

That universities differ from one another is – or should be – a critical consideration in the design of any successful performance monitoring and evaluation regime. Regrettably, most governments treat all of the universities in their purview alike. As a result, they try to apply the same objectives, performance criteria, targets, and funding formulas equally to all the universities they regulate. Such a regime, although easier for governments to design and administer, ignores the reality that universities are different and have different functions, missions, and mandates. It makes little sense for government to impose the same performance criteria on a University of Toronto or a UBC as it does on Algoma University or University of the Fraser Valley. It makes little sense to apply the same performance requirements to a research-intensive university as it does to a primarily undergraduate liberal arts university.

It makes little sense to expect the same graduation rates from a university that accepts lower achieving students as from one that admits only high-flying students.

The central point is that for a performance regime to be successful and reasonable it must accommodate the reality of institutional differentiation. There are many clever ways to incorporate this reality into a performance-based funding model, including the use of different indicators for different types of institutions, differential weightings of indicators in the funding scheme for universities with different mandates, and value-added, rather than absolute, indicators and targets. Failure to acknowledge the relevance and significance of institutional differentiation in the performance regime dooms it to failure. Conversely, acknowledging institutional differentiation has the promise of allowing each institution to do more of what it does best. Coupled with a well-designed performance system, accommodating differentiation has the capacity to offer students clarity as to which institutions will best serve their personal and professional aspirations and to improve the quality of the academic experience and the sustainability of the institutions.[21]

Recommendation for reform: Government introduction of transparent, performance-based funding regimes sensitive to the reality of institutional differentiation to regulate, manage, and monitor public universities

The rationale for government use of performance-based funding models to regulate, manage, and monitor public universities is a compelling one. Governments that desire more transparency and accountability from their public institutions and are keen to steer the work of universities to achieve societal and public goals will increasingly gravitate to the tool of performance-based funding. We should do it right. A close, collaborative, and trusting dialogue between governments and universities is needed before these schemes are developed and implemented, including a clear articulation of what outcomes we hope to achieve from the public university system and a rigorous, evidence-driven, and deep conversation about appropriate metrics and indicators.

Establishing such a regime requires appropriate sensitivity to the realities of how universities operate, their differences, and what one can expect them realistically to achieve. All of this is possible, but it necessitates a change in the mindset of governments toward their universities as well as increasing willingness on the part of universities to engage with government and appreciate its role and constraints.

chapter seven

Why Are Canadian Universities So Slow to Innovate?

The University of Al Quaraouiyine, founded in Morocco in 859, is considered by some to be the oldest degree-granting university. The oldest university in Europe is the University of Bologna, established in 1088. Oxford University is the oldest English-speaking university, created in 1096, and still going strong.[1] Several universities in the United States claim to be the oldest in that country, but Harvard, started in 1636, appears to have the strongest claim.[2] The University of New Brunswick in Fredericton is the oldest university in Canada, founded in 1785. Many other universities in Canada that are still operating today were established before Confederation, including University of King's College (1789), McGill (1821), University of Toronto (1827), Queen's (1841), and Université Laval (1852).[3]

The point is that universities have been around for a long time, and so there must be something about their nature, purpose, and structure that accounts for their longevity and apparent robustness. Some have suggested that one of the reasons for this is their capacity to insulate themselves from the volatile waves and tribulations of society and their capacity to resist change even when the whole world around them may be shifting. If so, this is an attribute that might be admired. At present, however, the apparent reluctance of universities to move and adapt quickly and to be more responsive – their seeming inability to initiate significant curriculum or program changes or reforms – is seen as a negative. Under their current structures and processes, it takes universities years to start a new program from the time the need for such a program is first recognized to the time it is actually initiated. In addition, it is almost impossible in most universities to kill a program, even one that has few or no students enrolled in it. The term most frequently applied to describe the pace of change at universities is "glacial," and even in this age of climate change, this moniker is not particularly complimentary.

Several years ago, I checked whether the program I had taken at McGill as an undergraduate still existed today, more than forty years later. It does. Although the course titles and the course content have changed, the overall structure of the program has remained the same, even down to the calendar copy describing the program to undergraduates.[4] The structure and organization of today's universities differ very little from what existed fifty years ago. In the great majority of instances, the names of departments, programs, and fields of study, and how these programs are organized, are remarkably similar to what has existed for decades. Have new programs and schools been introduced? Of course; but the overall curriculum in one of Canada's public universities today, particularly for disciplines that make up the core arts and sciences, would not seem foreign or odd to someone who graduated from that institution a half-century ago. How many institutions, organizations, or companies today look the same or operate in the same way as they did fifty years ago? If they had not adapted, they would not have survived. The lack of serious curriculum change stands in sharp contrast to the significant additions, deletions, and reorganizations we have seen on the research side of the university house.

We are also hearing angst and frustration about the lack of change in universities. Why are they not adapting or modifying their curricula, programs, organization, or modes of instruction to address students' skills gaps and lack of preparedness for jobs? Why do we still see the same slate of departments when we understand that finding solutions to critical societal issues such as climate change or income inequality calls for different organizational structures, such as multidisciplinary programs that bring together traditional disciplines like political science, economics, chemistry, and geography under one umbrella to expose students to the range of things they will need to know and master to solve these problems? We have seen new and creative reorganizations and amalgamations in research programs, but not in how the university is organized to teach. A suggestion to merge or amalgamate departments in the service of improved pedagogy is often seen as an attack on the sacred administrative structure of the academy. In the words of Bartlett Giamatti, "The ways people really think, teach and especially do research are not defined solely by departments and never have been. Of course, departments are necessary for bureaucratic and organizational purposes; of course, they serve to indicate larger zones of concern and common interest, but they must be shaped and perhaps reconceived. Departments must be administered, but not as if they were sacraments."[5] Is it so preposterous to contemplate an undergraduate curriculum structured around solutions to problems – a Department of Poverty Reduction or Climate Change Solutions – instead of the traditional departments that often operate in silos and create impediments to students who wish to learn in multi- and interdisciplinary ways? Professors affiliate with their disciplines and resist changes to their traditional administrative groupings. But this may not work well for students who are learning about the complex and discipline-intertwined challenges that face them and society today. As Clark Kerr said in *The Uses of the University*, "the professors' love of specialization has become the students' hate of fragmentation."[6]

When I was still at the University of Calgary, I wrote to about thirty of my presidential colleagues across Canada and asked them to tell me what they regarded as radical, significant, or transformative innovations in curriculum reform and undergraduate education in Canada. These are the things one does late on Friday afternoons when one seeks an interesting project to distract from the more transactional and mundane affairs of a university presidency. There was remarkable consensus in the many responses I got (apparently, other presidents also sought similar distractions). Two examples were offered by many. The first was the creation of Waterloo University as a co-operative education university, and the second was the introduction of problem-based learning as the basis for medical education in McMaster's Faculty of Health Sciences.

The University of Waterloo has its roots in the 1920s, when the Lutheran Synod established a seminary and college in Waterloo. Gerald Hagey was appointed president of Waterloo College in 1952, and he remained as head of the institution as it transitioned through a period of considerable growth and eventual incorporation as an independent University of Waterloo decreed by royal assent on 5 March 1959. The idea of co-operative education as the basis for the applied science and engineering curriculum was first enunciated by Ira Needles, the president of B.F. Goodrich Canada and a member of the Waterloo College Board. Described in a speech to a Rotary Club in 1956, and termed the "Waterloo Plan," the proposal, termed a "Co-Operative Plan of Education for Engineers and Technicians," presented a new way of educating engineers, with alternating terms of course work at the college and semesters in industry. Academic progress required successful completion of both the course and the work components. The impetus for this radical change in educating engineers was a seminal conference held several years earlier at St Andrews by-the-Sea and organized by prominent Canadian industrialists who cautioned that Canada was ill-prepared to meet future economic needs because of a lack of technical manpower. Its chief recommendation was for industries to work cooperatively with universities (hence, co-operative education or co-op) to meet this scientific, engineering, and technical shortfall.[7] The deliberations of that conference are eerily reminiscent of many gatherings today that also express concern about the dearth of Canadians in the STEM disciplines (science, technology, engineering, and mathematics) and advocate a closer collaboration between private sector industries and universities as the solution.

The idea of a medical school at McMaster University was first proposed by the university president, Harry Thode, in 1963. Perhaps the most instrumental act leading to the eventual opening of the school in 1969, with an entering class of just twenty students, was Thode's recruitment several years earlier of the founding dean, John Evans. Evans was young, in his mid-thirties, and early on, even before his official appointment began, had penned a memorandum that was to be the basis for the revolutionary medical curriculum. Evans quickly recruited a group of like-minded medical rogues and free thinkers who, unbridled by convention, were committed to the McMaster model. The fundamental underpinning of the curriculum was problem-based learning (PBL). Rather than educating medical students by having them sit initially in large classes organized into the traditional medical disciplines to be lectured at by a sage on the stage, PBL asked students, working in small groups led by a tutor, to self-learn by working through a carefully constructed problem designed to force students to think in a system-wide way. PBL was as revolutionary to medical education as the case method was to the education of business students. (Harvard's use of the case method in its business school may have influenced the design of PBL.) There were other revolutionary features to the PBL-based curriculum introduced by McMaster, including the use of non-expert tutors and – in contrast to traditional forms of evaluation –the elimination of exams; rather, student performance was assessed by a tutor, who evaluated a student's performance as satisfactory or unsatisfactory.[8]

Both co-op education and PBL have been enormous successes. They have been widely adopted and emulated internationally. Virtually every university now has some co-op programs that follow the Waterloo model. Millions of dollars have been allocated to promote more co-op learning in a host of disciplines in the belief that this does a better job of preparing students for their eventual jobs and of fostering the cognitive and behavioural skills that may be difficult to inculcate in the traditional classroom. Co-op education is the basis for Waterloo's high profile and reputation in the IT world and Silicon Valley. It is estimated that more than 500 higher education institutions worldwide use PBL in disciplines that go well beyond medicine. Other medical schools, Harvard's among them, have copied the McMaster curriculum.

There are important parallels between the Waterloo and McMaster examples that speak to the conditions that enable transformative and radical education innovations like these.

The most significant observation is that both initiatives, in spite of their ultimate glorious success, were met with considerable controversy, resistance, and even scorn from academics, other members of the engineering and medical communities, some community members, and other universities. These innovations were hardly welcomed or embraced. To the contrary. Their pedagogical innovations were criticized as inferior models of education that would produce substandard graduates. As described by historian Ken McLaughlin, chronicler of the development and emergence of the University of Waterloo, critics in the engineering profession suggested that the co-op plan of "interrupted education" was "shallow and disordered" and that the end result would be an "inferior engineer."[9] Critics of the proposed McMaster medical school curriculum were no less unkind.

So, how did these two innovations succeed in spite of considerable opposition? This is the second important observation. In both cases, the initiative was led and supported by an inspirational university president who provided unwavering support for and commitment to the vision. In the case of Waterloo this was Gerry Hagey, and for McMaster it was Harry Thode. Though neither of these individuals had "hands-on" involvement in the design and implementation of the revolutionary curricula, both were unhesitatingly supportive and committed to the innovation throughout the long and often frustrating years from conception to implementation. It was the president who often bore the scars of battles with community and academic colleagues that characterized the introduction of these curriculum innovations.

Third, the presidents were instrumental in recruiting a small group of key individuals who provided the on-the-ground detail work to design and implement the programs. In both cases, a core group of about five people did the hard slogging to make the idea and vision real. In Waterloo's case these academic leaders were known as the "Fearsome Five." For McMaster, John Evans recruited four other Founding Fathers, among them Fraser Mustard, a giant of Canadian health care.

These radical amendments in university education and pedagogy occurred in the 1950s and 1960s, a time, many current students would suggest, as remote as when dinosaurs roamed the earth. It is thought-provoking to learn that my query to university presidential colleagues revealed no more current examples that rival the Waterloo and McMaster examples. The only other contemporary example may be the innovative block design and topic-based undergraduate curriculum at Quest University, a private university in British Columbia.

The absence of daring initiatives in curriculum reform is surprising given the general perception that universities should be the crucible of bold ideas that challenge the status quo. There is also little downside risk to innovation at a university. Almost by definition, some, perhaps many, innovations will fail. Such is the nature of innovation. If a company takes a big gamble and fails, the company goes bankrupt and people lose their jobs and livelihood. What happens if a university attempts some innovation and it fails? The university does not go under – governments are not prepared to see a public university fail. Few, if any (except perhaps for the university president or some leaders of the initiative), would lose their jobs. Certainly, none of the tenured faculty would find themselves on the street. They would simply return to the teaching and research they were doing before at the same salaries and in the same working conditions they previously enjoyed.

The absence of innovation in higher education is not unique to Canada. Innovation can enhance a university's reputation, prestige, and profile. Many believe that Harvard is a great university because of its great wealth and all that it has allowed the university to obtain and create. Eyring and Christensen, having traced the history of education innovations at that university, argued though that "Harvard's great strength ... is a pattern of innovation that is continuous and focused on the university's great mission, without undue concern for either tradition or what other universities are doing."[10] Yet, as others who study innovations at universities have pointed out, "the history of the twentieth century was one in which postsecondary institutions tried to become more alike than different from one another."[11]

So, why are universities so slow to innovate, particularly in Canada? Why are they keener to emulate what others are doing instead of forging new, bold, and innovative paths and directions? Why are we not seeing examples in Canada of universities that embrace competency-based curriculum or customized, online digital programming for part-time learners, as at Western Governors University? Several possibilities come to mind.

Timid academic leadership. Some will argue that university leadership today is timid – less willing than presidents of yesteryear to take on bold, innovative initiatives. Some even suggest that the processes universities use to select their academic leaders actually weed out those with great leadership skills.[12] Perhaps so, although one must always be cautious about fond reminiscences about the way things used to be. This criticism may be unfair. University leaders, including presidents, do not have the authority and influence over their universities that they had in the past. The history of Waterloo and McMaster make it clear that Hagey and Thode were visionary leaders, but it is also illuminating to see the power, influence, and control they had in their institutions and the high regard in which they were held by the public, community, politicians, and even members of faculty. The bureaucracy and regulatory processes that now exist significantly fetter the ability of even the most courageous and bold university leader to initiate significant change. The Waterloo and McMaster examples also make it clear that governments were four-square behind these initiatives and supported them through legislation and, especially, resource allocation. Governments today are less nurturing and supportive than they have been in the past. A university presidency and the control and authority that senior university executives have today are quite different from what they were fifty years ago.[13] It is an open question whether Hagey and Thode could have realized their visions in today's environment. That said, there is no Canadian university president in recent memory who approximates the longevity, flair, and accomplishments of, for example, Michael Crow, the president of Arizona State University, who, over his almost twenty-year tenure, has transformed that university into one of the most progressive and innovative universities in the United States – a prototype for what he calls the "new American university."[14] Similarly, and regrettably, we have no contemporary example of the creation of a public university in Canada analogous to that of the University of Minnesota-Rochester that was established in 2007, an institution that is focused on health care programs; has no traditional departments; makes tenure decisions based on teaching, research, and research about teaching; offers its curriculum in a non-traditional "learning objects" style; charges low tuition fees; has a modest physical plant and student services; and is the most cost-effective public university in the state system.[15]

Governance. The traditional governance structure of universities is described as bicameral, the two governing bodies being a senate and a board of governors. In his book *University Leadership and Public Policy in the Twenty-First Century*, Peter MacKinnon, former president of the University of Saskatchewan, provides an excellent description of the respective roles of these two bodies.[16] Essentially, the senate is the senior academic body. It is dominated by rank-and-file academics, and its decisions traditionally reign supreme on academic matters, including the creation and dissolution of programs, admission standards, and tenure and promotion processes. The board of governors is the ultimate decision maker and authority on financial matters, including budgeting; resource allocation; the setting of tuition fees; the securing of loans, mortgages, or property; and renovations and the construction of new buildings.

In theory this is a clear division of authority. In practice, though, the waters are considerably muddier. First, there is, and should be, a linkage between academic decisions and resource allocation. It makes little sense for a senate to approve a new program only to have the board refuse to allocate any resources to it. Similarly, it makes little sense for a senate to cap or reduce enrolment if incremental student tuition is deemed necessary to keep the university financially sustainable. This has led some universities to add another management layer to these two bodies, often called a University Planning or University Budgeting Committee and typically consisting of membership from both senate and board to advise both bodies and presumably better align their decisions.

Perhaps the greatest change to the traditional bicameral governance structure has been the emergence of faculty unions. Faculty in virtually all Canadian universities are unionized. The exceptions are some of the most highly ranked universities in Canada, such as the University of Toronto and McGill, whose faculty are organized into "associations" that bear many, but not all, of the rights and responsibilities of a formal union. Unions now make university governance a "three-legged stool" as, through the

bargaining and collective agreement processes, unions now seek –
and in many cases have obtained – a role in matters that in the
past have been considered rights of senate or management. These
include the setting of salaries and workloads, various terms and
conditions of employment and tenure, and promotion processes.
A tripartite structure is not the most effective or efficient way of
running a large, complex institution like a modern public university. It means, though, that aside from the university executive
leadership, there are three other major voices in any decision to
initiate serious academic reform – senate, board, and union – and
these disparate voices often do not sing in unison or harmony.

These governance arrangements may also violate basic principles of performance management and accountability. In principle,
the person or organization charged with making a decision should
be accountable for that decision and bear the consequences, both
positive and negative, of that decision. That is not the general rule
in universities. The dichotomous roles of senate and board already
mean that one body can undermine the decisions of the other.
A prominent job of the university president is to make sure that
this does not happen. More importantly, those in senate, board,
or hybrid planning and budgeting committees are insulated from
the decisions they make. When I first got to the University of Calgary in 2001, even a quick perusal of the budget revealed that the
university was in dire financial condition and would have to make
some tough decisions and choices to maintain sound finances and
a balanced budget. The board agreed with my suggestion that we
embark on a three-year plan to repair the university finances. The
plan involved two years of modest deficits but a return to a balanced budget by year three. In year three, the University Budget
Committee implored me to minimize some of the tough decisions
that would return the university to a balanced financial state, their
argument being that if we had run deficits for two years why could
we not for a third? I responded by saying that the consequences
of that decision fell unequally on them and me. If we failed to live
up to the promise of a balanced budget by year three, they would
return to their offices and laboratories, they would continue to
receive the same salaries they had before, and they would continue

their teaching and research activities just as before. In contrast, the consequence to me was that the board would, rightly, fire me.

So how does this governance conundrum contribute to the inability of universities to initiate and expedite significant curriculum change?

First, it slows everything down tremendously. I have spared readers a description of the innumerable committees a proposed curriculum change must pass through at the department, faculty, senate, planning committee, and board levels before it can be approved. If John Evans and the Founding Fathers had had to navigate current approval structures, they might still be negotiating the introduction of PBL. It is not easy to delay a curriculum or program change for several years – what it typically takes to get a change through – but the bureaucratic and Byzantine nature of university governance makes it commonplace, even for routine or relatively minor program changes. By the time some of these curricular changes happen, the need or urgency for them may well have passed. Just witness the expansion of information technology programs in the late 1990s, which became vestigial once the programs actually got started because by then the IT bubble had burst. These snail-like approval processes not only slow things down, they also water them down. Everyone at every level has their say, and by the time a proposal has gone through the entire process, it may be so amended and compromised that the final product scarcely resembles what it was initially intended to be.

Second, it is not necessarily in the best interests of those who sit on the senate and board to see some curricular changes, especially significant ones like the starting of new faculties or other large new initiatives. Pedagogical innovations take resources, and the larger the initiative the more resources it will require. Those on senate appreciate that if resources flow to some new initiative it is not going to them. This inclination is exacerbated in times of resource constraints. Some might argue that boards, because their sole interest presumably is to defend and represent the public interest in the public university, might be immune to such considerations. But university boards today are more like representative bodies with membership from a variety of interest groups within the university – not just faculty but also staff groups, unions, under-graduates, and graduate students. These representatives often see their role as protecting the interests of their members; when an initiative arises that will consume resources or deflect faculty appointments to some other area, it is natural for stakeholders to worry about the impact this will have on their interest group. Sometimes board positions are held by government appointees who are more inclined to consider the presumed wishes of the government that appointed them rather than the best interests of the university, or by alumni who may pine to keep the university as it was in their day, or donors who themselves may have special interests.[17] In short, boards may not always be in the best position to assess or advance the strategic goals of the university, especially when an excursion into some bold new world is being considered.

Third, as MacKinnon has pointed out, unions are powerful forces within universities that may operate with a different mind-set than that of the university at large. Universities are, or at least should be, meritocracies. A new program or initiative means that some will be advantaged over others for the good of the academy. Unions are driven by egalitarian considerations and concerns that everyone be treated in the same way.

Finally, innovation means making choices. There are simply not enough resources in any university, no matter how good the times may be, to support all of the good ideas that arise in discussions of new programs or curriculum changes. Decisions have to be made. Priorities have to be set. Universities are predisposed to say yes to all these good ideas. Administrators, departments, senates, and boards do not like to say no to people's ideas and plans because they fear it will offend and because the ideas are often worthwhile. That is why the strategic plans of so many universities have far more "priorities" than can possibly be pursued and achieved at a reasonable level of quality. Universities have a difficult time saying no. As Clark Kerr, former president of the University of California, has noted, "in academic life, the power to say 'no' and the judgment to say it judiciously was much more important to the long-run quality of the endeavour than the power to say 'yes.' I came to agree that the easy 'yes' led to perdition, and the hard 'no' to distinction."[18] The easy "yes" leads to the spreading out of resources and absence of priorities, two consequences that inhibit innovation. The "no" is hard, but it enables consideration and implementation of new and innovative programs and curricula. Quite simply, as Krames distils in his book *Inside Drucker's Brain*, the best advice from one of the world's leading management gurus, Peter Drucker, is that "abandonment is the key to innovation – both because it frees the necessary resources and because it stimulates the search for the new that will replace the old."[19] To be more innovative, the administrative and governance bodies in universities have to get much better at abandoning the old and learning how to say no.

The inhibiting role of quality assurance processes. Quality assurance refers to processes used by universities and governments to assure themselves that universities pass a quality threshold and that the academic courses and programs offered by them surpass a desired quality level. In theory, this is a good thing to have. In practice, though, these processes can squelch attempts at academic innovation and transformative curricular change.

In their current form, quality assurance processes in Canada (often termed accreditation processes in the States) are highly bureaucratic and time consuming. Even after the years it takes for a university to approve a new program, the quality assurance process may take another number of years to approve it, an approval that is required for the university to receive funding for the program and the students enrolled in it. Even the most recent review of Ontario's Quality Assurance Council (which, by the way, is run by the universities themselves in violation of the generally accepted principle that a body should not evaluate itself) recommended that the council "lessen the bureaucratic and regulatory burden" inherent in its own processes and "increase transparency and accountability."[20]

The biggest problem is that the way most quality assurance and accreditation processes make their "quality" decisions is by asking whether the proposed new program or innovation looks like other programs that already exist.[21] As Brewer and Tierney write, "Accreditation fosters risk aversion and standardization, but by definition, aspiring new institutions [or programs] are start-up companies that must be risk takers and are often offering something new and different. Accreditation is a model that wants institutions to conform to norms, while new providers ... work against those norms."[22] The quality assurance mechanisms used in Canada to approve new programs or curricula suffer from the same problem.

I imagine how the following submission by John Evans to a current quality assurance body might be regarded:

> Every other medical school is a four-year program; our students will finish in three. Every other medical school starts by putting students in large lecture halls for two years with experts lecturing to them in the traditional disciplines (like anatomy, physiology, biochemistry). Our students will learn in small groups, will be guided by a tutor (who might be a non-expert), and will be expected to self-learn material to solve problems in a systems-like approach that will require them to integrate knowledge across the traditional disciplines. We will put them in clinical settings from day one. Oh, by the way, we will have no exams. A student's progress through the program will be based upon a satisfactory/unsatisfactory assessment by the group's tutor. The transcript they receive at the end of the program will look unlike anything else offered by other medical schools.

My suspicion is that in today's environment Evans would be laughed out the door, assuming he was ever invited in the first place. Approval decisions that ask whether any proposed new program resembles what already exists are not a recipe that encourages innovation. Rather, they inhibit it.

The quality assurance processes we now impose, especially given their time-consuming and bureaucratic nature, discourage innovative approaches to university education. One might also ask whether they are even necessary. Suppose that University of Toronto, McGill, UBC, University of Alberta, McMaster, or any one of a host of other Canadian universities wants to introduce a new program or teach in a different way. These universities are some of the most highly ranked in the world. Do we really think they would propose a new way of doing things that they believe to be of low quality or little worth? Do we really believe that some bureaucratic quality assurance process managed by perhaps less-qualified persons and/or functionaries is an effective way of assuring quality? The government has already accredited the public universities in its jurisdiction by granting them a charter to grant degrees. Presumably, therefore, the government has already decided they are of sufficient calibre to offer higher education in their province. If any one of these accredited universities wishes to try something new, why not just let them? If the government and public are concerned that some university does not have the ability to mount programs of reasonable quality, they should be asking themselves why that university was granted the right to operate in their jurisdiction in the first place.

We also should give a little credit to the ability of students to decide what programs are valuable and worthwhile to them. If students did not think Waterloo would graduate good engineers or McMaster good doctors, or if there were data showing the failure of these programs, then over time the enrolments in these programs would fall and the programs would fail and disappear. Although some might be hesitant to commit fully to a laissez-faire and free market quality assurance process, it should be noted that, whatever quality issues exist in the Canadian university system, a significant problem in our ability to deal with them may be the large issue of the lack of innovation and change. Quality assurance processes should worry less about policing – especially when so many of the variables they use to measure quality are inputs (e.g., are there adequate library resources? Do enough of the faculty have PhDs?) – and more about encouraging and enabling some much-needed experimentation and innovation in the higher education system.

How to Speed up Adoption of Pedagogical Innovations

What can we do to encourage more Waterloo- or McMaster-like experiments and innovations?

Organizational change requires a sense of urgency about the need for change to happen.[23] The creation of the University of

Waterloo was motivated by an urgent sense among Canadian industrialists that Canada and its economy would be uncompetitive unless we could educate more engineers and technologists. The creation of McMaster Medical School was motivated by its founders' urgent and deep sense of the inappropriateness of then-current methods of educating doctors and of the need for more doctors to be family physicians who were integrated in their communities. While some in the higher education world today have a similar sense of urgency, the absence of transformative education initiatives suggests that, in today's environment, a sense of urgency may no longer be sufficient to promote change at the level of a Waterloo or McMaster Medical School.

What may be needed is some external crisis. Crises, or a burning platform, motivate speedy change. The crises one often thinks of in the university context are financial ones. The chipping away of university resources, especially the reduction in government grants that was documented in earlier chapters, may not yet be of sufficient magnitude to motivate more excursions into innovative curricula and programming. More extreme reductions might be the stimulus needed. A desirable way to motivate change? No, but perhaps an effective one. Some have opined that a university bankruptcy would provide the signal and urgency for more innovation. This is something that is unlikely to be permitted in Canada.

The effect of the COVID pandemic on universities – the subject of chapter 10 – may represent a crisis of sufficient magnitude and scope to force change in Canada's university sector. No sane individual wants to motivate change in this way, but changes at universities as a result of the pandemic may fall into the category of "never letting a crisis go to waste."

Another possible stimulus for change might be to enable greater competition in the higher education sector in Canada. As noted earlier, Canada does not have a significant or material private university system. The Canadian higher education sector is also highly regulated, and many provinces have rules and regulations that make it difficult for private, non-traditional institutions to set up in their provinces. It is conceivable, if not probable, that the constraints on the importation or creation of new, non-traditional private higher education institutions will be relaxed in Canada or that public universities (or some components of them) that currently receive very little government funding will elect to go private to remove themselves from the shackles of government control and regulation.

Recommendation for reform: Enabling of greater competition in the higher education space by a relaxation of government regulation to permit easier and faster experimentation in universities and easier incorporation and establishment of non-traditional higher education providers

It would be unfortunate and regrettable if truly dire financial circumstances or a university failure were the impetus to motivate more rapid change. Breeding greater competition may be the most sanguine strategy to promote and encourage innovation and experimentation in Canada`s higher education sector. This will require governments to relax regulations and constraints that inhibit the creation of new institutions and the expansion of innovative institutions from other jurisdictions. The lesson of the University of Minnesota-Rochester is that the goal is to build large numbers of new, innovative, highly focused, low-cost public universities. Their success could encourage the creation of similar new institutions from scratch, given the difficulty of trying to reform current ones. The most significant barrier to the creation of such institutions will be the objections of existing universities and the straitjacket of undue government regulation. Such innovation will also require more belief in the ability of markets to influence higher education. Presumably, new initiatives that are viewed as valuable and worthwhile will succeed. Those that are not will fall by the wayside.

chapter eight

Are Canadian Universities Sustainable?

Universities Canada, the advocacy group representing Canada's universities, estimates that in 2019 approximately 1.4 million Canadians were enrolled in Canada's universities.[1] This massive education burden is shouldered by only slightly more than 100 universities across Canada. Canada would have 450 or so universities if it were to match the United States in the number of four-year degree-granting institutions per population.

These relatively few Canadian universities make an enormous contribution to individuals, to help them achieve their personal and professional aspirations, and to the country as it enjoys the public benefits we know university graduates return to society. These benefits will continue in the future only if these institutions are healthy and sustainable, a concern of many observers given the pressures and challenges universities currently face today.

Are Canadian Universities Sustainable?

The term "sustainability" in the university context is used in two interrelated ways.[2] First, in a strictly financial sense it refers to the balance between the university's revenues and its expenses. Simply put, does a university have enough money to cover its bills? If the institution has enough income to meet its ongoing expenses, then it is sustainable. If the university does not have enough income to meet its ongoing expenses, then it is unsustainable and, like other entities in the same situation, should go bankrupt.

In a university, the main sources of revenue are the grant of public funds it receives from its provincial government and the tuition and fees paid by students to attend the institution. Major expenses include, predominantly, salaries and benefits for employees (faculty and staff), the maintenance of the physical plant, and the procurement of needed material and supplies, including everything from laboratory equipment to library acquisitions to paper for the photocopying machines.

The second, loftier, and more appropriate question about "sustainability" in the university context refers to whether the institution has the resources and capacities required to maintain and sustain its desired high level of academic quality. If it does not have sufficient resources to mount and sustain the academic quality it wishes to offer, and the quality of the academic experience consequently suffers, then it is academically unsustainable.

Canadian universities are financially sustainable. We do not read about Canadian universities failing to make a payroll run, defaulting on loans, or going under. On those occasions where an institution is on the verge of one of these dire events (and such occasions do arise), the government typically steps in and advances future grant funds or excuses or covers obligatory payments. As one senior provincial minister of higher education once told me when asked if his government would allow a university to go bankrupt, "We would never allow a public university to go under." To paraphrase the attitude governments took regarding the possible failure of major financial institutions in the 2009 recession, apparently governments regard Canadian public universities as too important to fail. Canadian university administrators have also become very creative and expert in exercising the elasticity of their budgets to prevent a catastrophic financial failure.

By contrast, it is generally conceded that Canadian universities are *academically* unsustainable. A deep analysis by four knowledgeable veterans of the Ontario system in 2009 concluded that a steady decline into mediocrity was inevitable without some fundamental reforms to sustain academic quality in the Ontario university system.[3] This conclusion was reinforced in 2013 by an expert panel, which, following a review of plans submitted by all twenty Ontario universities, concluded that the Ontario university system is "not sustainable if the quality of the system is to be maintained."[4] There is no reason to think that the situation is different in any other province. Even the Ontario provincial government, an organization that typically is not predisposed to talk about unsustainability and quality concerns in its public sector, concluded that "The current system is unsustainable from a financial and quality perspective."[5] And, as Robert Campbell, then president of Mount Allison University, one of Canada's premier undergraduate universities, said in a 2011 conference titled *Transforming Canadian University Undergraduate Education*, "We all feel and know that the character of the undergraduate experience has deteriorated in our lifetimes, especially so in the last decades. And we know in our heart of hearts that this experience can and should be much better."[6]

Ironically, the reasons Canadian universities are academically unsustainable is precisely because of the manoeuvres they are required to make to keep themselves financially sustainable. In general, university annual revenues are increasing – by somewhere in the order of 4 to 5 per cent per year or more – because of increasing government grant, increased tuition revenue, and a host of other smaller revenue sources such as investment returns and philanthropy. But expenses are also increasing. There are the following non-trivial costs to accommodate: enrolment growth (which is almost always a requirement for securing additional government grant), which fuels the need for more instructors and facilities; inflationary increases in the cost of services, materials, and supplies, which are typically 1 to 2 per cent above the traditional Consumer Price Index; and salary and benefit increases for employees, which over the last decade or so have increased by about 1 to 2 per cent above the rate of inflation – a particularly demanding cost increase given that compensation represents about 75 per cent (or more) of a university's annual operating costs. In short, revenue increases are not keeping pace with the rise in expenses, leaving few or no financial resources to sustain or improve quality.

In responding to these realities, university administrators have made decisions that allow them to pay the bills, thus maintaining financial sustainability, but that diminish quality, with a predictable negative impact on academic sustainability. Decisions made in the service of financial sustainability include the following: hiring fewer instructors despite enrolment increases; transferring more of the instructional load from higher-paid tenured professors to part-time instructors; reducing library acquisitions and library hours; delaying the purchase of new laboratory equipment; reducing investment in technology and other digital systems; reducing the level of student services; offering fewer courses and increasing class sizes; and deferring needed maintenance and/or refurbishment of the physical plant. The extent of the erosion of infrastructure in Canada's universities is alarming. An October 2019 study by the Canadian Association of University Business Officers reports that the total deferred maintenance liability in Canadian universities has grown from $12.7 billion in 2014 to $17.2 billion in 2019, a 30 per cent increase. Thirty-six per cent of this maintenance backlog is deemed "critical or potentially critical," and the expectation is that the quality of the physical plant in Canadian universities will continue to diminish.[7]

The public university system in Canada is academically unsustainable, and the environment in which it operates has resulted in a downward spiral in quality over many years. This trend benefits no one. As various commentators have noted, there is a need for reform of Canada's public university system if quality is to be maintained or enhanced. So, what are some possible solutions to redress and reverse the quality decline?

Solutions to the Sustainability Challenge: Revenue Increases

More government funding: The traditional response in Canada to the sustainability problems universities face is to place the blame at the feet of government and to complain about inadequate government funding. One might think of this as the "Oliver" solution, which, like Oliver in the eponymous play, has university presidents going to government with hands outstretched and asking for "more." This approach is not unjustified, however, since the amount of public funding provided to universities in Canada has been relatively flat or in decline for many years. At this point, the public, although still the largest single contributor to university revenues, accounts on average for only about 47 per cent of university revenue, and for some universities the percentage is considerably less. The public is now a minority shareholder in Canada's public universities.[8] As James Duderstedt, a former president of the University of Michigan, once quipped, public (state) universities were once state funded, then became state assisted, and now are state located. The Canadian public university system is following suit.

Would increased government funding help universities? Of course, and there are compelling arguments for increased public support, especially in some provinces. There are several reasons, though, why increased government funding is unlikely to solve the university academic sustainability problem. First, by international standards, Canada is already funding its public universities more handsomely than many other countries. Canadian public universities still enjoy a higher percentage of public funding than US public universities, which have seen a far more dramatic decrease in government funding than Canadian institutions. Second, governments recognize that they have little control over how universities spend their funds, which are not necessarily allocated to activities that the government or students would want. For example, the decade or so after the Liberal government of Dalton McGuinty initiated Ontario's "Reaching Higher" initiative were golden years for funding increases in that province. Yet it was in those same years that concerns about the quality of the student experience became most acute. Although much of the incremental funding went to increasing student scholarships, a comprehensive analysis by the Ontario University Student Alliance showed that much also went to increasing the compensation of existing faculty rather than being used to hire new faculty to accommodate enrolment growth.[9] It is also likely that a non-trivial percentage of these incremental funds went to enhance the research infrastructure of universities – a non-core concern of provincial governments (and an issue I return to later). Third, governments have become increasingly frustrated and concerned with what they perceive to be the university's lack of responsiveness to issues such as job preparedness and skills gaps that are of prime concern to governments and students. As former Ontario Premier Dalton McGuinty, a great champion of education, once said in a meeting with the Toronto *Globe and Mail*'s editorial board, "Can I honestly say that I have got qualitative improvements as a result of these investments [in postsecondary education]? I don't think so, and we need to talk about that ... We have not demanded the same kinds of accountability that we have had with our hospitals and elementary and secondary schools."[10] Governments are also aware that a comprehensive, Canada-wide analysis of the relationship between universities' funding and performance has revealed that, at least within the funding ranges now provided in Canada, the performance of universities bears little correlation to the amount of funding they receive.[11] Finally, even if governments were inclined to provide more funding to public universities, the reality is that government coffers are strained, and other social issues, especially health care, now have greater call on the public purse. The need for additional health care funding is now the prominent concern of the public and governments, and the imperative to sustain (if not improve) a fragile and unsustainable health care system now boxes out the funding available from government to support public universities or address many other social needs. These trends will only be exacerbated as a result of the COVID pandemic; the financial and economic manoeuvres that will be necessary to address the huge deficits countries like Canada have incurred to keep their citizens and the economy going during COVID will likely limit the financial support governments can grant to our public universities.

Higher tuition: The tuition and fees paid by students are the other major revenue sources of universities. In fact, higher tuition has been the main source sustaining university revenues in light of government cutbacks. By 2017, tuition and fees accounted for an average 28 per cent of universities' annual revenues, rising to 50 per cent or more for many institutions, particularly smaller, less research-intensive ones. Over the last ten years, university income from student tuition and fees has increased by 76 per cent and from government by just 2 per cent. Over this period, increasing revenue from students has largely made up for the erosion of public funding. Student arguments for a greater say in how universities budget and spend their funds is reinforced by the fact that they are now becoming the majority shareholders in Canada's public university system.[12]

Why, then, do universities not employ the strategy of simply increasing tuition to assure themselves of adequate revenue to sustain the institution? Aside from the moral and public relations arguments against rapid tuition increases, the reality is that in Canada universities do not have the unfettered right to set tuition levels. Rather, governments regulate the tuition and fees universities can charge. In the past, at times of serious cutbacks in government funding, they allowed universities to increase tuition levels dramatically, thus enabling them to mitigate the consequences of reduced public funding. This, among other measures, allowed Alberta and Ontario universities, for example, to weather the dramatic Klein and Harris government cuts in the 1990s. But times have changed. The political dynamic now, resulting from a very effective student lobby and populist concerns, drives governments to limit the tuition increases they will permit, even as they may decrease public funding. Universities can now expect government to limit annual tuition increases to, at best, the rate of inflation or – as is more likely – to zero or less-than-inflation. At worst, in 2019, the Ontario government, at a time when it was decreasing public funding of its universities, cut tuition by 10 per cent. If the arguments being made in the United States for "free tuition" for public colleges and universities take hold in Canada, as they often do even though they may be quite inappropriate in this country, then universities might expect government to impose even greater restrictions on tuition increases. In short, it seems unlikely that substantially increased tuition revenues are in the cards, not even with the more limited deregulation of tuition for some programs that in the past allowed high-cost programs such as engineering, medicine, and law to boost their revenues through dramatic tuition increases.

Research funding: The mandate of universities is to educate and to conduct research. We read often about significant government programs that result in multimillion-dollar grants to universities to conduct research. Research and development activity in Canada is more dependent on the contribution of universities, compared to private research facilities or the private sector, than in every other OECD country. Regrettably, research funding provides no solution to the sustainability challenge. In fact, paradoxically, at least in terms of sustaining the quality of teaching programs, research makes the problem even worse.

Research funding is granted to universities on a competitive basis and is earmarked for the specific research desired by the research and granting funders. These funds are held in trust accounts, administered by the researcher, and can be used only for the designated purpose and activities that advance the aims of the research program. They cannot be used to support the general operations of the university. These research funds typically cover the *direct* costs of research: the salaries of the team (but not necessarily of the primary faculty researcher); the costs of conducting the research, such as the purchase of equipment, supplies, and materials; and travel and meeting expenses to enable the research team to engage with research colleagues, collaborate with others outside of their university who can advance the research program (research now is an international business), and attend conferences and meetings to report and disseminate their findings. But there is a significant cost of research to the university beyond these direct costs. These so-called *indirect costs* are the funds needed to maintain the research infrastructure that allows the research to happen, such as the buildings and laboratories used by the researchers; the heat, water, gas, and other utilities needed to support research activities; and the library resources and journal subscriptions that allow the researchers to stay at the top of their fields. These *indirect* costs are non-trivial, typically making up 40 per cent or more of the total costs. Canada, unfortunately, rarely covers the full indirect costs of research. Perversely, the largest research universities in Canada, such as University of Toronto, McGill, and UBC, receive the lowest percentage support of indirect costs as compared to less research-intensive universities. Yet, this extensive and expensive research infrastructure must be maintained. The unfortunate reality is that for Canadian universities, doing research is a losing financial proposition.

So, where do the funds to support the indirect costs of research come from? Government grants and some other grants from research funders are accompanied by a contribution to the indirect costs of the research program, although they typically do not cover the full indirect costs. Since we expect universities to do research, and we expect the most research-intensive universities to do the bulk of it, universities have no choice but to subsidize their research efforts by drawing from other sources of revenue, especially tuition and government grants, two sources of funds that in theory should be used exclusively to fund the education mission of universities. In short, the research mandate of the university is being subsidized by its education activities, so more research actually amplifies the challenge of maintaining a high-quality and academically sustainable education experience for students.

Philanthropy. Readers of Canada's newspapers regularly encounter large ads by universities thanking a generous donor for a philanthropic gift, often in the tens of millions of dollars. Universities vigorously pursue donations, benefactions, and gifts to help cover the costs of their operations or to create new programming. Campaigns to raise funds are now common among universities, and the targets of these multi-year efforts can be in the tens or hundreds of millions of dollars for the smaller and middle-sized universities, or the billions for the larger ones. The results are obvious; the endowments of Canadian universities have increased substantially.

Philanthropic giving has resulted in the building of some spectacular facilities, the recruiting or retention of world-class faculty, the funding of internationally recognized research, significant increases to scholarships and financial aid for students, and the development or improvement of academic programs. Canada's university system would be greatly diminished were it not for universities' intense engagement in fundraising. But despite these successes, it is unlikely, at least in the near future, that philanthropy will help much to ameliorate a university's sustainability challenge. Fundraising successes, especially for the large gifts, are episodic, while the sustainability challenge is chronic and ongoing. Furthermore, gifts, especially the large ones we read about, are often in the form of endowments that are intended to go on forever. So, the capital is never spent. Rather, to preserve the real value of the original endowment, only about 3 to 5 per cent – or $600,000 to $1 million of a $20 million donation – is spent annually. That is why one of Canada's most generous university donors, Seymour Schulich, argues for spending down the donation capital, or at least insisting on a significant annual spending rate, even if it erodes the real value of the original benefaction.[13] Finally, philanthropic giving and endowments in Canada's universities make up a relatively small proportion of revenue, especially when compared to the big American universities. In 2017, the three universities in Canada with the largest endowments were Toronto, McGill, and UBC, with endowments of approximately $2.4 billion, $1.65 billion, and $2.18 billion, respectively.[14] In contrast, the private universities of Harvard, Yale, and Stanford had accumulated endowments, in Canadian dollar terms, of $47 billion, $27 billion, and $33 billion, respectively.[15] Even public universities and small, private, liberal arts colleges in the States may have significantly larger endowments than the biggest Canadian institutions. More importantly, the Canadian institutions with the largest accumulated endowments are very large universities (Toronto has a student enrolment of more than 85,000 students; McGill has 41,000; UBC has 63,000), so the money available to spend per student is considerably smaller in Canada than in the United States (for comparison, Harvard has about 20,000 students, Yale has 15,000, and Stanford has 17,000).

So, philanthropy helps, and the efforts of universities to diversify their revenue base by pursuing donations are important. But donations alone are not yet and may never become large enough to make much of a dent in the ongoing efforts of universities to balance their revenues and expenses. We should also not ignore the tensions and concerns created on university campuses as more funding is sought from the corporate and private sectors.

Ancillary operations: Anyone who has visited a university campus recently will recognize that it runs some big businesses, such as residences, dining halls, parking lots, bookstores, and the occasional hotel. These so-called ancillary services bring in considerable amounts of revenue. Ancillary operations, though, are not designed to generate a profit that can be used by the university to defray the costs of academic programs and research. Rather, the requirement of these ancillary services is that they generate enough revenue to meet the expenses of mounting the activity. So, residence fees, for example, have to be sufficient to build the residence, staff it, maintain it in good working order, and maintain an adequate contingency fund to address future liabilities. Universities consider themselves lucky if these basic requirements are met. Often, they are not, which explains the increasing tendency for universities to outsource services such as student accommodation, dining halls, and bookstores in the hope that private sector management might relieve the university of the financial burden of running these operations. Notwithstanding universities' best efforts, there is commonly a constant battle between the university and student groups as the university charges students more and more every year to maintain these student services.

Increasing international enrolment: One of the few recent positive stories for revenue generation is the significant rise in enrolment by international students. The number of international students attending postsecondary institutions in Canada has risen dramatically, from about 60,000 students in 2000 to more than 300,000 in 2018. International students now constitute about 14 per cent of total postsecondary enrolments in Canada. This huge increase results from intense recruiting efforts by colleges and universities, especially in China and India; these two countries account for about half of all international enrolments.[16] Canada's comparative success in international recruiting relative to other countries also reflects the more recent hesitation of foreign students to study in other, previously more popular, destination countries such as the United Kingdom and the United States. Brexit and the policies of the Trump presidency have been a boon to international student enrolment in Canada.

While the motivation to enrol international students is purported to be a desire by Canadian institutions to provide domestic students with a more international and diverse campus life – and it does do this – a predominant reason for these intense international recruiting efforts is to raise additional revenue. International students pay higher tuition than Canadian students, as the amount they pay is intended to cover both the average tuition and the grant component of their education. Foreign undergraduate-level students pay on average three and a half times the Canadian tuition rate. But since the cost of adding an international student to the student population is a marginal cost, the higher tuitions they pay represent a windfall revenue source to the institution. For as long as this strategy is successful and Canada is able to increase its share of the international higher education business, the revenues accruing to universities are substantial – dramatic in the case of some institutions with a high percentage of international students.

The strategy of trying to remain sustainable by pursuing more revenue from foreign students has challenges and risks. International students create additional costs for the institution for things like language instruction, academic counselling, cultural acclimatization, and immigration services that go beyond the needs of domestic students. Also, as international enrolments rise there is increasing concern that fewer spots may be available for Canadian students. Finally, while there is no doubt that increased international fees represent a much-needed revenue infusion for cash-strapped universities, the funding is precarious and volatile. International enrolments, for a variety of reasons, can drop quickly.[17] Australia, a country that has pursued a very vigorous and successful international student enrolment strategy for years, has seen significant swings in international enrolments. Most recently, In February 2020, Australia banned entry to all foreigners from China in an attempt to stem the spread of the coronavirus, a move it understood would have significant revenue repercussions to its universities.[18] The intense concern among Canadian universities fearing a drop in international enrolments and the subsequent loss of international student tuition and fees as a result of the COVID-19 pandemic is realistic. Even before the pandemic, Canada had already experienced the liability of relying on international students. Several years ago, in response to a diplomatic spat with Canada, Saudi Arabia removed its trainees and funding from Canadian medical schools and hospitals, resulting in staffing shortages in our health care system and revenue drops for health care programs, especially physician training, that relied on Saudi revenue.

Sustainability requires that revenues and expenses are balanced and that there are sufficient resources to maintain the quality of academic programs that keep Canadian universities and their students competitive. For some time now, the actions Canadian universities have taken to pay their bills in an environment where expense growth is outstripping revenue growth have resulted in a steady erosion of the quality of the academic experience. There appears to be little runway left for increased revenues to solve the sustainability challenge. Although the specifics may vary from province to province, there is unlikely to be any appreciable increase in public funding from government (if anything, such funding will continue to erode); the political and public dynamic is not conducive to increased tuition revenue; and other potential sources of revenue, such as fundraising, ancillary operations, or international revenue, are not of the magnitude, structure, or certainty to appreciably affect sustainability.

The sustainability equation has two sides: increase revenues or decrease expenses. If the sustainability challenge is to be met, there is little choice but to consider strategies that will decrease expenditures or increase the productivity of existing faculty and staff within the boundaries of existing resources.

Solutions to the Sustainability Challenge: Expenditure Decreases

Salaries and benefits. Since compensation represents more than 70 per cent of annual university expenditures, the obvious first place to look to reduce costs is in salaries and benefits.

Salaries are paid to the following: *faculty* – full time and part time – who do the teaching and research; *administrators*, especially senior ones like presidents, vice-presidents, and deans; and *other staff*, who manage the university – everyone from the secretaries, to the IT staff, to the landscapers. Although there are typically twice as many "other staff" as "faculty," it is the wages paid to faculty and senior administrators that receive the greatest attention because these people are the highest paid in the university.

Canadian universities report regularly on administrator and faculty salaries, and the Canadian Association of University Teachers and Statistics Canada provide regular reports on the compensation paid to these individuals. The numbers provided in different reports do not match exactly as there are differences among these reports in terms of how people are classified and what compensation is reported. However, they do provide a good index of overall trends. We know even more now about the compensation paid to university personnel because of the many jurisdictions that now have "sunshine laws" that require disclosure of salaries of those in the broad public sector, including universities, who earn above some threshold, usually $100,000 per year or more. In Ontario, 85 per cent of faculty earn above the Sunshine List threshold.

Administrator salaries: Canadian university presidents earn well. As far back as 2011, there were presidents enjoying salaries and benefits exceeding half a million dollars per year, with many in the $400,000s. Presidents of even small universities, such as University of Regina, Brock, Lethbridge, and Trent, had salaries in the $300- and $400-thousand-dollar range.[19]

While these salaries surely position university presidents among the top 1 per cent of earners, in terms of financial compensation, the heads of Canadian universities are in the middle of the pack of university presidents internationally. A comparison of 2014 presidential salaries by Australia's National Tertiary Education Union showed that the average Canadian president earned $300,000 and those leading the top fifteen research-intensive universities in Canada (the so-called U-15) earned $440,000 (all in Australian dollars). In contrast, presidents of public and private universities in the United States earned $600,000 and $685,000 respectively. Australian university presidents earned an average of $860,000, and those leading their top eight research-intensive universities topped $1 million. Similarly, an analysis of 2016 presidential salaries showed that Canadian presidents' salaries lagged behind those in competitor countries. Presidents of Australian universities earned an average of $770,000 (all in Canadian dollars). Presidents of US public universities earned $660,000, and those leading universities in the United Kingdom averaged $510,000. In contrast, the average presidential salary in Canada's highest-paying province, Alberta, was $440,000, and Ontario presidential salaries averaged $365,000.[20]

While higher in absolute terms, the annual increases in presidential salaries have also lagged behind annual salary increases enjoyed by full-time faculty. Between 2003 and 2013, presidential pay rose by about 7 per cent, and average pay has levelled off even more or has even decreased. In contrast, during that same 2003–2013 period, salaries of full professors rose by 23 per cent, and salaries continue to increase, albeit at a reduced annual rate, for these professors. An analysis of salaries in Ontario derived from the annual required public salary disclosures reveals that presidential salaries rose by 4.8 per cent in the five-year period from 2006 to 2011 but actually decreased by 0.7 per cent in the subsequent five years from 2011 to 2016. In contrast, faculty salaries rose by 4.1 per cent in the three-year period from 2013 to 2016.[21]

The president's salary and overall contract are negotiated and approved by the university's board of governors, who are mindful of the competitive market for the top talent they seek to recruit to lead the institution. Recently, some provinces – such as Alberta and Ontario – have passed legislation to cap salaries paid to chief executives in the public sector, and this includes university presidents. There is concern that this may limit the pool of candidates willing to fill these senior administrative positions.

Universities are complex organizations, and there is a fair cohort supporting the management and administration of the university, aside from the university president. In university circles, particularly in the aftermath of the salary disclosures and media reports emanating from them, some point to what they perceive to be an inordinate increase in the number of administrators; the pejorative term used to refer to this phenomenon is "administrative bloat." Even though compensation for the total administrative staff has been increasing essentially at the same rate as salaries and benefits for faculty (since 2000, administrative compensation has increased by about 3.4 per cent above inflation and faculty compensation by about 3.2 per cent above inflation), a suggestion made not infrequently is that both the number and salaries of administrators should be reduced, with the ensuing salary savings diverted to provide greater direct support to the academic mission and activities of the university. This could be done. But supporters of this view may wish to consider the following: modern universities are complex organizations that regularly face increases to an already large and odious management, regulatory, and reporting burden imposed on them by government, students, and the public. Someone has to look after the management of these complex institutions, some of which boast annual budgets of more than a billion dollars per year and thousands of employees. As Stanley Fish, a very insightful commentator on the university, has pointed out, the faculty need the administrators because they are the ones that do the tough managerial tasks to keep the university afloat and ensure that faculty and university resources are managed properly so that faculty are able to stay focused on their primary jobs of teaching and research. Or, as he puts it so eloquently, "You need administrators to develop and put in place and, yes, administer the policies and procedures that enable those who scorn them [i.e., the faculty] to do the work they consider so much more valuable than the work of administration."[22] We should also remember that the efforts of some administrative staff actually bring additional revenue to the university. Aside from the president, these include fundraisers, government relations and marketing personnel, and international student recruiters. Without the additional revenue brought in by these people, the sustainability challenge faced by universities would be even more dire. Finally, although there is no doubt that expenditures on administration have increased, even if one were to dramatically cut the number of administrators or impose draconian cuts to their salaries, no matter how cathartic such actions might be to some, the overall financial impact of these manoeuvres might not make much of a dent in the substantial sustainability challenge faced by universities.[23]

Faculty salaries. In 2018, Canada's public universities employed 46,440 full-time faculty. It is not uncommon to hear some university faculty express the opinion that "the faculty are the university." As arrogant and self-centred as this may sound to some, the sentiment is correct. The reputation, profile, capacity, quality, worth, and contributions of any university are a direct reflection of the reputation, profile, capacity, quality, worth, and contributions of its faculty. As James Duderstadt, former president of the University of Michigan, wrote, "The principal academic resource of a university is its faculty. The quality and commitment of the faculty determine the excellence of the academic programs of a university, the quality of its student body, the excellence of its teaching and scholarship, its capacity to serve broader society through public service, and the resources it is able to attract from public and private sources."[24] One should be cautious about tinkering with any policy or practice that affects the quality, composition, or capacity of faculty, especially full-time tenured faculty.

The salaries and benefits paid to full-time faculty in Canada represent 34 per cent of the annual expenditures of the university, a number that has changed little over the years. The most junior professors – assistant professors – earn an average of $109,000. The most senior professors – full professors – average $171,000 per year. Not surprisingly, average faculty salaries depend on the type of university in which a professor works. Faculty teaching at so-called doctoral universities with a medical school and extensive graduate and professional programs (think University of Toronto, McGill, UBC, McMaster, etc.) earn an average of 20 per cent more than faculty working at primarily undergraduate institutions (think Acadia, Mount Allison, Trent, Bishop's, etc.). The differences between faculty salaries in different institutions can be dramatic. For example, the average professorial salary at the University of Toronto is $170,000. At Acadia it is $112,550. In spite of this earnings gap within Canada, salaries of faculty at our most research-intensive universities, which represent the largest, most prestigious, and most competitive international institutions, can trail salaries enjoyed by their peers at American universities by as much as 44 per cent, although faculty working at typically smaller, less comprehensive, and less research-intensive public Canadian universities out-earn their counterparts in US public institutions by 25 to 40 per cent.[25] The earnings gap between research-intensive US and Canadian institutions places some of Canada's best universities at a competitive disadvantage as they try to recruit top-ranked faculty from around the world. Perhaps this is the Canadian way, but it is why the government has introduced some funding programs, such as the Canada 150 Research Chairs Program, to try to level the playing field and help Canadian universities recruit world-class talent.[26] As noted earlier, full-time faculty salaries, through a combination of across-the-board increases and contractual provisions of funding "progress through the ranks" (seniority), have been increasing by about 2 to 3 per cent above the rate of inflation, although this varies across jurisdictions. At this point, adjusted for purchasing power parity, overall, Canadian full-time faculty appear to be the highest-paid faculty members in the world.[27]

The great majority of full-time faculty are on lifetime contracts. After a lengthy probationary period and a rigorous assessment of their contributions, they are granted tenure. Tenure was introduced at the turn of the twentieth century, and it is inextricably tied to the understood benefit to the academy and society of ensuring professors' academic freedom. The practical outcome of this policy, which is a common feature of employment for tenured faculty in almost all North American universities, is that even though academics are subject to regular performance reviews, they are very rarely fired, and the institution cannot terminate them simply for financial reasons or on the basis of organizational restructuring of programming. In practice, universities hold an iron-clad salary commitment to the tenured faculty cohort for the lifetime of their careers, which can be thirty-five years or more.

Prior to 2000, tenured faculty in many provinces were subject to mandatory retirement, which required them to retire at the age of sixty-five. The requirement for tenured faculty to retire at age sixty-five had been subject to challenge several times. In a 1990 landmark decision, the Supreme Court of Canada ruled, in *McKinney v. University of Guelph*, that while mandatory retirement might be taken as a violation of constitutional rights, it could be permitted because of the peculiar nature of the employment contract held by professors, specifically the life-long contract of tenure, and the need for the university to have some mechanisms to renew the faculty. The existence of mandatory retirement was crucial to universities to sustain themselves when faced with dramatic funding cuts – such as the Klein cuts in Alberta and the Harris cuts in Ontario – because they could introduce early retirement incentives for faculty who were facing imminent retirement anyway and thereby could reduce their faculty salary bill. In the absence of mandatory retirement, when faculty cannot be forced to retire, there is no incentive for faculty to take early or even age sixty-five retirement, and the fear of many a university administrator is that in the absence of mandatory retirement, early retirement incentives may not be effective, with perhaps the better faculty leaving and the less productive ones staying. The earlier Supreme Court ruling notwithstanding, universities continued to forward compelling arguments for the abolition of mandatory retirement, reflecting both human rights considerations and concern over the loss of talented faculty to jurisdictions where there was no mandatory retirement. Pressure to end mandatory retirement in all of Canada continued and eventually succeeded. Not unexpectedly, following eventual removal of mandatory retirement provisions in 2006, the number of faculty over age sixty-five has grown, exacerbating the sustainability challenge (because older professors earn more than junior professors) and limiting the opportunities for more hiring of junior faculty.

The requirement for mandatory retirement had been lost many years earlier in the American system. At the time of writing, the numbers of faculty over age sixty-five are increasing in Canada. In 2005, approximately 3 per cent of faculty were over age sixty-five. By 2018, that number had grown to 11 per cent. In Ontario, in 2005, before mandatory retirement was abolished, there were virtually no university professors over age sixty-five in the Ontario system. Now that percentage has risen to about 9 per cent. There has been a commensurate decrease in the number of junior professors in the system as a result.

There are indeed compelling arguments for not having mandatory retirement. But at least for the sustainability discussion, since older professors command higher salaries and typically continue to get salary increases, the abolition of mandatory retirement has exacerbated the salary problem of Canadian universities, not to mention limiting the opportunity for renewal of the professoriate.[28] The impact is not trivial. In Ontario, where the issue has been most closely studied, analyses show that if mandatory retirement had not been eliminated and faculty had continued to retire at age sixty-five, and if all of the retirees had been replaced by faculty age thirty-five and younger, universities could have maintained the same faculty complement as they now have but at a savings to the system of $89 million. Alternatively, with the continuation of mandatory retirement, the university system could have maintained the annual salary expenditure they had in 2016 but with an increase in faculty numbers of about 780 new professors, or about a 6 per cent increase in the total Ontario faculty complement.[29]

Limit salary increases to inflation or lower. Salary increases could be limited or capped to the rate of inflation or lower (of course, the same strategy could be equally applied to the salaries of all those, administrators included, who work in the university). The financial situation of Canada's universities would be quite different if salary increases over the last decade had not exceeded inflation.

Transfer more teaching to lower-paid academic staff. Expenses would be curbed if more teaching were done by instructors, who earn less than full-time faculty. Indeed, this is already happening as universities increasingly use part-time rather than full-time instructors to teach. These "sessional lecturers" (sometimes called contract academic staff) encompass a diverse group of instructors that includes working professionals (who provide disciplinary expertise, especially real-world experience), graduate students and postdoctoral fellows (where teaching opportunities represent part of their education and financial support), and a host of others, sometimes called itinerant or precarious workers, who earn by teaching one or more courses at one or more universities. In terms of sustainability, the important point is that part-timers are paid less than full-time faculty, so the more teaching done by part-timers the lower the overall instructional costs to the institution.

It is clear that this strategy is being used more and more by universities to maintain their program offerings in the face of increasing enrolments. The best data we have on the relative amount of the instructional load carried by part-time versus full-time faculty come from Ontario. (It is only recently that Statistics Canada, in spite of the voluminous data it accumulates on faculty numbers and salaries, has begun to measure the contribution of part-time instructors.) The Ontario Council of University Faculty Associations (OCUFA) estimates that the number of courses taught by part-time faculty has doubled since 2000.[30] At this point, according to the latest surveys by the Council of Ontario Universities (COU), part-timers make up 52 per cent of the academic workforce, and teach about 46 per cent of undergraduate students and 50 per cent of undergraduate courses.[31] For this strategy to really address the sustainability challenge, though, it must be coupled with a decrease in the number of tenured full-time faculty, a clear trend in the United States but one not evident in Canada, where full-time faculty numbers have remained stable or increased slightly. In addition, the increased reliance on sessional instructors or teaching-only faculty may be thought to undermine the historical argument that what distinguishes a university from a college is that the students are taught by teacher-scholars who are actively engaged both in transmitting knowledge and in research to advance the frontiers of knowledge in their disciplines.[32]

Increase productivity. If there is no additional revenue, expenses cannot be easily cut, the curriculum stays the same or more likely expands, and the number of students increases, a remaining strategy to support sustainability is to increase the productivity of the current workforce.

Productivity analyses are rarely embraced by universities but are increasingly the focus of governments and the public as part of their growing interest in what universities and their staff are doing with the public money they receive. There have been some attempts to increase productivity by amalgamating the corporate and back-room functions of several universities; negotiating buying consortia for everything from library acquisitions to paper clips; and outsourcing activities such as payroll and financial services, management of residences, and food services to the private sector. These strategies can save money and make universities more productive by freeing them to focus more of their time, attention, and resources on their core business of teaching and research. But the impact of these manoeuvres has been small. Not unlike the focus on faculty salaries, the productivity analyses that have received the greatest attention and have had perhaps the greatest impact on the quality of the academic experience are those that address the workloads of full-time faculty.

Full-time faculty are expected to teach, do research, and provide service to the institution and the profession. Although the distinction between these categories may be blurred, the usual expectation is that faculty will spend 40 per cent of their time on teaching, 40 per cent on research, and 20 per cent on service.

It is surprisingly difficult to answer what appears to be a simple question: "How much do university professors teach?" Historically, the amount faculty teach and whether teaching loads have changed over time have been closely guarded secrets, even though those within the university charged with the responsibility of assuring delivery of the curriculum – department heads, deans, and provosts – are surely aware of these data. Even now, when there are greater calls for disclosure and transparency on this issue, the answer depends very much on the type of institutions sampled, how "teaching" is defined and measured, which faculty are included in the sample, and which disciplines are studied. The ongoing debates in North Carolina, one of the earlier states pursuing these investigations, about how much teaching is done by tenure-stream and tenured faculty in the twelve campuses of the University of North Carolina provide an excellent example of the thorniness of this question and consequently the difficulty of generating solutions and new policies if changes are deemed to be in order.[33]

Analyses of faculty productivity and how much faculty teach are not new in the United States. Since the late 1980s, the National Center for Education Statistics has conducted national studies collecting information on faculty demographics, courses taught, and publications. For many years the United States has conducted a National Study of Instructional Costs and Productivity, also known as the Delaware Study, which provides data on faculty workload and corresponding financial data on faculty deployment and costs (a very small number of Canadian universities participate in this exercise).

Canada, more specifically Ontario, has entered the game of monitoring faculty workloads and contributions. One of the earliest systematic studies of teaching loads of Canadian full-time faculty was conducted by the Higher Education Quality Council of Ontario (HEQCO) in response to a government request for some analysis of the productivity of that province's university system. Data provided by four Ontario universities suggested that, overall, faculty were teaching an average of 3.4 courses per year. (A course is defined as a one-semester course. So, a professor teaching two courses in each of two semesters would have a workload of four courses.) Faculty in the sciences taught less than the average – 2.7 courses per year – and those in the humanities and social sciences taught more – 3.7 courses per year. Faculty members who were not active in research taught slightly more than those not active in research, but the difference was very small – less than a single one-semester course.[34] In a later study, HEQCO scoured publicly available data on the websites of ten Ontario universities in three departments – economics, chemistry, and philosophy – and generated an estimate of an average teaching load of 2.8 courses per year. Again, faculty not active in research taught slightly more (though less than one extra course) than research-active faculty.[35]

Subsequent extensive surveys by the Council of Ontario Universities (COU) of teaching loads in seventeen Ontario universities confirmed these teaching loads. It estimated that Ontario faculty teach an average of about 3.2 courses per year, with research-inactive faculty teaching less than one additional course to compensate for their lack of engagement in research.[36]

What do these data offer as possible solutions to allow universities to protect their sustainability by doing more with the resources they currently have?

One way is to simply increase the teaching loads of all faculty. There is a general perception that the teaching loads of full-time faculty have decreased over the years. There are more than 45,000 faculty members in Canada. If every full-time faculty member taught just one more course per year, there would be a significant increase in teaching capacity in Canada's universities without any additional hirings. This would certainly go a long way to decreasing the reliance on the use of part-time faculty.

But an increase in every faculty member's teaching load is a blunt instrument. There is also no suggestion that faculty in Canada are teaching less than their peers in other jurisdictions, and we do not wish to disadvantage Canadian faculty by jeopardizing the amount of time they devote to research. We could employ more surgical strategies. About 40 per cent of faculty receive some amount of relief from teaching to give them more time for research or administrative work. A more hard-nosed approach to how many faculty members are granted teaching release and for what purposes could increase teaching capacity and resources in the university. Finally, we could insist on equity of workloads for faculty. As was noted before, faculty work on an expectation of a 40 per cent commitment to research, 40 per cent to teaching, and 20 per cent to service. Yet, workload studies tell us that somewhere between 10 and 15 per cent of full-time faculty have no demonstrable research output. Given the 40–40–20 work expectation, it seems reasonable that research-inactive faculty should teach double what research-active faculty do, but they do not. The productivity implications of not insisting on equitable workloads are significant. In Ontario, if research-inactive faculty members taught twice the teaching load of their research-active colleagues, the overall teaching capacity of the full-time professoriate would increase by about 10 per cent, a teaching impact equivalent to adding about 1,500 additional faculty members across the province. Similarly, the COU workload reports tell us that between 17 and 20 per cent of full-time faculty make no service contribution, a commitment that should represent 20 per cent of their workloads, with no evidence of additional contributions in other areas to compensate for this lack.

An analysis of faculty workloads at University of Texas's flagship campus in its public system, UT Austin, underscores the potentially significant contribution a productivity perspective can make toward solving some of higher education's sustainability woes. It shows that a small portion of professors teach a majority of students and that a minority of faculty secure the majority of research funding.[37] This pattern is likely reflected in Canadian universities as well. The finding suggests that workloads can be redistributed without affecting the teaching or research mission and accomplishments of the university, accompanied perhaps with a substantial cost savings to the institution, to government (in the form of grants), and to students (in the form of reduced tuition).

In short, the funding mechanisms, regulatory regimes, and overall competitive environment of Canada's universities challenge the sustainability of these institutions. By contrast with examples in the United States, we are not seeing, and are unlikely to see, financial failures, bankruptcies, or universities going under. The Canadian public are unlikely to allow that to happen. Nova Scotia, in a planned and careful manner, has instituted a set of logical policies and reforms over many years to assist universities to meet their financial challenges based on the assumption that if a university, even with these strategies, were still unable to pay its bills, the province would allow it to fail. But, when push came to shove, even these hard-nosed plans got set aside when there was concern that a public university was going under.

Canadian universities are doing what they can to meet their financial challenges. But requests for more government funding are unlikely to provide the answer, for the reasons identified above. Why don't we see more activity in universities on solutions on the expenditure side, such as increasing teaching loads, or, at a minimum, insisting on equitable work contributions from faculty? The cynic will point out that as long as the problem is cast as a revenue problem – a failure of government to provide adequate funding – the erosion of quality can be blamed on government. But focusing on expenditure solutions requires the university to look inward and tackle any suboptimal policies, practices, and actions (or inactions) that may contribute to the erosion of quality. These are hard discussions and not ones a university looks forward to or is keen to promote or advertise.

Sustaining the quality of the Canadian public university system and ensuring that all of its students get the very best university education possible are important goals, and worries about public relations, politics, or who is to blame should not prevent action to achieve these goals. Solutions will require a collaborative, trusting, and productive relationship between universities and governments, something that is now in short supply.

We should not minimize the impact of the financial and academic sustainability challenges faced by Canadian universities. Ensuring that universities have the resources necessary to maintain the quality of their programs will require change. Some of that will involve creative efforts to diversify and increase the revenue base beyond the traditional sources of government grants and tuition. Some of it will require a re-examination of the pattern and nature of expenditures and efforts to decrease them, either through cost cutting, mitigation of expenditure increases, or improved productivity. These are actions that individual institutions can choose to take. Universities will need some assistance in making these changes. And, as some have suggested, there may not be a lot to be gained by squeezing individual institutions, especially given that governments regulate many of their financial inputs and outputs. Overcoming the sustainability challenge may require systemic changes in the way that governments manage and fund the public university systems in their province, the central issue discussed in chapter 6.

Recommendation for reform: Public disclosure of the workloads of faculty coupled to an equity-of-workload policy

Universities need no encouragement to lobby government and the public for more resources. This is already a highly developed and preferred strategy for addressing the financial challenges faced by the university system. But, as argued here, the opportunities for revenue solutions to sustainability challenges are limited. Solutions to the university's sustainability challenges are going to require some analysis of university expenditures.

Currently, there is little public debate or discussion in university circles about expenditure issues (although there is a lot of discussion in the back rooms). It is easier for universities to take on the government than to engage publicly in the divisive and difficult discussions required to reflect on and amend their internal processes.

Governments are increasingly attentive to the expenditure issues of universities. Part of this derives from their increased attention, in general, to how public institutions spend public funds and how governments can hold them accountable. In the current dynamic, governments are increasingly willing to intervene in the operations of public institutions. Universities are not exempt from these encroachments on their autonomy. If universities do not begin to attend to their expenditure and productivity issues, governments surely will step in. This is not desirable. What would be helpful is some sort of "nudge" to encourage universities to address these challenges. Public disclosure of faculty workloads might represent a useful nudge to accomplish this. Transparency about faculty productivity and about inequities in faculty contributions could lead to probing questions by government, students, and the public that will focus increased attention on these matters.

A senior university administrator once quipped to me that, in the eyes of the public, university faculty work 24/7 – twenty-four weeks a year and seven hours a week. My university experience, and even a quick perusal of the annual contributions in teaching, research, and service, will reveal a very different picture of what faculty do and accomplish. Not every faculty member will contribute in exactly the same way. It is reasonable that some may bias their time and contribution to teaching, research, or service. But universities can insist that, however their contribution is configured, every faculty member contributes equitably to the work of the academy. The data we have so far reveal that this is not always the case, and that the productivity and sustainability benefits of an equitable contribution by all can be substantial. Public disclosure of faculty workloads in teaching, research, and service would celebrate the accomplishments of Canadian university faculty and open the door to ensuring a more equitable distribution of effort and accomplishment in the institution.

chapter nine

Are Canadian Universities High Quality?

The topic that should dominate any serious analysis of Canada's or any other country's university system is the issue of quality. What is the quality of Canada's universities and the academic experience they offer to their students, and how does the quality of Canada's universities compare to that of other universities around the world? Physics has the concept of a "unified theory or principle." For universities, the unified principle is "quality." In higher education, quality is the issue that matters the most. Quality is what underpins all other aspects of and questions about universities. If the quality of a university or a university system is subpar or inadequate, it does not matter whether it is financially sustainable, how many students it enrols, how well it is managed or regulated, or how beautiful its buildings and physical plant may be.

These assertions about the primacy of "quality" in any assessment of a university system presuppose or require that we understand how to measure the quality of higher education institutions. The problem is that we don't. There are many opinions – and considerable debate – about how to measure the quality of a university. No consensus exists, and the debates and arguments about how to measure quality are often heated, even rancorous. This is good because it reflects people's appreciation of the significance and centrality of the quality question and the implications of identifying an institution as of low or high quality.

Two main strategies have been used to assess quality. The first and most commonly recognized method is to develop ranking systems that include variables that are presumed to reflect quality, or at least to provide reasonable proxies of it. The second is to assess quality by linking the outcomes and accomplishments of a university to its advertised or desired purposes and goals. I consider each of these approaches in turn.

University Rankings

There are many university ranking systems. Some of them rank universities around the world; others rank universities within a country or jurisdiction. Some of them rank the university as a whole; others restrict themselves to specific disciplines or fields of study. Wikipedia provides a useful review of the various international and national ranking systems.[1]

The ranking schemes that receive the greatest attention are those that attempt to compare universities across the world or all the universities in the same country.

The most recognized and influential global rankings of universities are the international Academic Rankings of World Universities (ARWU), the Quacquarelli Symonds (QS) World University Rankings, and the Times Higher Education (THE) World University Rankings.

The ARWU (also known as the Shanghai Ranking) was initiated from Shanghai Jiao Tong University in 2003. It is heavily biased toward research accomplishments, particularly in the natural sciences. It measures variables such as the number of articles the faculty have published in prestigious journals such as *Nature* and *Science*, the number of alumni and staff that have been awarded the prestigious Nobel Prizes and Fields Medals, and the number of highly cited researchers. Recent versions of this ranking also disaggregate overall university rankings into academic subject categories.

The QS World University Rankings scheme began in 2004. It is based heavily on assessments of the reputation of universities based on a survey of more than 94,000 individuals in higher education and more than 45,000 employers. The sole student- or teaching-related measures are the faculty-to-student ratio and the ratio of international students enrolled in the university. In 2011, in an attempt to provide a more granular analysis of a university's quality, QS broke down its global assessment of a university into subjects and disciplines.

The THE World University Rankings scheme was originally part of the QS ranking scheme but broke off from it in 2010 and partnered with Thomson Reuters with a new and expanded set of indicators. It also is biased toward research accomplishments and incorporates a strong reputational component offered by more than 10,000 academics in 133 countries.

The most recent versions of these three international rankings systems paint quite a consistent picture of how Canada's universities rank relative to universities internationally. In the 2019 AWRU ranking, which ranked 1,000 universities worldwide, the top 100 universities included the University of Toronto (no. 24), followed by University of British Columbia (UBC) (no. 35), and McGill and McMaster (tied at no. 90). The University of Alberta ranked in the 101–150 range, and the University of Calgary, Université de Montréal, University of Ottawa, and University of Waterloo ranked in the 151–200 category.[2] The 2020 QS Ranking identifies University of Toronto as the top-ranked Canadian university (no. 29), followed by McGill (no. 35), and UBC (no. 51). The only other Canadian universities breaking the top 200 were University of Alberta (no. 113), Université de Montréal (no. 137), McMaster (no. 140), and Waterloo (no. 173).[3] The 2020 THE rankings also identified University of Toronto as the top-ranked Canadian university (no. 18), followed by UBC (no. 34), McGill (no. 42), and McMaster (no. 72) in the top 100. The University of Alberta (no. 136) and the University of Ottawa (no. 141) also make it into the top 200.[4]

In sum, there are three Canadian universities – Toronto, UBC, and McGill – that consistently rank among the top 100 in the world. It is not clear that these ranking systems were needed to point that out. Other Canadian universities, like University of Alberta, Université de Montréal, and McMaster University, also consistently rank highly. While Canada does not dominate the world rankings like some universities in the States and other countries, it is important that we have some highly ranked universities; they establish

Canada's "chops" on the world university scene and serve as a magnet for international students, an effect that spills over to other higher education institutions in Canada.

In Canada, the university ranking scheme with the greatest reach and influence is published annually by *Maclean's* magazine. The annual university rankings issue is to *Maclean's* what the swimsuit issue is to *Sports Illustrated*. It is the most hotly anticipated issue of the year, the biggest seller, and the issue most likely to be pilfered from the library. The ranking scheme differentiates among three categories of Canadian universities: Medical/Doctoral – the most research-intensive ones that also have a medical school; Comprehensive – those that are also research-intensive with a broad range of programs that include graduate studies but do not have a medical school; Primarily Undergraduate – typically, smaller universities with a focus on baccalaureate degree programs for the undergraduate. The rankings within these categories differ little from year to year. Any significant change in ranking of a particular university in one year is regarded with suspicion. The ranking system uses a variety of indicators – some related to teaching and others to research. Fifteen per cent of a university's position in the *Maclean's* rankings is based on assessments by people who are presumably knowledgeable about these universities and their graduates – that is, faculty and senior administrators in the universities themselves, high school guidance counsellors, and business people. It is unclear how these individuals form their opinions, what evidence they use to generate them, and how objective they are. Nevertheless, these reputational judgments end up ranking universities into categories of "highest quality," "most innovative," and "leaders of tomorrow."[5]

For better or worse, these rankings are important to universities and influence their thinking, actions, and resource allocation, all in an attempt to improve their standing. The ranking offers bragging rights (and advertising and branding copy) to those universities that rank highly and generates complaints about methodological shortcomings by those who rank poorly. A university's ranking influences student decisions about which university to attend, as well as parents' and the public's perceptions of the worth and quality of a university. This is especially so for international students.

In spite of the prominence and influence of these rankings, however, there are several reasons to question whether they really say much about the quality of a university, at least with regard to the things that are meaningful to most students, parents, and the governments that support these institutions.

First, as noted, the rankings are heavily influenced by measurements and outcomes related to research. The research mandate and contributions of Canada's universities are certainly important. Research capacity and accomplishments are significant to potential graduate students, who often select a university, a program, and faculty mentors based upon their research profile and status. Having universities that are highly ranked in the research world is also important to the nation, as the basis on which a country competes with others around the world for the best students and faculty – and in today's world, the global competition for talent is fierce and critical.[6] These few institutions also serve as magnets for companies and industries that are looking to locate their research, manufacturing, and service arms in regions that offer the most plentiful supply of the best talent. The research performed in universities contributes to a nation's economic vitality, health, and competitiveness. That is why the aspiration of so many Asian countries is to propel more and more of their universities into a top 100 position in international rankings.[7] But it is not clear that issues of research matter much to many undergraduates. Undergraduates may never get exposed to or be taught by the high-flying research stars. There is also little evidence, despite the assertions of many universities, that better researchers make better teachers. In fact, as Pocklington and Tupper, two Canadian academics and policy makers concluded in 2002, "university research often detracts from the quality of teaching. We regret the continuing elevation of research and the systematic neglect of the quality of instruction ...," and "university research ... is often specialized and far removed from the needs of undergraduate students."[8]

As Kevin Carey pointed out in an insightful analysis of rankings systems, the three essential elements that determine the lion's share of a university's ranking are wealth, fame, and exclusivity.[9] Wealth is reflected in the size and holdings of its library, the number of faculty stars, the beauty and grandeur of the buildings and physical plant, the size of the endowments, and the resources available per student. Fame captures their reputation and prestige, largely dependent on the amount of research they do, the star power of their faculty, and their research revenue. Exclusivity is determined by how hard it is to get into the university, how many applicants they reject, and the entering average needed to be admitted. Most universities have internalized these elements of success for high rankings and have amended their practices accordingly. The Canadian university system is quite homogeneous and united in its pursuit of wealth, fame, and exclusivity. It takes real courage to buck this trend, to be like an Arizona State University, which, as its strategic plan clearly enunciates, wants to be known for the students it includes and how they succeed, not by the students it excludes.[10] Do fame, wealth, and exclusivity relate in some way to quality? Perhaps so, but they are at best proxy measures that are loosely linked to the quality of a university, if at all.

Second, it is understood by all that the ranking systems are incomplete and methodologically flawed. They are based on an arbitrary set of indicators – those deemed most important by the ranking architects – and, as noted before, they tend to be biased in favour of research measures and inputs. Worse yet, these exercises amalgamate scores on these indicators to construct league tables that rank the overall university relative to others. The methodology by which these scores are collapsed into league tables is highly suspect. Universities that question the scientific basis of these league table rankings have valid concerns. Expressions of these concerns are voiced most forcefully by those low in the rankings, thus leaving them open to the criticism that their scientific concerns are simply a way of explaining away their low rankings. In Canada, however, there was an eruption of protests, although short-lived, about the *Maclean's* ranking systems that led to a principled boycott of the exercise in 2006 by a host of Canadian universities, including some of the highest ranked.[11]

Third, the quintessential academic activity of a university is education. Ironically, the most influential ranking systems do a very poor job of measuring what matters most to most students – how good an education they are getting, what and how well they are learning, and how their education sets them up for future success. When these rankings do migrate into issues of teaching and learning they rely mostly on input measures like class sizes and student-to-faculty ratios. It is not clear how these surrogate variables relate to the quality of the undergraduate curriculum. Ranking systems may measure student-related variables such as student satisfaction or how students and others rate the "academic quality" of an institution. While the information is good to have, it is a stretch to make inferences and judgments about the quality of teaching and learning based on these measures, particularly judgments about the central questions of how well universities teach, the quality of the learning environment, and how much and what their students learn.

It is not that measuring the quality of teaching, learning, and academic programs is impossible. The Teaching Excellence Framework (TEF), now renamed the Teaching Excellence and Student Outcomes Framework, was initiated in the United Kingdom by the Office for Students in 2016 as a companion process to the Research Excellence Framework that had been used for some time to measure research excellence and contributions. The TEF is designed specifically to measure teaching and learning excellence. The process collects data from a number of surveys and other measurement exercises to assess variables such as dropout rates, employment outcomes of graduates, and student satisfaction. This information is then evaluated by an independent expert panel who also consider a narrative submitted by the institution that provides context to its teaching and learning performance and that takes into account the mandate of the institution and the makeup of its student body. On the basis of these data, the panel awards the institution a ranking of gold, silver, or bronze. Most importantly, an institution's ranking influences the amount by which they can impose tuition increases in the future. Like all performance measurement and ranking systems, there are methodological worries about some of the indicators and how they are interpreted and used to generate the overall assessment. Nevertheless, the TEF is outstanding relative to other instruments in its attempt to specifically isolate and evaluate the teaching and learning components of a higher education institution.[12]

If the current ranking systems are so deficient, why do they receive so much attention and profile? The answer is simple. Universities are highly competitive. They are driven by the pursuit of prestige and reputation. The ranking systems are among the few mechanisms available now to attest to a university's presumed quality or competitive standing. In spite of all of the understood inadequacies and limitations of the various ranking systems, they are all universities now have to advertise their worth, reputation, and quality. As someone once sagely pointed out, if rankings did not exist the universities would have invented them. This is unfortunate. There must be a better way of measuring the worth, value, and quality of a university, especially their teaching, curricula, and learning programs. Fortunately, there is such a "better way," and it relies on tying the university's accomplishments to the purposes and objectives of a university education.

Measuring Quality by Linking It to Purpose and Outcomes

The International Organization for Standardization (ISO) is a non-governmental body established in 1947. It has 164 member countries and is the largest and most influential organization in the world that establishes international standards for performance.[13] It defines quality as "The totality of features and characteristics of a product or service that bear on its ability to satisfy stated or implied needs." Essentially, to the ISO, the definition of quality is inextricably linked to the requirements or needs to be fulfilled.[14] Simply put, high quality exists when the product, service, or process fulfils all of the identified needs and requirements in a timely and satisfactory manner. Low quality exists when the product, service, or process fails to fulfil those needs and requirements, or does so to an inadequate degree.

This definition of quality feels right given that different people have different needs and requirements depending on a range of circumstances. Consider two people, each of whom wants to purchase a new car. Person 1 wants a car that is great on mileage, small, relatively cheap, and inexpensive to maintain. Person 2 wants a spacious car with a living-room ride – one that screams luxury and prestige – and price is irrelevant. Person 1 buys a Toyota Corolla. Person 2 buys a Jaguar XJ. They can both conclude that they obtained a high-quality vehicle. Why? Because both cars fulfil the needs and requirements they were looking to satisfy.

Assessing the quality of a university is no different. A student enrols in a particular university because of a particular need. That need may be a credential that will lead to a good job, or a vibrant social life, or a campus of a certain size or culture that fits their requirements and desires, or the opportunity for a study experience abroad. As long as the student's needs and requirements are satisfied by the university, then the student can rightfully conclude that they have had a quality university experience. By this metric, based on student satisfaction scores, Canadian universities are high quality. A 2019 survey by the Canadian University Student Consortium reported that 87 per cent of first-year Canadian students thought that their university met or exceeded their expectations.[15] Surveys in previous years confirm the overall satisfaction of most students during or right after their university studies with their university experience, their university, and their program of study.

But there are other stakeholders in a public university system. A government has certain requirements and needs and, as has been discussed in previous chapters, these revolve mainly around whether graduates fulfil labour market needs and demands and the economic impact of the institution. Employers who hire the university graduates also have requirements, which are centred mostly on their need for a talented and skilled workforce with the appropriate education, knowledge base, and skill set to do the available jobs. As has been discussed earlier, there is concern among governments, employers, the public, and students themselves that universities may not be doing an adequate job of preparing students for today's jobs and their future careers.

The other significant stakeholder in this discussion is the university itself. The university needs and wants graduates who are well educated and well equipped to succeed in the world, professionally and personally. It wants graduates who have acquired the information and the cognitive and behavioural skills required to succeed in their chosen professions, to construct successful personal lives, and to contribute positively to society.

It is now that the reader's thinking should migrate back to the discussion of learning outcomes. Learning outcomes represent the knowledge and skills a graduate should have – what a graduate should know and be able to do. This principle of measuring quality linked to desired outcomes essentially distils into a demonstration of whether the university is graduating students who have actually achieved the learning outcomes identified as desirable by the university, employers, and society. Universities and others can claim that their institution of higher education is high quality if their students graduate with the knowledge, skills, and attributes the university purports to teach its students. If students have these attributes then it is reasonable to conclude that the institution has done a high-quality job. If they do not, quality needs to improve. The challenge of assessing quality given this perspective is twofold. First, universities must clearly articulate what knowledge and skills graduates should have. Second, universities must be able to provide evidence that this knowledge and these skills have in fact been acquired. Derek Bok, former president of Harvard, clearly describes this two-stage process of quality determination, as follows:

> A better way to evaluate the strengths and weaknesses of our colleges is to begin – where all serious debates about education must – with a careful look at the purposes to be achieved. Once the aims of the enterprise are defined, we can examine each purpose in turn to determine how far our colleges have progressed toward accomplishing their goals.[16]

Historically, there has been considerable debate in universities about the purposes, goals, or desired outcomes of a university education and the knowledge and skills graduates should have. Different universities will have different views, and this is quite appropriate given their different mandates and the differences in the students and societal roles they serve. All will likely agree that reasonable literacy, numeracy, critical thinking, problem solving, and communication skills are outcomes they all seek. Institutions will differ on the extent to which they emphasize such things as moral development and citizenship, scientific literacy, a tolerance for diversity, or knowledge of the great books.

The important point is that one cannot make statements about quality with any confidence until one has clearly identified the needs and requirements that are to be fulfilled or the purposes of the specific university. Once that is done, the second step is to provide convincing evidence of the degree to which the specified needs and requirements are being fulfilled. As has been discussed earlier, this is where our university evaluation systems fail and why it is difficult to make statements with any degree of confidence or validity about the quality of a university. Universities and their leaders are not hesitant to make assertions about the knowledge and skills university graduates will have, but there is a dearth of compelling evidence that would convince a sceptic that they actually possess them. Emerging research also makes one sceptical about universities' track record in helping students develop critical thinking, literacy, and numeracy skills. Is this true for some, perhaps many, graduates? Surely. But for a non-trivial proportion of graduates, the evidence suggests not. Given the central purpose of a public university system – the production of an educated and informed citizenry – we can only make assertions that are meaningful and useful to students and the public once universities do a better job of measuring, validating, and credentialing the learning outcomes that a university education purports to foster and develop.

The point has been made repeatedly throughout this book that a dominant need of students who choose to attend university is to obtain the education and credential required to secure and succeed in a good job. Based on a review of the eventual labour market outcomes of graduates from more than 4,500 US colleges and universities, Anthony Carnevale at the Center on Education and Workforce at Georgetown University has developed a ranking system of universities that relies less on the institution's prestige and more on the degree to which it improves the future job prospects and earnings of its graduates. The top-scoring institutions in this ranking system are not necessarily the same as the institutions that score highest on the more traditional measures of wealth, fame, and exclusivity.[17] Other ranking systems have adopted a "value-added" approach that, acknowledging the diversity and different characteristics of the student bodies at different institutions, attempts to capture more precisely the degree to which the university education at a particular institution has improved or enhanced student outcomes and fortunes. Specifically, they estimate what a student might have been expected to earn if they had not attended university (calculated on the basis of a set of assumptions and data related to student characteristics and demographics) and what they eventually did earn in the jobs they secured following graduation.[18] Again, these schemes end up identifying a suite of highly ranked institutions that are not necessarily the same as those ranked highly on the basis of more traditional measures. If provinces proceed with performance-based assessments of universities based on outcomes related to the jobs students get after graduation, then these data will also provide the capacity to evaluate the quality of a university based on these metrics.

Any attempt to assess the quality of a university or a university system will necessarily reflect a set of values and attitudes about universities and their purposes. If all that matters to someone is whether a university prepares one adequately for jobs, then their assessments of quality will revolve around post-graduation labour market successes and earnings. If to someone else the essence of a university is to prepare moral, engaged citizens, then their assessment of a university's quality will centre on indicators that measure these attributes. If to others the central accomplishment of a university is to increase their prestige or international competitiveness, then the measures they select will index these purposes. For any quality-assessment exercise, the closer the measure is to the intended outcome, and the less it relies on proxy or surrogate measures of the desired outcome, the better. But one cannot escape the general lesson that there is no absolute or right measure of quality. Rather, the determination of the quality of an institution will depend on what the one doing the evaluation thinks the university is there to do and accomplish.

Recommendation for reform: A comprehensive consultation on the roles and expected contributions of Canada's public university system. This consultation should be: (1) national, (2) led by thought leaders and influencers who are not in government or the universities, (3) focused on the purposes of undergraduate education, and (4) linked to the development and implementation of new policies and funding schemes to achieve desired goals.

The Canadian public university system is too important to the future of the country to be based on the results of a fragmented, disjointed, or informal conversation about its current state and what the country expects of it. There are often calls for a national conversation about the state and future of Canada's health care system and how it can be reformed. A similar conversation about Canada's universities is no less urgent. Some will argue that, in contrast to health care, the absence of a ministry of higher education at the federal level impedes this important conversation. They are right. But allowing thirteen separate conversations about university education, one in each province and territory, is not a way to consider and initiate the reforms needed in Canada's public university system. In any case, the federal government has already shown itself to be quite adept at imposing itself and directing and steering discussion about public universities' roles of research, student aid, and skill development.

This national dialogue must, of course, involve government and the universities. But it is best if it is not led or dominated by them. Rather, it might work best if such an exercise were driven by thought leaders and influencers outside the university. This exercise cannot be seen merely to serve the interests of government or the universities. Rather, it should be an exercise in defining what the country expects from the public universities that are supported by the public purse. It should be an exercise that allows Canadians to express at a high level their aspirations and concerns for the future. It is then up to those who manage the higher education system and public universities to fashion policies, actions, and reforms to address these concerns and help others achieve their goals.

I have little doubt that such a consultation would underscore the continuing and growing concern of the country about the economy and jobs. It is inevitable that the discussion will emphasize the recurring question of whether, and how, universities are preparing graduates for their future careers. This is why it might be best at the outset to be clear that the emphasis of this consultation should be on the academic programming and curricula our universities offer.

There is little point in initiating any consultation unless it is tied to a commitment to action based on the results of the national discussion. The consultation will have been seen as an empty exercise unless it leads to new policies, processes, or actions in the university sector. Linking the results of the discussion to funding is one way of signalling the seriousness of the consultation.

In 2017, the Ontario university system, under the leadership of David Lindsay, the president of their advocacy group, the Council of Ontario Universities (COU), made a move in this direction. It engaged thousands of Ontarians by asking them what their ideas, concerns, hopes, and aspirations were for the future. It is not surprising that the issues for those sampled centred on jobs, the economy, health care, the environment, and access to higher education.[19] This exercise was admirable and to be applauded. It was disappointing in several ways, however. First, the response of the Ontario universities to this public engagement was largely to advertise what they were already doing in these spheres, how successful these efforts had been, and the need for more resources if the country wanted them to do more. Notwithstanding the validity of such arguments, they told us little that was new or likely to address the concerns of students, employers, and government. Second, there was no commitment to change – at least change that would reflect the views of those outside the academy – and to being accountable for doing better.

chapter ten

Canada's Public Universities in a Post-COVID World

If this book is about anything, it is about the need to critically examine the parlous state of Canada's public university system and consider how it can improve and overcome its current challenges. This examination will necessarily suggest changes to the existing public higher education system. However, as will be clear from the discussion in previous chapters, change in higher education is difficult and slow. Never once when I was thinking about the processes and speed of change did I, or anyone else for that matter, ever contemplate the impact of a global pandemic.

The COVID-19 pandemic has illuminated deficiencies and challenges in Canada's health care system. It has equally revealed liabilities and issues in our public university system. This crisis also demonstrates the attitude and inclinations of the country toward our public university system. It is noteworthy and encouraging that some of the relief packages mounted during the pandemic have considered and specifically targeted the impact of COVID-19 on Canada's universities and its students. The Canada Emergency Student Benefit is a $9 billion program that offers aid, $1,250 per month for four months, to recently graduated and in-course university students. Additional monies were allocated to enrich the financial aid program targeted to First Nations students. Changes were also made to the Canada Student Loans Program to increase financial support to students and make it easier for graduated students to repay their loans.[1] As Alex Usher has pointed out, these changes, particularly the Canada Emergency Student Benefit, represent by far the largest infusion of money into student aid programs that the country has ever made.[2] Canada also appears to be one of the few countries that has offered programs specifically to address the impact of COVID-19 on students. This says much about the prominence in Canada of concerns about postsecondary students and, presumably, the health of the university system.

COVID has also resulted in unprecedented job losses. It is not clear what jobs will be available and in what numbers after the pandemic is over. One can anticipate a large demand for the retraining and reskilling of displaced workers – an imperative to which Canada's universities can and should respond. A recent survey of workers whose employment has been affected by COVID reveals that about 34 per cent of them believe they will need more education to replace their lost jobs and that 64 per cent of those who will seek some upskilling and reskilling would be looking to use that opportunity for a career change, putting further pressure on the need for massive retraining programs, given the millions who have lost their jobs during the pandemic.[3] The demand for upskilling programs should lead to a new willingness by universities to entertain different ways of aligning their programs with jobs and labour markets. As Ryan Craig, a world authority on innovative ways of closing the gap between university education and the workplace has observed, there will be a tendency to look to a "magic bullet" solution for training more workers. And, as he further notes, the magic bullet governments will likely choose for "putting millions of Americans [or Canadians] back to work is pouring billions of additional dollars into existing higher education and workforce training programs."[4] Will this help? Sure. But the magnitude of the challenge of putting the enormous number of unemployed workers back to work post-COVID should also lead universities to consider processes and programs that align their education better, faster, and more efficiently with the needs of emerging labour markets. This will require a level of institutional and pedagogical innovation that exceeds what we are demonstrating now.

It seems inevitable, also, that there will be a focus on the need to educate more health care workers. Health care programs have always been a preferred destination for Canadian students. But the need for more qualified workers to sustain a more robust Canadian health care system, and to replace workers who may choose to leave these professions because of their traumatic experiences during the pandemic, will place a demand on programs to graduate not only doctors and nurses but also the host of applied health care professionals, such as medical laboratory technicians, respiratory therapists, and diagnostic cytologists, who are essential to a modern health care system.

A sense of urgency is required for change, and never has a sense of urgency been greater and more widely and deeply felt than now, in the midst of COVID-19. A possible positive outcome of this pandemic might be the impetus it gives to reform and innovation in higher education. At the very least, the challenges it brings should force universities to change simply to stay alive in the post-COVID environment.

The starkest issue facing universities as a result of COVID is the cancellation of in-person classes and the shuttering of campuses. It is not clear when universities will be able to reopen fully. The only option at present is a move to online delivery of courses, evaluations, and all other university functions. Two things are apparent. First, although Canada can claim only one fully online university, the fragile Athabasca University, the great majority of universities have already ventured, to a greater or lesser extent, into the world of digital and online delivery of courses and programs. This is not surprising. One would certainly have expected the explosion and greater availability of computers, the Internet, and information technology to have moved universities to exploit this resource in the service of pedagogy. Second, the digital learning capacities in our universities and the public system are fragmented, uncoordinated, and inadequate to take over curriculum delivery in any meaningful way.

Even before COVID, the Ontario government had commissioned an analysis of digital and online learning in the province. This examination revealed that the government's support of online learning was "unfocussed and disorganized," with "little coordination or clear direction from government toward an overall provincial purpose or goal"; as a result, "institutions have sharp and differing opinions about [online learning] and the contributions and activities of other entities."[5] At the individual university level in Ontario, there is simply not enough expertise or current capacity to offer the curriculum at a high-quality level through online or Zoom capacity, even with the paid-for version. There is no reason to think the situation is any better in any other province.

Moving a course from in-person to online learning involves much more than simply transmitting a video feed of a lecturer standing in front of a camera. This primitive use of technology was how the introductory chemistry course I took more than fifty years ago at McGill was offered. Considerable expertise is required to create and design effective online learning courses, and even the most motivated professors and well-intentioned universities are going to need a lot of assistance in order to move to an online format. It is unlikely that any single university can recruit all of this necessary help on its own. Rather, as Usher has argued, this may be a time for universities to collaborate on the development of online courses, particularly for the introductory courses that they all offer.[6] Ironically, this exact suggestion is what dominated early thinking in Ontario when the previous government initiated a significant investment to promote digital and online learning. Alas, that sensible strategy was never adopted – it is hard to get universities to overcome their competitive nature and to collaborate across institutions – and the funds for online learning got distributed, largely on a proportional basis, to the province's colleges and universities.

The need for the capacity to operate online is evident not only in course delivery. Other university functions – including the recruitment and admission of students, counselling, evaluations, and the identification of at-risk students – will also require innovative and effective use of information technology and online services.[7] Arizona State University is a leader in the innovative use of online services throughout the institution.[8] No Canadian university compares, although, to be fair, few US ones do either.

The second significant impact of COVID on universities is a serious financial challenge. The balance sheet of many higher education institutions is propped up by fees from international students. The precariousness of this strategy was discussed earlier, but the liability of trying to remain sustainable by relying on this opportunistic revenue source has now become apparent. In spite of their best efforts to convince international students that a Canadian educational experience is worth it, the reality is that travel restrictions, visa concerns, and the perceived lowering of quality because of the transition to online learning are causing a significant drop in international enrolments. Many institutions, particularly those that relied heavily on international student revenue to keep the lights on, are in serious financial trouble. The loss of international student revenue may well exceed the financial hit resulting from government cutbacks. Institutions that are heavily reliant on international tuitions and fees will face a serious cash flow challenge that, in the absence of some government assistance, and in the real world, would lead to closure.[9]

In the post-COVID era, government will also be required to engage in dramatic financial manoeuvres to address the large deficits resulting from the assistance packages being used to redress the dramatic effects of economic shutdowns and massive job losses. It seems unlikely that additional government support for universities will be at the top of governments' agendas as these restorative measures are initiated. The only exception might be infrastructure funding, a traditional stimulus for the university sector, which over the last several years in Canada has included funding targeted specifically to upgrade and enhance facilities. I have argued earlier that provincial governments are reluctant to see any of their public universities fail. It may be that the financial duress that is sure to come to universities in the post-COVID era may lead some governments to acknowledge that some universities are simply no longer sustainable and allow them to close.

In addition, governments that were already contemplating reforms to their university systems, might hunker down post-COVID and delay introduction of new policies such as performance-based funding. Ontario has already announced that it will delay implementation of its new performance-based funding scheme for one year, a move encouraged by the faculty associations in Ontario. Similarly, Alberta is delaying implementation of its performance-based funding system, although it maintains that it is still committed to implementation of this new policy regardless of COVID.[10]

Finally, the voices of students and their views about higher education will become more prominent as universities consider different strategies to adapt to the COVID and post-COVID environment. Recent surveys of students indicate that students are still looking for, and prefer, a traditional college experience – living and/or taking classes on campus, and engaging in face-to-face interactions with professors and other students. Students do not see online programming as a suitable alternative to these personal contacts.[11] Also, and not surprisingly, if universities move to online and non-residential programming, students will expect to pay less tuition. In the United Kingdom, some universities have voluntarily advertised a lowering of fees under the current COVID restrictions, a move that has garnered them some relationship and reputational credits and kudos. For the moment, Canadian universities seem to have been largely spared from the more robust discussion of tuition reductions and rebates that is happening south of the border. One American law firm has already initiated three class-action lawsuits to obtain partial refunds for students because of semesters that have been cut short, courses that have been moved online, and other losses such as unused meal plans.[12] Some have also renewed calls to eliminate tuition from US higher education institutions as an appropriate response to COVID.[13] It is inevitable that such discussions will migrate to Canada, adding to the financial difficulties the universities face. If nothing else, this dynamic will empower students (some of whom are already complaining about their university experience and its costs) and force universities to consider more intensely the consequences of failing to provide what students regard as value for money.

Some have suggested that the "new normal" post-COVID may look remarkably similar to the old normal pre-COVID. Perhaps so. But it is difficult to imagine that the shocks administered to universities by the pandemic will not have some impact on how they organize and deliver programs in the future, and how they engage with students. Times like these underscore the relevance of the suggestion made in the previous chapter for a national discussion on the expected and needed role and contribution of Canada's university sector as the country emerges from the ravages of the pandemic. Public universities represent some of the most important institutions a country has to support its citizenry, grow its economy, and contribute to a civil society. These institutions have responded well in the past to national challenges – just think of how they contributed to the education of returning soldiers and to the growth of the economy following World War II. The present challenge represents both an obligation and an opportunity, and our public universities have an important contribution to make once more. Their potential contribution is too important to allow their futures to be determined in an ad hoc or reactive way, or to have this important conversation fragmented into a set of intra-provincial discussions.

Recommendation for reform: Adoption by the Canadian public university system of policies that permit greater institutional differentiation, leading to a more diverse and innovative set of higher education institutions

It is hard to predict exactly how the massive disruptive force of the COVID pandemic will influence the structure and design of Canada's public university system. As Yogi Berra once said, "It's tough to make predictions, especially about the future." Perhaps the actions taken by universities to deal with the impact of the pandemic on them will lead them to embrace and encourage a different, more diverse, and more focused array of institutions than we currently see in the Canadian public university system. Yes, there is some limited differentiation in Canada's public system. But overall, institutions in the system are quite homogeneous and not strongly committed to innovation. The enhanced post-pandemic demand for retraining and upskilling will surely lead people to ask whether it is really necessary to go to school full time for four years to get the re-education they need. There will be a far greater demand for shorter and more vocationally oriented programs. There will be an appetite for micro-credentialing attesting to a student's skill set and preparedness for certain jobs and careers. There will be greater demand for short courses or training programs that bridge the gap between a university education and a first-time job. It is to be hoped that universities will pivot to these demands, both to respond to societal need and as a source of revenue. Indeed, some have already taken some steps in this direction. But, as was noted earlier, the pace of innovation and change in universities is slow. If today's universities do not move expeditiously, others will step into this space, whether from the public or the private sphere, leading to a greater diversity of higher education institutions in Canada than currently exists. This would not be a bad thing. In fact, it should be encouraged.

chapter eleven

Conclusion: A Recipe for Reform

Canada has a good, perhaps a very good, public higher education system. But given the importance of this sector to the future
of the country, we should aspire to nothing less than a great system. Relative to other countries, Canada has a small population
spread out over a large expanse. Some of our traditional sources of
wealth – natural resources and manufacturing – are diminishing.
Economically, we rely heavily on exports, especially to the United
States and China; however, as recent events have shown dramatically, the world has become increasingly competitive. Countries
have become more protectionist, and trade is now a geopolitical
weapon that countries use to exert their influence or punish other
countries. We are a more vulnerable country than we were before.

These trends have been recognized for some time. We have also
understood for some time that the world economy is increasingly
knowledge based. A country's human capital – the talents and
skills of its residents – can be as powerful and influential as its
armies and gold reserves. The future of Canada, and that of other
countries, rests in the minds and education level of its citizens. In
a world like this, surely the quality of education a country provides to its citizens and the quality of the people it graduates are
paramount. In Canada, that is the great responsibility held by the
public education system at all levels, including by its public colleges and universities

Moving from good to great is not easy. As Jim Collins points out
in his book *Good to Great*, good is the enemy of great, and moving

to greatness requires us to confront some brutal facts.[1] Canada sometimes suffers from complacency – good is good enough, we say. This is not the attitude we should have about our universities. For the country to thrive, we should aspire to nothing less than a great, world-leading, set of public universities. No one likes confrontation or bad news. But ignoring the stark reality of the current state of Canada's universities is a recipe for ensuring that we never become great. The analyses offered in this book are part of confronting reality. This is done in an effort not to blame or shame but rather to improve and become great.

This book began with Woodrow Wilson's admonition about the difficulty of creating change in universities, especially of reforming and amending the undergraduate curriculum. It is messy to move a graveyard. Some history is lost, toxic fumes may be released, people can get hurt, and it is expensive and time consuming. Some readers may conclude that trying to move the graveyard is too radical or too dangerous a goal. They may propose that less dramatic interventions are sufficient – mow the lawn, straighten the fallen headstones, liberalize the policies about who can be buried and the type of monument that can be erected, and create a more park-like environment to which the community is welcomed.

Whether one prefers more radical solutions to the challenges faced by Canada's universities or more incremental ones, some change is necessary. As described in this book, the Canadian university system as currently structured is unsustainable, and its trajectory is downward, not up. COVID has exacerbated and amplified all of the challenges universities face and has created a need for greater and faster change and reform. But even in the absence of the current pandemic, for all of the reasons discussed in this book, Canada's public university system needs to change and get even better.

This book suggests a number of recommendations for reform. They fall into four broad categories: (1) increasing awareness of the state and contributions of Canada's universities, (2) broad system reforms, (3) curriculum reform, and (4) improving equity of access.

Increasing awareness of Canada's universities: Canadians take their universities for granted. And why shouldn't they? Whatever body blows universities are subject to as a result of government action, media reports, student protests, or pandemics, there is no shortage of university presidents and administrators who continue to claim that they are offering a high-quality, if not world-class, experience to their students. Universities appear to continuously grow to accommodate student and societal demand. Universities are reluctant to speak in public about the quality challenges or internal issues they face. When they do complain, the proposed remedy is almost always more public funding.

For reasons described earlier, it is unlikely that in the current environment more government funding is coming to the universities, and other revenue solutions are quite limited. Part of the solution set will require changes in the way universities operate and relate to the public and their governments. Changes are inevitable. They can be imposed by government or decided upon unilaterally by the institutions. These are not optimal solutions. It would be better if changes and reforms came as a result of a purposeful and harmonious conversation between the relevant parties, including, and perhaps especially, parents and students.

An informed conversation about possible changes is needed. That is the logic underlying the recommendation of a national consultation on Canada's public university system. We need clear-headed thinking and articulate statements about the role of Canada's public universities, what Canada expects from them, and which of these expectations are shared and achievable. The essential elements of this national consultation are described in Chapter 9.

Recommendation: A comprehensive consultation on the roles and expected contributions of Canada's public university system. This consultation should be: (1) national, (2) led by thought leaders and influencers who are not in government or the universities, (3) focused on the purposes of undergraduate education, and (4) linked to the development and implementation of new policies and funding schemes to achieve desired goals.

Positive change will also require openness and transparency about what universities currently do and what they are currently contributing. That is the rationale for the recommendation that universities publish a scorecard that informs the country about some of their current operations, issues, and achievements, particularly with regard to the relationship of a university education to jobs – an area of dominant concern for students, the public, and government.

Recommendation: Public disclosure of information showing the relationship between institution, field of study, and future earnings

Public disclosure of faculty workloads will reveal the contributions of one of universities' most important resources, their faculty. These public reports will dispel many of the myths about what university professors do and, by making public information of interest to many, demonstrate the willingness of universities to be transparent. It may also assist efforts within the university to assure equity of workload.

Recommendation: Public disclosure of the workloads of faculty coupled to an equity-of-workload policy

Broad system reforms: As described earlier, Canada's public universities have some degree of autonomy but are also highly regulated by government. Change in the university sector will require a collaborative effort between institutions and government. Even for the most courageous and bold universities, significant change often requires the blessing, approval, or at least benign neglect of their governments. The internal politics of universities also make it necessary for governments to provide cover for the universities, or at least collaborate with them, to enable universities to succeed at some of the changes they might contemplate. Simply put, the relationships public universities have with their governments are important, and the enormous control governments have over the higher education environment can enable or discourage change. These observations underlie the recommendation that governments establish a purposeful, useful, and informative, performance-based monitoring and funding system for their universities. Doing so will provide clarity to institutions about what is expected of them and send clear messages to potential students about what they can expect from their university. If designed appropriately, with due attention to institutional differentiation, performance management can be an important stimulus for improvement.

Recommendation: Government introduction of transparent, performance-based funding regimes sensitive to the reality of institutional differentiation to regulate, manage, and monitor public universities

We need more innovation and experimentation in our higher education system. This can come from greater experimentation or innovation in existing public institutions or from the enabling of other non-traditional higher education institutions. Canada's higher education system would be improved, and students would be better served, by a more differentiated and diverse array of institutions. Government relaxation of current regulatory policies is needed to enable new developments and allow new institutions to be created and flourish.

Recommendation: Adoption by the Canadian public university system of policies that permit greater institutional differentiation, leading to a more diverse and innovative set of higher education institutions

Recommendation: Enabling of greater competition in the higher education space by a relaxation of government regulation to permit easier and faster experimentation in universities and easier incorporation and establishment of non-traditional higher education providers

It is the job of governments to assure the quality and value of these new higher education entities, and governments should be diligent in doing so. But these new entities should also be subject to diligent performance monitoring, using sound and proper performance objectives, and monitoring of outcomes, using appropriate performance metrics and indicators.

Curriculum reform: A central theme of this book is the need to modernize undergraduate programs. A quick perusal of the strategic plans of many universities suggests that a quality undergraduate experience is one of their primary objectives. Universities' stated goals notwithstanding, there is a ubiquitous free-floating concern that the research activities of universities have come to exert an undue influence on the universities' attention, hiring and promotion processes, and resource allocation. It is time to reclaim the central purpose of the university – its curriculum and its education programs – especially at the undergraduate level. Different universities will approach curriculum reform in different ways – this is sensible and expected given the differences in their mandates, their programs, and the students they accept. This book puts forward the view, however, that a central consideration in any curriculum reform exercise is the recognition that the acquisition of cognitive and behavioural skills is at least as relevant as the acquisition of disciplinary knowledge. This does not reflect a view that universities are there primarily to prepare students for work; nor is it in response to the many and vocal complaints about a skills gap of university graduates. Rather, it is based on the observation that the acquisition of skills and attributes that will serve students well in their personal lives and make them better people and citizens has always been, and continues to be, a dominant objective of a university education. In today's world, the importance of this objective is magnified. Disciplinary knowledge and content change rapidly. Skills are enduring. Hence, the following recommendation:

Recommendation: Rebalancing of university programs and curricula from a dominant focus on information and content to an increased emphasis on the teaching, evaluation, and credentialing of cognitive and behavioural skills

People take seriously what universities credential. The following initiative could help reify and reinforce the rebalancing of curricula from content to skills.

Recommendation: The granting of university graduation credentials that complement the current traditional transcript and that document the skills and competencies a student has acquired

Improving equity of access: One of the great accomplishments of the Canadian public university system is the wide access it provides. Ensuring access has been a dominant policy goal of the public university system and the governments that support it, and should remain so. It does not matter how great a university system is, it is all for naught unless students have access to it, especially those who would derive the greatest benefit from it. The dominant access challenge now is to ensure that all Canadians have an equitable opportunity to attend and succeed in university. This underlies the next recommendation:

Recommendation: To close the equity of access gap, preferential allocation of funds to programs for elementary and secondary school students who are currently under-represented in colleges and universities to influence them to consider, and prepare them to succeed at, higher education

Some will argue that, in higher education, broad access is incompatible with high quality. This argument should be rejected. We have excellent examples in Canada of institutions that are undeniably world class and yet, in contrast to what we see in the United States, are also very big and widely accessible. Such a model – of an excellent, accessible, large university – is also strongly recommended by Michael Crow of Arizona State University. The most highly ranked universities in Canada – such as the University of Toronto, UBC, McGill, and McMaster – provide evidence that broad access and access equity can be successfully achieved by large universities in Canada. Going to university, for a whole host of reasons, is well worth it. The more who go, the better.

Thanks for reading.

Notes

Epigraph

1 Christopher Eisgruber, "I Opposed Taking Woodrow Wilson's Name off Our School. Here's Why I Changed My Mind," *Washington Post*, 27 June 2020: https://www.washingtonpost.com/opinions/2020/06/27/i -opposed-taking-woodrow-wilsons-name-off-our-school-heres-why-i -changed-my-mind/?utm_campaign=wp_todays_headlines&utm_medium =email&utm_source=newsletter&wpisrc=nl_headlines.

2 Axtell, *The Making of Princeton University*; Berg, *Wilson*, chapters 5 and 6.

1. Introduction: Why This Book, by Me, Now?

1 Kennedy, *Academic Duty*, 287.

2 Kerr, *The Uses of the University*, 30.

3 University of Calgary, "Presidential Legacy," *University of Calgary Alumni Magazine* (Fall/Winter 2010), 46.

4 Government of Ontario, "Higher Education Quality Council of Ontario (HEQCO) Act. 2005, S.O. 2005, Chapter 28, Schedule G" (2005): https:// www.ontario.ca/laws/statute/05h28.

5 Paul Basken, "Westerners Sceptical of Value of Higher Education – Global Poll," *The World University Rankings*, 29 June 2020: https://www .timeshighereducation.com/news/westerners-sceptical-value-higher -education-global-poll.

2. Is Going to University Worth It?

1 https://www.economist.com/leaders/2015/03/26/theworld-is-going -to-university.

2 http://thielfellowship.org/.

3 Statistics Canada, "Labour Market Outcomes for College and University Graduates, 2010–2015," *The Daily* (November 2019): https://www150 .statcan.gc.ca/n1/daily-quotidien/191204/dq191204a-eng.htm.
4 Marc Frenette, "An Investment of a Lifetime? The Long-term Labour Market Premiums Associated with a Postsecondary Education," *Analytical Studies Branch Research Paper Series*, no. 359, *Statistics Canada Catalogue no. 11F0019M*, Statistics Canada (2014): https://www150 .statcan.gc.ca/n1/pub/11f0019m/11f0019m2014359-eng.htm; John Zhao, Sarah Jane Ferguson, Heather Dryburgh, Carlos Rodriguez, and Laura Gibson, "Does Education Pay? A Comparison of Earnings by Level of Education in Canada and Its Provinces and Territories. Census in Brief," *Statistics Canada Catalogue no. 98–200-X2016024*, Statistics Canada (2017): https://files.eric.ed.gov/fulltext/ED585233.pdf.
5 Yuri Ostrovsky and Marc Frenette, "The Cumulative Earnings of Postsecondary Graduates over 20 Years: Results by Field of Study," *Economic Insights. Statistics Canada Catalogue no. 11–626-X* (2014): https:// www150.statcan.gc.ca/n1/pub/11-626-x/11-626-x2014040-eng.htm.
6 Karim Moussaly-Sergieh and Francois Vaillancourt, "Extra Earning Power: The Financial Returns to University Education in Canada," *E-brief*, C.D. Howe Institute (2009): https://www.cdhowe.org/sites/default/files /attachments/research_papers/mixed/ebrief_79.pdf; Martin Hicks, and Linda Jonker, "Still Worth It after All These Years," Higher Education Quality Council of Ontario (2015): http://www.heqco.ca/SiteCollection Documents/Still_Worth_It_EN.pdf; Daniel Boothby and Torben Drewes, "The Payoff: Returns to University, College and Trades Education in Canada, 1980 to 2005," *E-brief*, C.D. Howe Institute (August 2010): https:// www.cdhowe.org/sites/default/files/attachments/research_papers /mixed//ebrief_104.pdf; Statistics Canada, "Does Education Pay? A Comparison of Earnings by Level of Education in Canada and Its Provinces and Territories," *Statistics Canada – Catalogue no. 98-200-X2016024* (November 2017): https://www12.statcan.gc.ca/census-recensement /2016/as-sa/98-200-x/2016024/98-200-x2016024-eng.cfm; Statistics Canada, "Estimated Gross Annual Earnings and Student Debt of Post-Secondary Graduates in Canada: An Interactive Tool" (November 2019): https://www150.statcan.gc.ca/n1/pub/71-607-x/71-607-x2019025 -eng.htm; Government of British Columbia, "The Cost and Return on Investment of Post-Secondary Education": https://www2.gov.bc.ca/gov /content/education-training/post-secondary-education/data-research /cost-of-post-secondary-education; Joel Schlesinger, "The High Price of Higher Learning," *Globe and Mail*, 8 November 2019: https://www .theglobeandmail.com/featured-reports/article-the-high-price-of-higher

-learning/; Jennifer Ma, Matea Pender, and Meredith Welch, "Education Pays 2019: The Benefits of Higher Education for Individuals and Society," *College Board, Trends in Higher Education Series* (2019): https://research .collegeboard.org/pdf/education-pays-2019-full-report.pdf.

7 Anthony P. Carnevale and Ban Cheah, "From Hard Times to Better Times: College Majors, Unemployment and Earnings," Georgetown University Center on Education and the Workforce (2015): https:// 1gyhoq479ufd3yna29x7ubjnwpengine.netdna-ssl.com/wp-content /uploads/HardTimes2015-Report.pdf.

8 Marc Frenette, "Are the Career Prospects of Postsecondary Graduates Improving?" *Analytical Studies Branch Research Paper Series, no. 415. Statistics Canada Catalogue no. 11FOO19M,* Statistics Canada (2019): https:// www150.statcan.gc.ca/n1/en/pub/11f0019m/11f0019m2019003-eng .pdf?st=Vg-GCiBF; Hicks and Jonker, "Still Worth It after All These Years."

9 Alex Berezow, "Humanities Enrollment Is in Free Fall," American Council on Science and Health (31 July 2018): https://www.acsh.org/news/2018Z/07 /31/humanities-enrollment-free-fall-13243; Michael Nietzel, "Whither the Humanities: The Ten-year Trend in College Majors," *Forbes*, 7 January 2019: https://www.forbes.com/sites/michaeltnietzel/2019/01/07/whither-the -humanities-the-ten-year-trend-in-college-majors/#3ed2cd2664ad.

10 Kery Murakami, "Liberal Arts Pay Off in the Long Run," *Inside Higher Ed* (14 January 2020): https://www.insidehighered.com/news/2020/01/14 /long-term-look-return-investment-reveals-positive-indicators-liberal-arts.

11 Anthony P. Carnevale, Ban Cheah, and Andrew R. Hanson, "The Economic Value of College Majors," Georgetown University, Center on Education and the Workforce (2015): https://1gyhoq479ufd3yna29x7ubjn -wpengine.netdna-ssl.com/wp-content/uploads/The-EconomicValue-of -College-Majors-Full-Report-web-FINAL.pdf; Carnevale and Cheah, "From Hard Times to Better Times"; Anthony P. Carnevale, Megan Fasules, Stephanie A. Bond Hule, and David Troutman, "Major Matters Most: The Economic Value of Bachelor's Degrees from the University of Texas System," Georgetown University Center on Education and the Workforce (2017): https://cew.georgetown.edu/wp-content/uploads /UT-System.pdf.

12 Chris Belfield, Jack Britton, Frank Buscha, Lorraine Dearden, Matt Dickson, Laura van der Erve, et al., "The Impact of Undergraduate Degrees on Early-Career Earnings," Institute for Fiscal Studies: Economic and Social Research Council (2018): https://www.ifs.org.uk/publications/13731.

13 Kristyn Frank, Marc Frenette, and Rene Morissette, "Labour Market Outcomes of Young Postsecondary Graduates, 2005–2015," Statistics Canada, *Economic Insights, no. 050, Catalogue no. 11-626-X* (2015):

https://www150.statcan.gc.ca/n1/en/pub/11-626-x/11-626-x2015050
-eng.pdf?st=9abHfxol.

14 Ross Finnie, "Barista or Better? Where Post-Secondary Education Will Take You," *Policy Magazine* (September/October 2016): 47–50: http://www
.policymagazine.ca/pdf/21/PolicyMagazineSeptemberOctober-2016
-Finnie.pdf.

15 https://opportunityinsights.org/; Raj Chetty, John Friedman, Emmanuel Saez, Nicholas Turner, and Danny Yagan, "Mobility Report Cards: The Role of Colleges in Intergenerational Income Mobility," *National Bureau of Economic Research (NBER) Working Paper 23618* (July 2017): https://www
.nber.org/papers/w23618.pdf.

16 Equality of Opportunity Project, "Which Colleges in America Help the Most Children Climb the Income Ladder?": http://www.equality-of
-opportunity.org/college/; *New York Times*, "Economic Diversity and Student Outcomes at City College of New York," *The Upshot* (18 January 2017): https://www.nytimes.com/interactive/projects/college-mobility
/city-college-of-new-york.

17 https://www.brookings.edu/blog/social-mobility-memos/2018/01/11
/raj-chetty-in-14-charts-big-findings-on-opportunity-and-mobility-we
-should-know/.

18 Marc Frenette, "Do Youths from Lower- and Higher-Income Families Benefit Equally from Postsecondary Education?" *Statistics Canada, Analytical Studies – Research Paper Series, Catalogue no. 11FOO19M, no. 24* (April 2019): https://www150.statcan.gc.ca/n1/pub/11f0019m
/11f0019m2019012-eng.htm.

19 Kenny Chatoor, Emily MacKay, and Lauren Hudak, "Parental Education and Postsecondary Attainment: Does the Apple Fall Far from the Tree?" Higher Education Quality Council of Ontario (2019): http://www.heqco.
ca/SiteCollectionDocuments/Formatted%20Parental%20Ed%283%29.pdf.

20 Philip Oreopolous and Uros Petronijevic, "Making College Worth It: A Review of the Returns to Higher Education," *The Future of Children* (2013): 41–65: https://www.nber.org/papers/w19053.pdf; Harvey P. Weingarten, Martin Hicks, Linda Jonker, Carrie Smith, and Hillary Arnold, "Canadian Postsecondary Performance: Impact 2015," Higher Education Quality Council of Ontario (2015): http://www.heqco.ca/SiteCollectionDocuments
/HEQCO_Canadian_Postsecondary_Performance_Impact2015.pdf.

21 Preston Cooper, "Job Losses Hit Those without College Degrees the Hardest," *Forbes*, 12 May 2020: https://www.forbes.com/sites
/prestoncooper2/2020/05/12/job-losses-hit-workers-without-college
-degrees-the-hardest/#690c58e17e87.

22 U.S. Department of Education, "Secretary DeVos Delivers on Promise
    to Provide Students Relevant, Actionable Information Needed to Make
    Personalized Education Decisions" (November 2019): https://www
    .ed.gov/news/press-releases/secretary-devos-delivers-promise-provide
    -students-relevant-actionable-information-needed-make-personalized
    -education-decisions; Kery Murakami, "Many Non-profit College
    Programs Would Fail Gainful Test," *Inside Higher Ed* (16 January 2020):
    https://www.insidehighered.com/news/2020/01/16/profit-programs
    -not-only-ones-would-fail-gainful-employment-test; Center on Education
    and the Workforce, "A First Try at ROI: Ranking 4,500 Colleges,"
    Georgetown University Center on Education and the Workforce (2019):
    https://cew.georgetown.edu/cew-reports/CollegeROI/; Lilah Burke,
    "U.S. Releases Earnings Data for Thousands of College Programs,"
    Inside Higher Ed (21 November 2019): https://www.insidehighered.com
    /news/2019/11/21/federal-government-releases-earnings-data
    -thousands-college-programs.

3. Who Goes to University, and Do All Have an Equal Chance to Attend?

1 Fiona Deller, Amy Kaufman, and Rosanna Tamburri, "Redefining Access
    to Postsecondary Education," Higher Education Quality Council of
    Ontario (2019): http://www.heqco.ca/SiteCollectionDocuments
    /Formatted-Access%20Paper.pdf.
2 Statista, "Number of Students Enrolled in Universities in Canada from
    2000 to 2018": https://www.statista.com/statistics/447814/university
    -enrollment-in-canada/; Universities Canada, "Facts and Stats": https://
    www.univcan.ca/universities/facts-and-stats/; Alex Usher, "The State
    of Postsecondary Education in Canada," Higher Education Strategy
    Associates, 2019: http://higheredstrategy.com/wp-content/uploads
    /2019/08/HESA-Spec-2019-Final_v2.pdf.
3 Statistics Canada, "Education Indicators in Canada: The Evolution of
    College and University Participation Rates among 18- to 24-year-olds in
    Canada" (2 June 2020): https://www150.statcan.gc.ca/n1/daily-quotidien
    /200602/dq200602b-eng.htm.
4 Nicholas Köhler, "In Defence of White Male Students," *Maclean's*,
    19 November 2009: https://www.macleans.ca/news/canada/in-defence
    -of-white-male-students/.
5 Joe Friesen, "Summer Enrolment up at Universities Despite Online Shift
    during Pandemic," *Globe and Mail*, 18 May 2020: https://www

.theglobeandmail.com/canada/article-summer-enrolment-up-at
-universities-despite-online-shift/.

6 Maritime Provinces Higher Education Commission, "University Enrolment
2018–2019," *Trends in Maritime Higher Education*, 17, no. 1 (January 2020):
http://www.mphec.ca/media/192719/Annual-Digest-2018-2019.pdf.

7 OECD iLibrary, "Education at a Glance 2019," *OECD Indicators* (2019):
https://www.oecd-ilibrary.org/docserver/f8d7880d-en.pdf?expires
=1586967964&id=id&accname=guest&checksum=18936BF2FC818076B9
D0AD16EE0A590D; Statistics Canada, Council of Ministers of Education
Canada, "Education Indicators in Canada: An International Perspective,"
Tourism and the Centre for Education Statistics, *Statistics Canada
Catalogue no. 81-604-X* (10 December 2019): https://www150.statcan.
gc.ca/n1/en/pub/81-604-x/81-604-x2019001-eng.pdf?st=iLbJWkre.

8 Alex Usher, *The State of Postsecondary Education in Canada, 2019,* Higher
Education Strategy Associates , Chapter 5, "Tuition and Student Aid":
http://higheredstrategy.com/wp-content/uploads/2019/08/HESA
-Spec-2019-Final_v2.pdf.

9 U.S. Department of Education, "Federal Pell Grant Program": https://
www2.ed.gov/programs/fpg/index.html.

10 Auditor General of Ontario, "Annual Report. Ontario Student Assistance
Program" (2018), Chapter 3, Section 3.10: https://www.auditor.on.ca
/en/content/annualreports/arreports/en18/v1_310en18.pdf; Ontario
Newsroom, "Free Tuition for Hundreds of Thousands of Ontario
Students" (29 March 2017): https://news.ontario.ca/opo/en/2017/03
/free-tuition-for-hundreds-of-thousands-of-ontario-students.html.

11 Marc Frenette, "Postsecondary Enrolment by Parental Income: Recent
National and Provincial Trends," *Statistics Canada, Economic Insights,
no. 070, Catalog 11-626-X* (April 2017): https://www150.statcan.gc.ca/n1
/en/pub/11-626-x/11-626-x2017070-eng.pdf?st=qIYN0J5j.

12 Marc Frenette, "Why Are Youth from Lower-income Families Less
Likely to Attend University? Evidence from Academic Abilities, Parental
Influences, and Financial Constraints," *Statistics Canada. Catalogue
no. 11F0019MIE — No. 295* (February 2007): https://www150.statcan.gc.ca
/n1/en/pub/11f0019m/11f0019m2007295-eng.pdf?st=G2Kh5HvC.

13 Ruben Ford, Taylor Shek-wai Hui, and Cam Nguyen, "Postsecondary
Participation and Household Income," Higher Education Quality Council
of Ontario (2019): http://www.heqco.ca/SiteCollectionDocuments
/Formatted%20SRDC%20PSE%20Access%20and%20Income.pdf.

14 Ross Finnie, Stephen Childs, and Andrew Wismer, "Under-represented
Groups in Postsecondary Education in Ontario: Evidence from the

Youth in Transition Survey," Higher Education Quality Council of
Ontario (2011): http://www.heqco.ca/SiteCollectionDocuments
/UnderRepdGroupsENG.pdf.

15 Huizi Zhao, "Postsecondary Education Participation of Under-
represented Groups in Ontario: Evidence from the SLID Data," Higher
Education Quality Council of Ontario (2012): http://www.heqco.ca
/SiteCollectionDocuments/HEQCO%20SLID%20Eng.pdf.

16 Ken Chatoor, Emily MacKay, and Lauren Hudak, "Parental Education
and Postsecondary Attainment: Does the Apple Fall Far from the Tree?"
Higher Education Quality Council of Ontario (2019): http://www.heqco
.ca/SiteCollectionDocuments/Formatted%20Parental%20Ed%283%29.pdf.

17 Canadian Millennium Scholarship Foundation, "Changing Course:
Improving Aboriginal Access to Post-Secondary Education in Canada,"
Millennium Research, Note #2, (September 2005): https://library.carleton
.ca/sites/default/files/find/data/surveys/pdf_files/millennium_2005
-09_rn-2_en.pdf.

18 Statistics Canada, "The Educational Attainment of Aboriginals in
Canada: National Household Survey (NHS) 2011," *Statistics Canada,
Catalogue no. 99-012-X2011003* (2013): https://www12.statcan.gc.ca/nhs
-enm/2011/as-sa/99-012-x/99-012-x2011003_3-eng.pdf; Indigenous and
Northern Affairs Canada, "Indigenous Youth: Post-Secondary Education
and the Labour Market" (2018): https://www.aadnc-aandc.gc.ca/DAM
/DAM-INTER-HQ-AI/STAGING/texte-text/post_secondary_education
_and_lm_1452001640143_eng.pdf; Assembly of First Nations, "First
Nations Post-Secondary Education: Fact Sheet" (2016): https://www.afn
.ca/wp-content/uploads/2018/07/PSE_Fact_Sheet_ENG.pdf.

19 Matthew Calver, "Closing the Aboriginal Educational Attainment Gap
in Canada: Assessing Progress and Estimating the Economic Benefits,"
Centre for the Study of Living Standards (June 2015): http://www.csls.ca
/reports/csls2015-03.pdf.

20 Marc Frenette, "What Explains the Educational Attainment Gap between
Aboriginal and Non-Aboriginal Youth?" Canadian Labour Market and
Skills Researcher Network, *Working Paper 78* (June 2011): http://www
.clsrn.econ.ubc.ca/workingpapers/CLSRN%20Working%20Paper%20no
.%2078%20-%20Frenette.pdf.

21 Alex Usher, "A Little Knowledge Is a Dangerous Thing: How Perceptions
of Costs and Benefits Affect Access to Education," Educational Policy
Institute (2005): https://files.eric.ed.gov/fulltext/ED499870.pdf.

22 University of Toronto, Institutional Data Hub: https://data.utoronto.ca
/performance-indicators/education-pathways/financial-support/.

23 Boris Palameta and Jean-Pierre Voyer, "Willingness to Pay for Post-Secondary Education among Under-represented Groups," Social Research and Demonstration Corporation (2010): http://www.srdc.org/media/195595/WTP_SRDC_execsum_EN.pdf.

24 People for Education, "Roadmaps and Roadblocks: Career and Life Planning, Guidance, and Streaming in Ontario's Schools" (2019): https://peopleforeducation.ca/wp-content/uploads/2019/02/Roadmaps_roadblocks_WEB.pdf.

25 Pathways to Education: https://www.pathwaystoeducation.ca/.

26 Philip Oreopoulous, Robert S. Brown, and Adam Lavecchia, "Evaluating Student Performance in Pathways to Education," *E-Brief*, C.D. Howe Institute (22 January 2015): https://www.cdhowe.org/sites/default/files/attachments/research_papers/mixed/E-Brief_203.pdf.

27 Fiona Deller and Rosanna Tamburri, "Early Supports for Accessing Postsecondary Education: Good, Bad or Indifferent?" Higher Education Quality Council of Ontario (2019): http://www.heqco.ca/SiteCollectionDocuments/Formatted-Access%20Early%20Interventions.pdf.

28 *New York Times*, "Some Colleges Have More Students from the Top 1 Percent Than the Bottom 60: Find Yours," *The Upshot*, 18 January 2017: https://www.nytimes.com/interactive/2017/01/18/upshot/some-colleges-have-more-students-from-the-top-1-percent-than-the-bottom-60.html.

29 Carnevale, Schmidt, and Strohl, *The Merit Myth*.

4. What Should Students Learn at University, and Are They Learning It?

1 Giamatti, *A Free and Ordered Space*, 47–58.

2 Bok, *Our Underachieving Colleges*, chapter 3, 58.

3 Fish, *Save the World on Your Own Time*, 12–13.

4 Holly Zanville, "Competency Frameworks: Blueprints for Strong Learning Structures," Lumina Foundation (27 July 2017): https://www.luminafoundation.org/news-and-views/competency-frameworks-blueprints-for-strong-learning-structures; Fiona Deller, Sarah Brumwell, and Alexandra MacFarlane, "The Language of Learning Outcomes: Definitions and Assessments," Higher Education Quality Council of Ontario (2015): http://www.heqco.ca/SiteCollectionDocuments/The%20Language%20of%20Learning%20Outcomes-Definitions%20and%20Assessments.pdf.

5 Cliff Adelman, Peter Ewell, Paul Gaston, and Carol Geary Schneider, "The Degree Qualifications Profile: A Learning-Centered Framework

for What College Graduates Should Know and Be Able to Do to Earn the Associate, Bachelor's or Master's Degree," Lumina Foundation (2011): https://www.luminafoundation.org/files/resources/dqp.pdf; Association of American Colleges and Universities (AACU), "College Learning New Global Century" (2008): https://secure.aacu.org/AACU /PDF/GlobalCentury_ExecSum_3.pdf; Ontario Ministry of Training, Colleges and Universities (MTCU), "Ontario Qualification Framework" (2009): http://www.tcu.gov.on.ca/pepg/programs/oqf/; Ontario Ministry of Training, Colleges and Universities, "Essential Employability Skills" (2009): http://www.tcu.gov.on.ca/pepg/audiences/colleges /progstan/essential.html.

6 Mary Catherine Lennon, Brian Frank, James Humphreys, Rhonda Lenton, Kirsten Madsen, Abdelwahab Omri, and Roderick Turner, "Tuning: Identifying and Measuring Sector-based Learning Outcomes in Postsecondary Education," Higher Education Quality Council of Ontario (2014): http://www.heqco.ca/SiteCollectionDocuments/Tuning%20 ENG.pdf.

7 Australian Council for Educational Research (ACER), "Assessment of Higher Education Learning Outcomes (AHELO)" (11 January 2019): https://www.acer.org/au/aheloau/what-is-ahelo; Organisation for Economic Co-operation and Development (OECD), "Testing Student and University Performance Globally: OECD's AHELO" (2014): https://www.oecd.org/education/skills-beyond-school /testingstudentanduniversityperformancegloballyoecdsahelo.htm.

8 Harvey P. Weingarten, "Managing for Quality: Classifying Learning Outcomes," Higher Education Quality Council of Ontario (13 February 2014): http://blog-en.heqco.ca/2014/02/harvey-p-weingarten-managing -for-quality-classifying-learning-outcomes/?_ga=2.103317635.222180343 .1574347086-1391902665.1572968862; Organisation for Economic Co-operation and Development (OECD), "The Future of Education and Skills: Education 2030" (2018): https://www.oecd.org/education/2030 /E2030%20Position%20Paper%20(05.04.2018).pdf.

9 Sylvia Hurtado, Kevin Egan, John H. Pryor, Hannah Whang, and Serge Tran, "Undergraduate Teaching Faculty: The 2010–2011 HERI Faculty Survey," Higher Education Research Institute, UCLA (2012): https://www.heri.ucla. edu/monographs/HERI-FAC2011-Monograph.pdf; E.B. Stolzenberg, Kevin Eagan, H.B. Zimmerman, J. Berdan Lozano, N.M. Cesar-Davis, M.C. Aragon, and C. Rios-Aguilar, "Undergraduate Teaching Faculty: The HERI Faculty Survey 2016–2017," Higher Education Research Institute, UCLA (2019): https://www.heri.ucla.edu/monographs/HERI-FAC2017-monograph.pdf.

10 Alan Harrison, "Skills, Competencies and Credentials," Higher Education Quality Council of Ontario (2017): http://www.heqco.ca /SiteCollectionDocuments/Formatted_Skills%20Competencies%20and %20Credentials.pdf.

11 Jamie Merisotis, "Assessment Is the Key in the Quest for Quality," Lumina Foundation (10 March 2015): https://www.luminafoundation. org/news-and-views/reassessing-assessment; Elena Silva, "Measuring Skills for 21st Century Learning," *Phi Delta Kappan* (May 2009), 630–4: https://journals.sagepub.com/doi/pdf/10.1177/003172170909000905.

12 Max Blough, "Universities Should Educate – Employers Should Train," *Globe and Mail*, 3 September 2013: https://www.theglobeandmail.com /opinion/universities-should-educate-employers-should-train /article14078938/.

13 Bok, *Our Underachieving Colleges*, 45.

14 Scott Jaschik, "University of California Board Votes down SAT and ACT," *Inside Higher Ed* (22 May 2020): https://www.insidehighered.com /admissions/article/2020/05/22/university-california-votes-phase-out -sat-and-act.

15 Benjamin, *Collective Goods and Higher Education Research*, chapter 9.

16 National Institute for Learning Outcomes Assessment: https://www .learningoutcomesassessment.org/.

17 Council for Aid to Education: https://cae.org/; Benjamin, Klein, Steedle, Zahner, Elliot, and Patterson, *The Case for Critical Thinking Skills and Performance Assessment*.

18 Association of American Colleges and Universities, "Liberal Education and America's Promise": https://www.aacu.org/leap.

19 Wabash National Study of Liberal Arts Education: https://centerofinquiry .org/wabash-national-study-of-liberal-arts-education/.

20 Office for Students, "Learning Gain": https://www.officeforstudents.org .uk/advice-and-guidance/teaching/learning-gain/research-into -learning-gain/.

21 Weingarten, Hicks, and Kaufman, *Assessing Quality in Postsecondary Education*; Cecile Hoareau McGrath, Benoit Guerin, Emma Harte, Michael Frearson, and Catriona Manville, "Learning Gain in Higher Education," Higher Education Funding Council of England (2015): https://www.officeforstudents.org.uk /media/11b42adc-534c-481e-91e9-aa87fbddff62/learning-gain-rand-report .pdf; Alexandra MacFarlane and Sarah Brumwell, "The Landscape of Learning Outcomes Assessment in Canada," Higher Education Quality Council of Ontario (2016): http://www.heqco.ca/SiteCollectionDocuments /The-Landscape-of-Learning-Outcomes-Assessment-in-Canada.pdf;

Camille B. Kandiko Howson, "Final Evaluation of the Office for Students Learning Gain Pilot Projects," Office for Students (July 2019): https://www.officeforstudents.org.uk/media/20ffe802-9482-4f55-b5a0-6c18ee4e01b1/learning-gain-project-final-evaluation.pdf.

22 Harvey P. Weingarten, Sarah Brumwell, Kenny Chatoor, and Lauren Hudak, "Measuring Essential Skills of Postsecondary Students: Final Report of the Essential Adult Skills Initiative," Higher Education Quality Council of Ontario (2018): http://www.heqco.ca/SiteCollectionDocuments/FIXED_English_Formatted_EASI%20Final%20Report%282%29.pdf.

23 Arum and Roksa, *Academically Adrift*.

24 Roger Benjamin, "Does College Matter? Measuring Critical-thinking Outcomes Using the CLA," Council for Aid to Education (January 2013): https://cae.org/images/uploads/pdf/Does_College_Matter.pdf.

25 Ross Finnie, Michael Dubois, Dejan Pavlic, and Eda Suleymanoglu, "Measuring Critical-thinking Skills of Postsecondary Students," Higher Education Quality Council of Ontario (2018): http://www.heqco.ca/SiteCollectionDocuments/Formatted_PAWS_FINAL_FIX.pdf.

26 Creso Sá, Andrew Kretz, and Kristjan Sigurdson, "The State of Entrepreneurship Education in Ontario's Colleges and Universities," Higher Education Quality Council of Ontario (2014): http://www.heqco.ca/SiteCollectionDocuments/Entrepreneurship%20report.pdf.

27 Scott Stirrett, "When Hiring New Grads, Employers Should Ignore Grade Point Average," *Globe and Mail*, 2 July 2019: https://www.theglobeandmail.com/business/commentary/article-when-hiring-new-grads-employers-should-ignore-grade-point-average/; Jonathan Lister, "Corporate Canada Is Facing a Soft Skills Deficit – What Can We Do about It?" *Globe and Mail*, 5 November 2019: https://www.theglobeandmail.com/business/careers/leadership/article-corporate-canada-is-facing-a-soft-skills-deficit-what-can-we-do/.

28 Glassdoor, "15 More Companies That No Longer Require a Degree – Apply Now": https://www.glassdoor.com/blog/no-degree-required/.

29 Jill Scott, Brian Frank, and Natalie Simper, "Ten Recommendations for Undertaking Institutional Assessment," in Deller, Pichette, and Watkins, *Driving Academic Quality*, chapter 2, 29–53; Steve Joordens, "Learning Outcomes at Scale: The Promise of Peer Assessment," in Deller, Pichette, and Watkins, *Driving Academic Quality*, chapter 1, 13–29; Weingarten, Hicks, and Kaufman, *Assessing Quality in Postsecondary Education*.

30 ADoc, "PhDetectives: Revealing PhD Competencies and Employment Trends in Canada" (2020): https://static.wixstatic.com/ugd/c19fb8_8dbeb092f207469f80e0194025f837ac.pdf.

31 Employment and Social Development Canada, "Guide to Essential Skills Profiles": https://www.canada.ca/en/employment-social-development /programs/essential-skills/profiles/guide.html.

32 Social Research and Demonstration Corporation (SRDC), "A Comprehensive Review and Development of Measurement Options for Essential Skills Initiatives. Phase 1 – Inventory of Measures" (September 2018): http://www.srdc.org/media/553000/oles-measurement-phase-1 -report.pdf.

33 Katharine O'Grady, Marie-Anne Deussing, Tanya Scerbina, Yitian Tao, Karen Fung, Vanja Elez, and Jeremy Monk, "Measuring Up: Canadian Results of the OECD PISA 2018 Study," Council of Ministers of Education, Canada (CMEC) (2019): https://www.cmec.ca/Publications /Lists/Publications/Attachments/396/PISA2018_PublicReport_EN.pdf.

5. The Relationship between University Education and Jobs

1 Higher Education Quality Council of Ontario (HEQCO), "Edu-data: Where Graduates Work" (2015): http://blog-en.heqco.ca/2015/11 /edudata-where-graduates-work/.

2 Prism Economics and Analysis, "Labour Market Trends and Outlooks for Regulated Professions in Ontario," Higher Education Quality Council of Ontario (2016): http://www.heqco.ca/SiteCollectionDocuments /Labour%20Market%20Trends%20and%20Outlooks%20for%20Regulated %20Professions%20in%20Ontario.pdf.

3 The Expert Panel on STEM Skills for the Future, "Some Assembly Required: STEM Skills and Canada's Economic Productivity," Council of Canadian Academies (2015): https://cca-reports.ca/wp-content/uploads /2018/10/stemfullreporten.pdf.

4 Keynes, *The General Theory of Employment, Interest, and Money*, Preface, 7.

5 JPMorgan Chase, "JPMorgan Chase Makes $350 Million Global Investment in the Future of Work" (18 March 2019): https://www.jpmorganchase.com /corporate/news/pr/jpmorgan-chase-global-investment-in-the-future-of -work.htm.

6 Royal Bank of Canada, "Humans Wanted: How Canadian Youth Can Thrive in the Age of Disruption" (March 2018): https://www.rbc.com /dms/enterprise/futurelaunch/_assets-custom/pdf/RBC-Future-Skills -Report-FINAL-Singles.pdf; Andy Blatchford, "Royal Bank Study Says Focus on 'Human Skills' Needed to Navigate Workplace Automation," *Globe and Mail*, 25 March 2018: https://www.theglobeandmail.com

/report-on-business/royal-bank-study-says-focus-on-human-skills
-needed-to-navigate-workplace-automation/article38349296/.

7 Sophie Borwein, "The Great Skills Divide: A Review of the Literature," Higher
Education Quality Council of Ontario (2014): http://www.heqco.ca
/SiteCollectionDocuments/Skills%20Part%201.pdf; Canadian Council of
Chief Executives, "Preliminary Survey Report: The Skill Needs of Major
Canadian Employers" (January 2014): http://www.ceocouncil.ca/wp-content
/uploads/2014/01/Preliminary-report-on-skills-survey-Jan-20-2014-2.pdf.

8 Conference Board of Canada, "Employability Skills": https://www
.conferenceboard.ca/edu/employability-skills.aspx; Scott Stirrett,
"It's Human Skills – Not Technical Skills – That We Need the Most in
Today's Work Force," *Globe and Mail*, 8 August 2017: https://www
.theglobeandmail.com/report-on-business/small-business/talent/its
-human-skills-not-technical-skills-that-we-need-the-most-in-todays-work
-force/article35854379/?utm_medium=Referrer:+Social+Network
+/+Media&utm_campaign=Shared+Web+Article+Links.

9 World Economic Forum, "The Future of Jobs: Employment, Skills and
Workforce Strategy for the Fourth Industrial Revolution" (January 2016):
http://www3.weforum.org/docs/WEF_Future_of_Jobs.pdf; World
Economic Forum, "What Are the 21st Century Skills Every Student
Needs?" (March 2016): https://www.weforum.org/agenda/2016/03
/21st-century-skills-future-jobs-students/.

10 Mona Mourshed, Diana Farrell, and Dominic Barton, "Education to
Employment: Designing a System That Works," McKinsey Center for
Government, McKinsey & Co. (2012): https://www.mckinsey.com/~
/media/McKinsey/Industries/Social%20Sector/Our%20Insights
/Education%20to%20employment%20Designing%20a%20system%20
that%20works/Education%20to%20employment%20designing%20a%20
system%20that%20works.ashx.

11 *Inside Higher Ed*, "The 2014 Inside Higher Ed Survey of College and
University Chief Academic Officers" (conducted by Gallup) (January
2014): https://www.insidehighered.com/news/survey/pressure-provosts
-2014-survey-chief-academic-officers; Allie Grassgreen, "Ready or Not,"
Inside Higher Ed (26 February 2014): https://www.insidehighered.com
/news/2014/02/26/provosts-business-leaders-disagree-graduates
-career-readiness; Julian L. Alssid, "A New Gallup Survey Says Colleges
and Employers Disagree about How Workforce-ready Graduates Are –
Who Is Right? "*Huffpost*, 29 April 2014: https://www.huffpost.com
/entry/a-new-gallup-survey-says-_b_4862669.

12 Institute for Competitiveness and Prosperity, "The Labour Market Shift: Training a Highly Skilled and Resilient Workforce in Ontario" (2017): https://www.competeprosper.ca/uploads/The_labour_market_shits _in_Ontario_Sept_2017.pdf.

13 Brandon Busteed, "University Academic Leaders Are Losing Confidence in Student Work Readiness – and That's Good News," *Forbes*, 23 January 2020: https://www.forbes.com/sites/brandonbusteed/2020/01/23 /university-academic-leaders-are-losing-confidence-in-student-work -readiness–and-thats-good-news/#2609071c28c7; James Patterson, "Survey: Only 22% of Americans Say Colleges Prepare Workers for Future Work," *Education Dive* (1 July 2019): https://www.educationdive .com/news/survey-only-22-of-americans-say-colleges-prepare-workers -for-future-jobs/557966/.

14 Will Nott, "Almost Half of Learners in Top Study Destinations Say Higher Ed Failed to Prepare Them for Their Career," *The PIE (Professionals in International Education) News* (27 November 2019): https://thepienews .com/news/almost-half-of-learners-in-top-destinations-say-higher-ed -failed-to-prepare-them-for-their-career-survey/; and https://www .pearson.com/content/dam/global-store/global/resources/Pearson _Global_Learner_Survey_2019.pdf.

15 Danielle Lenarcic Biss and Jackie Pichette, "Minding the Gap? Ontario Post-secondary Students' Perception of the State of Their Skills," Higher Education Quality Council of Ontario (2018): http://www.heqco.ca /SiteCollectionDocuments/Formatted_%20Student%20Skills%20Survey _FINAL.pdf.

16 York University, "Study Finds More Than Half of University Students Feel They Need Better Basic Skills to Succeed," York Media Relations (25 April 2019): http://news.yorku.ca/2019/04/25/study-finds-more -than-half-of-university-students -feel-they-need-better-basic-skills-to -succeed/.

17 OECD, "Education and Skills Online Technical Documentation," *OECD Publishing* (2015; updated October 2016), 66–8 and 71–3: http://www .oecd.org/skills/ESonline-assessment/assessmentdesign/technical documentation/.

18 Aoun, *Robot-Proof*, Introduction, xvii.

19 Janet Lane and T. Scott Murray, "Literacy Lost: Canada's Basic Skills Shortfall," Canada West Foundation (December 2018): https://cwf.ca/wp -content/uploads/2018/12/2018-12-CWF_LiteracyLost_Report_WEB-1.pdf.

20 Roger Pizarro Milian, Brad Seward, David Zarifa, and Scott Davies, "Skills, Signals and Labour Market Outcomes: An Analysis of the 2012

Longitudinal and International Study of Adults," Higher Education Quality Council of Ontario (2019): http://www.heqco.ca /SiteCollectionDocuments/Formatted%20RIES_Skills%20and%20Labour %20Market%20Outcomes.pdf.

21 Guido Schwerdt and Simon Wiederhold, "Literacy and Growth: Evidence from PIAAC," DataAngel (2018): http://www.dataangel.ca/docs /LiteracyandGrowth_revised_October2018.pdf.

22 Strada Institute for the Future of Work, "The New Geography of Skills" (10 December 2019): https://www.stradaeducation.org/report/the -new-geography-of-skills/?utm_campaign=New%20Geography%20of %20Skills&utm_content=108463595&utm_medium=social&utm_source =facebook&hss_channel=fbp-83868748397; Royal Bank of Canada (RBC), "Upskills: A Future Launch Initiative" (2019): https://www.rbcupskill. ca/; Daniel Munro, Cameron MacLaine, and James Stuckey, "Skills – Where Are We Today? The State of Skills and PSE in Canada," Conference Board of Canada (2014): https://www.conferenceboard.ca/temp /e3c9d9cf-1a7e-4cf6-b5e9-fc379d80d3cc/6603_Skills-WhereAreWeAt %20-%20RPT.pdf; Alison Doyle, "Employment Skills Listed by Job," The Balance Careers (30 July 2019): https://www.thebalancecareers.com /employment-skills-listed-by-job-2062389.

23 Business-Higher Education Roundtable: http://bher.ca/.

24 Future Skills Canada and the Future Skills Centre: https://www.canada .ca/en/employment-social-development/programs/future-skills.html; https://fsc-ccf.ca/.

25 Craig, *A New U*; Doug Lederman and Paul Fain, "A New U: Faster and Cheaper Alternatives to College," *Inside Higher Ed* (22 August 2018): https://www.insidehighered.com/digital-learning/article/2018/08/22 /qa-ryan-craig-author-new-book-faster-cheaper-college.

26 Zakaria, *In Defense of a Liberal Education*, 51.

27 Giamatti, *A Free and Ordered Space*, 109–18.

28 Michael T. Nietzel, "Whither the Humanities: The Ten-year Trend in College Majors," *Forbes*, 7 January 2019: https://www.forbes.com /sites/michaeltnietzel/2019/01/07/whither-the-humanities-the-ten -year-trend-in-college-majors/#6f085a9864ad; Universities Canada, "The Future of the Liberal Arts: Report" (2016): https://www.univcan.ca/the -future-of-the-liberal-arts-report/.

29 Jackie Pichette and Elyse Watkins, "Competency-Based Education: Driving the Skills Measurement Agenda," Higher Education Quality Council of Ontario (2018): http://www.heqco.ca/SiteCollectionDocuments /Formatted_CBE%20Paper_REVISED.pdf.

30 Western Governors University: https://www.wgu.edu/; R. Mendenhall, "What Is Competency-Based Education?" *Huffpost*, 5 November 2012: https://www.huffpost.com/entry/competency-based-learning-_b_1855374.

31 Competency-Based Education Network (C-BEN): https://www.cbenetwork. org/; Charla Long, "Better Data on Competency-Based Education," *Inside Higher Ed* (5 December 2019): https://www.insidehighered.com/views /2019/12/05/essay-need-better-data-whatworks-competency-based -education; Tom Lindsay, "New Study: Less Expensive Competency-Based Education Programs Just as Good as Traditional Programs," *Forbes*, 27 March 2018: https://www.forbes.com/sites/tomlindsay/2018/03/27/new-study -less-expensive-competency-based-education-programs-just-as-good-as -traditional-programs/#3c50394d674d.

32 Simon Fraser University, "FASS Forward Microcredit Courses": https:// www.sfu.ca/fass/students/current-students/undergraduate-students /fassforward.html?utm_source=Academica+Top+Ten&utm_campaign =6a277dfbca-EMAIL_CAMPAIGN_2020_02_27_06_39&utm_medium=email &utm_term=0_b4928536cf-6a277dfbca-51507781; Ontario Tech University, "University Announces Bold Tech Talent Initiative to Bridge the Skills Gap" (2020): https://news.ontariotechu.ca/archives/2020/02/university -announces-bold-ontario-tech-talent-initiative-to-bridge-the-skills-gap.php.

33 Paul Fain, "Experimenting with Competency," *Inside Higher Ed* (13 January 2015): https://www.insidehighered.com/news/2015/01/13 /feds-move-ahead-experimental-sites-competency-based-education; Paul Fain, "Feds Drop Experiment on Competency-Based Ed," *Inside Higher Ed* (16 December 2019): https://www.insidehighered.com/quicktakes/2019 /12/16/feds-drop-experiment-competency-based-ed.

34 Paul Fain, "IBM Looks beyond the College Degree," *Inside Higher Ed* (29 October 2019): https://www.insidehighered.com/digital-learning /article/2019/10/29/interview-ibm-official-about-companys-new-collar -push-look; Glassdoor, "15 More Companies That No Longer Require a Degree – Apply Now" (14 April 2018): https://www.glassdoor.com/blog /no-degree-required/; Ray Schroeder, "What Matters More? Skills or Degrees?" *Inside Higher Ed* (10 July 2019): https://www.insidehighered .com/digital-learning/blogs/online-trending-now/what-matters-more -skills-or-degrees.

35 Brandon Busteed, "Americans Rank a Google Internship over a Harvard Degree," *Forbes*, 6 January 2020: https://www.forbes.com/sites /brandonbusteed/2020/01/06/americans-rank-a-google-internship-over -a-harvard-degree/#7bd8750731b9.

36 Rhea Kelly, "Competency-Led Hiring on the Rise," *Campus Technology* (4 February 2020): https://campustechnology.com/articles/2020/02/04 /competency-led-hiring-on-the-rise.aspx?admgarea=news.
37 Strada Consumer Insights & Gallup, "Hiring for Success. Employer Survey on Finding the Best Talent for the Job" (17 April 2019): https://www .stradaeducation.org/report/hiring-for-success/.
38 Mikhail Zinshteyn, "How the Skills Gap Is Changing the Degree Path," *Education Dive* (17 February 2020): https://www.educationdive.com /news/how-the-skills-gap-is-changing-the-degree-path/572382/; Gallagher, *The Future of University Credentials*; Paul Fain, "Beyond the Transcript," *Inside Higher Ed* (13 July 2015): https://www.insidehighered .com/news/2015/07/13/project-create-models-broader-form-student-transcript; Greg Toppo, "The Record of Everything You've Forgotten," *Inside Higher Ed* (4 February 2019): https://www.insidehighered.com /news/2019/02/04/colleges-experiment-experiential-transcripts.
39 Alan Harrison, "Skills, Competencies and Credentials," Higher Education Quality Council of Ontario (2017), 2: http://www.heqco.ca /SiteCollectionDocuments/Formatted_Skills%20Competencies%20and %20Credentials.pdf.
40 Reich, *The Work of Nations*, 171–234.
41 Reich, *I'll Be Short*, 65.

6. How Should a Government Manage Its Public University System?

1 Barber, *How to Run a Government So That Citizens Benefit and Taxpayers Don't Go Crazy*.
2 Harvey P. Weingarten, "Goals vs Strategies: A Postsecondary Primer," Higher Education Quality Council of Ontario (26 January 2016): http:// blog-en.heqco.ca/2016/01/harvey-weingarten-goals-vs-strategies-a -postsecondary-primer/.
3 Harvey P. Weingarten, "How Do Governments Really Make Higher Education Policy, and How Can Universities Influence the Policies Governments Make: An Experience-based Analysis," in Axelrod, Trilokekar, Shanahan, and Wellen, *Making Policy in Turbulent Times*, 85–98.
4 Harvey P. Weingarten and Martin Hicks, "Performance of the Ontario (Canada) Higher Education System: Measuring Only What Matters," in Curaj, Deca, and Pricopie, *European Higher Education Area*, 471–85: https:// doi.org/10.1007/978-3-319-77407-7_29.

5 Harvey P. Weingarten and Martin Hicks, "Measurement of Postsecondary Performance in Canada: Moving beyond Inputs and Funding to Outputs and Outcomes," in Hazelkorn, Coates, and McCormick, *Research Handbook on Quality, Performance, and Accountability in Higher Education*, 498–508; Harvey P. Weingarten, Martin Hicks, Linda Jonker, Carrie Smith, and Hillary Arnold, "Canadian Postsecondary Performance: Impact 2015," Higher Education Quality Council of Ontario (2015): http://www .heqco.ca/SiteCollectionDocuments/HEQCO_Canadian_Postsecondary _Performance_Impact2015.pdf; Organisation for Economic Co-operation and Development (OECD), "Enhancing Higher Education System Performance: Report on Benchmarking Higher Education System Performance: Conceptual Framework and Data" (2017): https://www .oecd.org/education/skills-beyond-school/Benchmarking%20Report.pdf.

6 Statistics Canada, "Education and Labour Market Longitudinal Platform" (March 2019): https://www.statcan.gc.ca/eng/about/pia/generic /educationlabour; Canadian Research Data Centre Network, "ELMLP (Education and Labour Market Longitudinal Linkage Platform)": https:// crdcn.org/datasets/elmlp-education-and-labour-market-longitudinal -linkage-platform.

7 Joe Friesen, "New Metrics for Ontario University and College Funding Include Employment and Graduation Rate," *Globe and Mail*, 16 April 2019: https://www.theglobeandmail.com/canada/article-new-metrics -for-ontario-university-and-college-funding-include/; Ryan White, "Alberta Unveils New Performance-Based Funding Structure for Post-secondary Institutions," *Calgary Herald*, 20 January 2020: https://calgary. ctvnews.ca/province-unveils-new-performance-based-funding -structure-for-post-secondary-institutions-1.4775212; CBC News, "New Brunswick MLAs Ponder Performance-Based Funding for Universities," 7 February 2020: https://www.cbc.ca/news/canada/new-brunswick /cbc-nb-political-panel-podcast-university-funding-1.5455391.

8 Alex Usher, "Performance-Based Funding 101: The Performance Indicators," Higher Education Strategy Associates (23 April 2019): http:// higheredstrategy.com/performance-based-funding-101-the-indicators/.

9 Weingarten, Hicks, and Kaufman, *Assessing Quality in Postsecondary Education*.

10 Rosovsky, *The University: An Owner's Manual*, 164–5.

11 Amy Y. Li, "Lessons Learned: A Case Study of Performance Funding in Higher Education," *Third Way* (25 January 2019): https://www.thirdway .org/report/lessons-learned-a-case-study-of-performance-funding-in -higher-education?mod=article_inline.

12 M. Kate Callaghan, Kasey Meehan, Kathleen M. Shaw, Austin Slaughter,
    Dae Y. Kim, Virginia R. Hunter, et al., "Implementation and Impact of
    Outcomes-based Funding in Tennessee," *Research for Action* (July 2017):
    https://8rri53pm0cs22jk3vvqna1ub-wpengine.netdna-ssl.com/wp
    -content/uploads/2017/07/RFA-OBF-in-Tennessee-Full-Brief_updated
    -July-2017.pdf.

13 Marc Spooner, "Performance-Based Funding in Higher Education,"
    Canadian Association of University Teachers, *CAUT Education Review*
    (October 2019): https://www.caut.ca/sites/default/files/caut-education
    -review-performance-based_funding_in_higher_education.pdf; Alex Usher,
    "Funding for Results in Higher Education," *E-Brief*, C.D. Howe Institute
    (17 September 2019): https://www.cdhowe.org/sites/default/files
    /attachments/research_papers/mixed/e-brief_295.pdf; Cheryl D. Blanco,
    "Essential Elements of State Policy for College Completion: Outcomes-
    based Funding," Southern Regional Education Board (September 2012):
    https://www.sreb.org/sites/main/files/file-attachments/outcomes
    _based_funding.pdf?1465333498; Mary Ziskin, Don Hossler, Karyn
    Rabourn, Osman Cekic , and Youngsik Hwang, "Outcomes-based Funding:
    Current Status, Promising Practices and Emerging Trends," Higher
    Education Quality Council of Ontario (2014): http://www.heqco.ca
    /SiteCollectionDocuments/Outcomes-Based%20Funding%20ENG.pdf.

14 Harvey P. Weingarten, "Outcomes-based Funding: Part 1. Successful
    Models Start with Psychology 101," Higher Education Quality Council of
    Ontario (3 December 2014): http://blog-en.heqco.ca/2014/12/harvey
    -p-weingarten-outcomes-based-funding-part-1-successful-models-start
    -with-psychology-101/.

15 Carnegie Classification of Institutions of Higher Education: https://
    carnegieclassifications.iu.edu/classification_descriptions/basic.php;
    Carnegie Classification of Institutions of Higher Education, Wikipedia:
    https://en.wikipedia.org/wiki/Carnegie_Classification_of_Institutions
    _of_Higher_Education.

16 *U.S. News & World Report*, "National Liberal Arts Colleges": https://
    www.usnews.com/best-colleges/rankings/national-liberal-arts-colleges.

17 *Maclean's*, "University Rankings 2020" (3 October 2019): https://www
    .macleans.ca/education/university-rankings/university-rankings-2020/.

18 U-15 Group of Canadian Research Universities: http://u15.ca/.

19 Jennifer Lewington, "Why a Group of Small Universities Believe the
    Future Is Theirs," *Maclean's*, 14 March 2017: https://www.macleans.ca
    /education/why-a-group-of-small-universities-believes-the-future
    -is-theirs/.

20 Clark Kerr, "A Master Plan for Higher Education in California," in *The Gold and the Blue*, Volume 1: chapter 12, 172–91.
21 Harvey P. Weingarten and Fiona Deller, "The Benefits of Greater Differentiation of Ontario's University Sector," Higher Education Quality Council of Ontario (26 October 2010): http://www.heqco.ca/SiteCollectionDocuments/DifferentiationENG.pdf.

7. Why Are Canadian Universities So Slow to Innovate?

 1 Nonprofit colleges online, "10 Oldest Universities in the Western World": https://www.nonprofitcollegesonline.com/10-oldest-universities-in-the-western-world/.
 2 Wikipedia, "First University in the United States": https://en.wikipedia.org/wiki/First_university_in_the_United_States.
 3 Good University Ranking Guide, "Oldest Universities in Canada": https://whichuniversitybest.blogspot.com/2011/12/oldest-universities-in-canada.html.
 4 Harvey P. Weingarten, "Undergraduate Programs: Plus ça change …," Higher Education Quality Council of Ontario (7 September 2017): http://blog-en.heqco.ca/2017/09/harvey-p-weingarten-undergraduate-programs-plus-ca-change/.
 5 Giamatti, A *Free and Ordered Space*, 144.
 6 Kerr, *The Uses of the University*, 11.
 7 McLaughlin, *Waterloo*; McLaughlin, *Out of the Shadow of Orthodoxy*.
 8 Greenlee, *McMaster University. Vol. 3, 1957–1987*, chapter 6; Servant, *Revolutions and Re-iterations*.
 9 McLaughlin, *Waterloo*, 62.
10 Henry J. Eyring and Clayton M. Christensen, "The Innovative University: Changing the DNA of Higher Education," Washington: American Council on Education (2011), 11: https://www.acenet.edu/Documents/Changing-the-DNA-of-Higher-Ed.pdf; Christensen and Eyring, *The Innovative University*, Part 2.
11 Dominic J. Brewer and William G. Tierney, "Barriers to Innovation in U.S. Education," in Wildavsky, Kelly, and Carey, *Reinventing Higher Education*, 33.
12 Dennis M. Barden, "Self-destructive Tendencies, Part 1," *The Chronicle of Higher Education* (19 May 2006): https://www.chronicle.com/article/Self-Destructive-Tendencies/46788.
13 Paul, *Leadership under Fire*; Judith Woodsworth, "Setting Strategic Direction from the Presidential Suite: Hurdles and Successes," in Axelrod, Trilokekar, Shanahan, and Wellen, *Making Policy in Turbulent Times*, 117–36.

14 Crow and Dabars, *Designing the New American University*, 240–310.
15 Kevin Carey, "The Mayo Clinic of Higher Education," in Wildavsky, Kelly, and Carey, *Reinventing Higher Education*, 225–39.
16 MacKinnon, *University Leadership and Public Policy in the Twenty-First Century*, 91–110.
17 David Friedman and Ryan Craig, "The Problem with College Governance? Alumni," *Inside Higher Ed* (13 March 2017): https://www .insidehighered.com/views/2017/03/13/colleges-and-universities -should-recruit-more-nonalumni-and-donors-boards-essay.
18 Kerr, *The Gold and the Blue*, Volume One, 25.
19 Krames, *Inside Drucker's Brain*, 33.
20 Ontario Universities Council on Quality Assurance: https://oucqa. ca/; Ontario Universities Council on Quality Assurance, "Review of the Quality Assurance Framework and Quality Council," Council of Ontario Universities (Spring 2018): https://oucqa.ca/the-quality-council/review -of-the-quality-assurance-framework-and-quality-council/.
21 Harvey P. Weingarten, "Quality Assurance: A Simple Process That We Overly Complicate," Higher Education Quality Council of Ontario (9 January 2018): http://blog-en.heqco.ca/2018/01/harvey-p-weingarten -quality-assurance-a-simple-concept-that-we-overly-complicate/.
22 Brewer and Tierney, "Barriers to Innovation in U.S. Higher Education," 28.
23 Kotter, *Leading Change*; Kotter, A *Sense of Urgency*.

8. Are Canadian Universities Sustainable?

1 Universities Canada: https://www.univcan.ca/universities/facts-and-stats/.
2 Organisation for Economic Co-operation and Development (OECD), "On the Edge: Securing a Sustainable Future for Higher Education" (2004): http://www.oecd.org/education/imhe/33642717.pdf; Harvey P. Weingarten, Martin Hicks, and Greg Moran, "Understanding the Sustainability of the Ontario Postsecondary System and Its Institutions: A Framework," Higher Education Quality Council of Ontario (2016). http://www.heqco.ca/SiteCollectionDocuments/Report%20-%20 Understanding%20the%20Sustainability%20of%20the%20Ontario%20 Postsecondary%20System.pdf.
3 Clark, Moran, Skolnik, and Trick, *Academic Transformation*; Harvey P. Weingarten, "The Diminishing Quality of Ontario's Universities: Can the System Be Fixed?" Higher Education Quality Council of Ontario (31 October 2011): http://blog-en.heqco.ca/2011/10/the-diminishing -quality-of-ontarios-universities-can-the-system-be-fixed/.

4 Higher Education Quality Council of Ontario, "Quality: Shifting the Focus. A Report from the Expert Panel to Assess the Strategic Mandate Agreement Submissions" (2013): http://www.heqco.ca /SiteCollectionDocuments/FINAL%20SMA%20Report.pdf.

5 Ontario Ministry of Finance, "Report of the Commission on the Reform of Ontario's Public Services. Chapter 7. Post-Secondary Education," Government of Ontario (2010): https://www.fin.gov.on.ca/en /reformcommission/chapters/ch7.html.

6 Association of Universities and Colleges of Canada (AUCC), "The Revitalization of Undergraduate Education in Canada" (2011): https:// www.univcan.ca/wp-content/uploads/2015/11/revitalization-of -undergraduate-education-in-canada-march-2011.pdf.

7 Canadian Association of University Business Officers (CAUBO), "Deferred Maintenance at Canadian Universities" (October 2019): https://www .caubo.ca/wp-content/uploads/2019/07/Building-the-Case-for-Funding -in-Deferred-Maintenance.pdf.

8 Statistics Canada, "Financial Information of Universities and Degree-granting Colleges, 2017/2018" (24 July 2019): https://www 150.statcan.gc.ca/n1/en/daily-quotidien/190724/dq190724a-eng.pdf ?st=yulO0aq-; Alex Usher, "Canadian University Finances, 2017–2018," Higher Education Strategy Associates (12 September 2019): http:// higheredstrategy.com/canadian-university-finances-2017-18/.

9 Martin Pin and Sam Andrey, "Rising Costs: A Look at Spending in Ontario Universities," Ontario University Student Alliance (November 2011): https://d3n8a8pro7vhmx.cloudfront.net/ousa/pages/97 /attachments/original/1473427886/2011-11_-_Rising_Costs_document .pdf?1473427886.

10 Karen Howlett, "McGuinty Gives Ontario Colleges and Universities an F in New Spending," *Globe and Mail*, 19 April 2010: https://www .theglobeandmail.com/news/national/mcguinty-gives-ontario-colleges -and-universities-an-f-in-new-spending/article4314356/.

11 Harvey P. Weingarten, Martin Hicks, Linda Jonker, Carrie Smith, and Hillary Arnold, "Canadian Postsecondary Performance: Impact 2015," Higher Education Quality Council of Ontario (11 March 2015): https:// heqco.ca/pub/canadian-postsecondary-performance-impact-2015/.

12 See references in endnote 8.

13 Schulich, *Life and Business Lessons*, 243–5.

14 Jessica Brice, "Universities with the Highest Endowments in Canada 2019," *Maclean's*, 5 May 2019: https://www.universitymagazine.ca /universities-with-the-highest-endowments-in-canada-2019/; Wikipedia,

"List of Canadian Universities by Endowment": https://en.wikipedia
.org/wiki/List_of_Canadian_universities_by_endowment.

15 Wikipedia, "List of Colleges and Universities in the United
States by Endowment": https://en.wikipedia.org/wiki/
List_of_colleges_and_universities_in_the_United_States_by_endowment.

16 Statistics Canada, "Canadian Postsecondary Enrolments and Graduates,
2017/2018" (19 February 2020): https://www150.statcan.gc.ca/n1
/daily-quotidien/200219/dq200219b-eng.htm; Statistics Canada, "Study:
International Student Enrolment in Postsecondary Education Programs
Prior to COVID-19" (15 June 2020): https://www150.statcan.gc.ca/n1
/daily-quotidien/200615/dq200615b-eng.htm.

17 Alex Usher, "Canadian Universities Have Become Addicted to the Revenues
Brought in by International Students. But How Much Should They Subsidize
Our Institutions?" *Policy Options* (29 August 2018): https://policyoptions
.irpp.org/magazines/august-2018/canadas-growing-reliance-on
-international-students/; Alex Usher, "Danger Ahead," Higher Education
Strategy Associates (10 June 2019): http://higheredstrategy.com/danger-
ahead/; Charles Beach and Frank Milne, "Ontario Post-Secondary Education
Funding Policies: Perverse Incentives and Unintended Consequences,"
Queen's Economics Department Working Paper # 1424 (October 2019):
https://www.econ.queensu.ca/sites/econ.queensu.ca/files/wpaper/qed
_wp_1424.pdf; Joe Friesen, "In Cape Breton, a Dramatic Rise in International
Students Has Transformed a School and a Community," *Globe and Mail*,
9 October 2019: https://www.theglobeandmail.com/canada/article-how
-the-world-came-to-cape-breton-university/.

18 John Ross, "Universities Reel as Australia Bans Entry to Chinese," *Times
Higher Education* (2 February 2020): https://www.timeshighereducation.
com/news/universities-reel-australia-bans-entry-chinese.

19 Josh Dehass, "Leaders of Western, Calgary, Alberta and Waterloo top
$500K," *Maclean's*, 28 October 2013: https://www.macleans.ca/education
/uniandcollege/leaders-of-western-calgary-alberta-and-waterloo-top
-500k/; Alex Usher, "Presidential Compensation," Higher Education
Strategy Associates (18 September 2017): http://higheredstrategy.com
/presidential-compensation/.

20 Paul Kniest, "Australian Universities Top World Ranking ... for VC Pay,"
National Tertiary Education Union (16 March 2017): http://www.nteu
.org.au/article/Australian-universities-top-world-rankings...-for-VC-pay
-(Advocate-24-01)-19415.

21 Harvey P. Weingarten, Linda Jonker, Amy Kaufman, and Martin Hicks,
"University Sustainability: Expenditure," Higher Education Quality Council

of Ontario (2018): http://www.heqco.ca/SiteCollectionDocuments /Formatted_University%20Core%20Expenditures_FINAL__ENGLISH.pdf.

22 Stanley Fish, "First, Kill All the Administrators," *The Chronicle of Higher Education* (21 March 2003): https://www.chronicle.com/article/First-Kill -All-the/45128.

23 Alex Usher, "Administrative Bloat, 2020 Edition," Higher Education Strategy Associates (18 February 2020): https://higheredstrategy.com /administrative-bloat-2020-edition/.

24 Duderstadt, *A University for the 21st Century*, 149.

25 Alex Usher, "Counter-intuitive Faculty Salary Data," Higher Education Strategy Associates (4 February 2020): https://myemail.constantcontact. com/One-Thought-to-Start-Your-Day–Counter-intuitive-Faculty-Salary -Data.html?soid=1103080520043&aid=Vo1TnTI9gnM; Alex Usher, "More Fun with Faculty Salary Data," Higher Education Strategy Associates (5 February 2020): https://myemail.constantcontact.com/One-Thought -to-Start-Your-Day–More-Fun-with-Faculty-Salary-Data.html?soid =1103080520043&aid=OWhh4NcFoSA; Statistics Canada, "Number and Salaries of Full-time Teaching Staff at Canadian Universities (Final), 2018/2019" (25 November 2019): https://www150.statcan.gc.ca/n1/en /daily-quotidien/191125/dq191125b-eng.pdf?st=MSjeO1mW.

26 Canada 150 Research Chairs program: https://www.canada150.chairs -chaires.gc.ca/home-accueil-eng.aspx.

27 Altbach, Reisberg, Yudkevick, Androushchak, and Pacheco, *Paying the Professoriate*: https://www.routledge.com/Paying-the-Professoriate-A -Global-Comparison-of-Compensation-and-Contracts/Altbach-Reisberg -Yudkevich-Androushchak-Pacheco/p/book/9780415898072.

28 J. McChesney and Jaqueline Bischel, "The Aging of Tenure-track Faculty in Higher Education: Implications for Succession and Diversity," College and University Professional Association for Human Resources (January 2020): https://www.cupahr.org/wp-content/uploads/CUPA-HR-Brief -Aging-Faculty.pdf.

29 Weingarten, Jonker, Kaufman, and Hicks, "University Sustainability: Expenditures."

30 Ontario Council of University Faculty Associations (OCUFA), "OCUFA Response to the Latest Faculty at Work Report" (February 2018): https:// ocufa.on.ca/assets/2018-02-15-OCUFA-Faculty-at-Work-response.pdf.

31 Council of Ontario Universities, "Faculty at Work: The Composition and Activities of Ontario Universities' Academic Workforce" (2018): https:// cou.ca/wp-content/uploads/2018/01/Public-Report-on-Faculty-at-Work -Dec-2017-FN.pdf.

32 Karen Foster and Louise Birdsell Bauer, "Out of the Shadows: Experiences of Contract Academic Staff," Canadian Association of University Teachers (September 2018): https://www.caut.ca/sites/default/files/cas_report.pdf.

33 Jay Schalin, "Faculty Teaching Loads in the University of North Carolina System," The John William Pope Center for Higher Education Policy (August 2014): https://files.eric.ed.gov/fulltext/ED555619.pdf.

34 Higher Education Quality Council of Ontario, "The Productivity of the Ontario Public Postsecondary System Preliminary Report" (December 2012): http://www.heqco.ca/SiteCollectionDocuments/HEQCO%20Productivity%20Report.pdf.

35 Linda Jonker and Martin Hicks, "Teaching Loads and Research Outputs of Ontario University Faculty Members: Implications for Productivity and Differentiation," Higher Education Quality Council of Ontario (2014): http://www.heqco.ca/SiteCollectionDocuments/FINAL%20Teaching%20Loads%20and%20Research%20Outputs%20ENG.pdf.

36 Council of Ontario Universities, "Faculty at Work: A Preliminary Report on Faculty Work at Ontario Universities, 2010–2012" (26 August 2014): https://cou.ca/wp-content/uploads/2015/04/OCAV-Faculty-at-Work.pdf; Council of Ontario Universities, "Faculty at Work" (January 2018).

37 Richard Vedder, Christopher Matgouranis, and Jonathan Robe, "Faculty Productivity and Costs at the University of Texas at Austin," Center for College Affordability and Productivity (May 2011): https://files.eric.ed.gov/fulltext/ED536155.pdf; Alex Usher, "Faculty Productivity," Higher Education Strategy Associates (7 December 2011): http://higheredstrategy.com/faculty-productivity/.

9. Are Canadian Universities High Quality?

1 Wikipedia, "College and University Rankings": https://en.wikipedia.org/wiki/College_and_university_rankings; Wikipedia, "Rankings of Universities in the United States": https://en.wikipedia.org/wiki/Rankings_of_universities_in_the_United_States; Wikipedia, "Rankings of Universities in Canada": https://en.wikipedia.org/wiki/Rankings_of_universities_in_Canada.

2 Academic Ranking of World Universities, "ShanghaiRanking's Academic Ranking of World Universities 2019 Press Release" (15–17 October 2019): http://www.shanghairanking.com/index.html.

3 Seeta Bhardwa, "ShanghaiRanking Academic Ranking of World Universities 2019 Results Announced," THE World University Rankings

(15 August 2019): https://www.timeshighereducation.com/student/news/shanghairanking-academic-ranking-world-universities-2019-results-announced; QS World University Rankings (2020): https://www.topuniversities.com/university-rankings/world-university-rankings/2020.

4　Ellie Bothwell, "THE World University Rankings 2020. Results Announced," *Times Higher Education* (11 September 2019): https://www.timeshighereducation.com/news/world-university-rankings-2020-results-announced; THE World University Rankings, "World University Rankings" (2020): https://www.timeshighereducation.com/world-university-rankings/2020/world-ranking#!/page/2/length/100/sort_by/rank/sort_order/asc/cols/stats.

5　Mary Dwyer, "*Maclean's* University Ranking 2020: Our Methodology," *Maclean's*, 3 October 2019: https://www.macleans.ca/education/macleans-university-rankings-2020-our-methodology/.

6　Merisotis, *America Needs Talent.*

7　Richard C. Levin, "Top of the Class: The Rise of Asia's Universities," *Foreign Affairs* 89, no. 3 (May/June 2010): 63–75.

8　Pocklington and Tupper, *No Place to Learn*, 7.

9　Kevin Carey, "College Rankings Reformed: The Case for a New Order in Higher Education," *Education Sector Reports* (September 2006): https://www.issuelab.org/resources/533/533.pdf.

10　Crow and Dabars, *Designing the New American University*, 60.

11　Caroline Alphonso, "Universities Boycott *Maclean's* Rankings," *Globe and Mail*, 15 August 2006: https://www.theglobeandmail.com/news/national/universities-boycott-macleans-rankings/article1102197/.

12　Office for Students, "What Is the TEF?": https://www.officeforstudents.org.uk/advice-and-guidance/teaching/what-is-the-tef/; Seeta Bhardwa, "What Is the TEF? Results of the Teaching Excellence Framework 2019," THE World University Rankings (19 June 2019): https://www.timeshighereducation.com/student/blogs/what-tef-results-teaching-excellence-framework-2019; Andrew Gunn, "The UK Teaching Excellence Framework (TEF): The Development of a New Transparency Tool," in Curaj, Deca, and Pricopie, *European Higher Education Area*, 505–26; Roger King, "Governance and Power through Indicators: The UK Higher Education Teaching Excellence and Student Outcomes Framework," in Weingarten, Hicks, and Kaufman, *Assessing Quality in Postsecondary Education*, 67–83.

13　International Organization for Standardization: https://www.iso.org/home.html.

14 International Organization for Standardization, "What Is Quality?": http://
www.fao.org/3/W7295E/w7295e03.htm.

15 Moira Macdonald, "First-year Students Are a Relatively Satisfied
Bunch, Survey Says," *University Affairs* (7 October 2019): https://www
.universityaffairs.ca/news/news-article/first-year-students-are-a
-relatively-satisfied-bunch-survey-says/.

16 Bok, *Our Underachieving Colleges*, 57.

17 Anthony Carnevale, "Future Earnings over Prestige: A New Measuring
Stick for Higher Education," *The EvoLLLution* (12 April 2016): https://
evolllution.com/attracting-students/todays_learner/future-earnings
-over-prestige-a-new-measuring-stick-for-higher-education/; Center on
Education and the Workforce, "Ranking ROI of 4,500 US Colleges and
Universities," Georgetown University (2019): https://cew.georgetown
.edu/cew-reports/CollegeROI/.

18 Jonathan Rothwell, "Using Earnings Data to Rank Colleges: A Value-
added Approach Updated with College Scorecard Data," Brookings
(29 October 2015). https://www.brookings.edu/research/using-earnings
-data-to-rank-colleges-a-value-added-approach-updated-with-college
-scorecard-data/; Jonathan Rothwell and Siddharth Kulkarni, "Beyond
College Rankings: A Value-added Approach to Assessing Two- and Four-
year Schools," Metropolitan Policy Program at Brookings (April 2015):
https://www.brookings.edu/wp-content/uploads/2015/04/BMPP
_CollegeValueAdded.pdf; *The Economist*, "The Value of University: Our
First-ever College Rankings" (29 October 2015): https://www.economist
.com/graphic-detail/2015/10/29/our-first-ever-college-rankings.

19 Council of Ontario Universities, "Partnering for a Better Future
for Ontario" (2017): https://ontariouniversities.ca/wp-content/
uploads/2019/01/COU_Partnering-for-a-Better-Future-for-Ontario_
Summary-Report.pdf.

10. Canada's Public Universities in a Post-COVID World

1 Bill Curry and Kristy Kirkup, "Ottawa Creates New Benefit to Help
Students, Recent Graduates without Summer Jobs Due to COVID-19
Pandemic," *Globe and Mail*, 22 April 2020: https://www.theglobeandmail
.com/politics/article-ottawa-creates-new-benefit-to-help-students
-without-summer-jobs/.

2 Alex Usher, "Coronavirus (20) – So, That Student Support Package,"
Higher Education Strategy Associates (23 April 2020): https://myemail
.constantcontact.com/One-Thought-to-Start-Your-Day–Coronavirus–20

–So–that-Student-Support-Package.html?soid=1103080520043&aid
=oe-6772aqYQ.

3 Allison Dulin Salisbury, "Do Laid-off Workers Want to Reskill? The
Answer Is Yes," *Forbes*, 16 April 2020: https://www.forbes.com/sites
/allisondulinsalisbury/2020/04/16/do-laid-off-workers-want-to-reskill
-the-answer-is-yes/#7dfc4b751bed.

4 Ryan Craig, "Can America Still Do Hard Things?" *Gap Letter* (22 May
2020): https://mailchi.mp/gapletter/can-america-still-do-hard-things
-2609980?e=a8ee5690b7.

5 Higher Education Quality Council of Ontario, "Government's Role
in Digital Learning: Review and Recommendations for the Ontario
Ministry of Colleges and Universities" (2020): http://www.heqco.ca
/SiteCollectionDocuments/Formatted_digital%20learning_FINAL.pdf.

6 Alex Usher, "Coronavirus (12) – A National Effort in On-line Education,"
Higher Education Strategy Associates (7 April 2020): http://
higheredstrategy.com/coronavirus-12-a-national-effort-in-online
-education/.

7 Laura Pappano, "College Is Hard. Iggy, Pounce, Cowboy Joe and Sunny
Are Here to Help," *New York Times*, 8 April 2020: https://www
.nytimes.com/2020/04/08/education/college-ai-chatbots-students.html
?campaign_id=9&emc=edit_NN_p_20200409&instance_id=17491&nl
=morning-briefing&regi_id=93678127&section=whatElse&segment
_id=24428&te=1&user_id=d6cb24c2517c9f4c202d1679271874b4.

8 Arizona State University: https://www.asu.edu/.

9 Joe Friesen, "Universities, Colleges Face Potential Budget Crunch as They
Assess Impact of COVID-19 on International Student Enrolment," *Globe
and Mail*, 10 April 2020: https://www.theglobeandmail.com/canada
/article-universities-colleges-face-potential-budget-crunch-as-they
-assess/; Michael Savage, "Universities Brace for Huge Losses as Foreign
Students Drop Out," *The Guardian*, 11 April 2020: https://www
.theguardian.com/education/2020/apr/11/universities-brace-for-huge
-losses-as-foreign-students-drop-out; Christopher Ziguras and Ly Tran,
"The Coronavirus Outbreak Is the Biggest Crisis Ever to Hit International
Education," *The Conversation* (6 February 2020): https://theconversation
.com/the-coronavirus-outbreak-is-the-biggest-crisis-ever-to-hit
-international-education-131138.

10 Ontario Confederation of University Faculty Associations (OCUFA),
"Now Is Not the Time for Destabilizing Performance Funding" (15 April
2020): https://ocufa.on.ca/blog-posts/now-is-not-the-time-for
-destabilizing-performance-funding/?utm_source=Academica+Top

+Ten&utm_campaign=c4be183637-EMAIL_CAMPAIGN_2020_04_16_07
_54&utm_medium=email&utm_term=0_b4928536cf-c4be183637
-51507781; Janet French, "Pandemic Delays New Alberta University
Funding Model Indefinitely," CBC News, 3 June 2020: https://www.cbc
.ca/news/canada/edmonton/pandemic-delays-university-funding
-model-1.5595570.

11 Richard A. Hesel, "What Prospective Freshmen Think about the Fall,"
Chronicle of Higher Education (30 April 2020): https://www.chronicle.com
/article/What-Prospective-Freshmen/248681.

12 Mary Curnock Cook, "A Student-centric Bailout for Universities," Higher
Education Policy Institute (15 April 2020): https://www.hepi.ac.uk/2020
/04/15/a-student-centric-bailout-for-universities/; John Byrne, "Should
Colleges Discount Tuition because of the Shift to Internet Classes?"
Forbes, 30 March 2020: https://www.forbes.com/sites/poetsandquants
/2020/03/30/should-colleges-discount-tuition-because-of-the-shift-to
-internet-classes/#12bc8d5837d0; Greta Anderson, "Students Turn to
Courts for Refunds," *Inside Higher Ed* (20 April 2020): https://www
.insidehighered.com/news/2020/04/20/students-sue-universities-tuition
-and-fee-refunds.

13 Claire Bond Potter, "The Only Way to Save Higher Education Is to Make
It Free," *New York Times*, 5 June 2020: https://www.nytimes.com/2020/06
/05/opinion/sunday/free-college-tuition-coronavirus.html.

11. Conclusion: A Recipe for Reform

1 Collins, *Good to Great*.

Selected Bibliography: Books Cited in the Text

Altbach, Philip, Liz Reisberg, Maria Yudkevick, Gregory Androushchak, and Ivan Pacheco, eds. *Paying the Professoriate: A Global Comparison of Compensation and Contracts.* New York: Routledge, 2012.

Aoun, Joseph E. *Robot-Proof: Higher Education in the Age of Artificial Intelligence.* Cambridge, MA: The MIT Press, 2017.

Arum, Richard, and Josipa Roksa. *Academically Adrift: Limited Learning on College Campuses.* Chicago: The University of Chicago Press, 2011.

Axelrod, Paul, Roopa Desai Trilokekar, Theresa Shanahan, and Richard Wellen, eds. *Making Policy in Turbulent Times: Challenges and Prospects for Higher Education.* Montreal and Kingston: McGill-Queen's University Press, 2013.

Axtell, James. *The Making of Princeton University: From Woodrow Wilson to the Present.* Princeton, NJ: Princeton University Press, 2006.

Barber, Michael. *How to Run a Government So That Citizens Benefit and Taxpayers Don't Go Crazy.* London: Penguin Random House UK, 2016.

Benjamin, Roger. *Collective Goods and Higher Education: Pasteur's Quadrant in Higher Education.* New York: Routledge Taylor and Francis Group, 2019.

Benjamin, Roger, Stephen Klein, Jeffrey Steedle, Doris Zahner, Scott Elliot, and Julie Patterson. *The Case for Critical-Thinking Skills and Performance Assessment.* New York: Council for Aid to Education, 2013.

Berg, A. Scott. *Wilson.* New York: G.P. Putnam's Sons, 2013.

Bok, Derek. *Higher Learning.* Cambridge, MA: Harvard University Press, 1986.

Bok, Derek. *Our Underachieving Colleges.* Princeton, NJ: Princeton University Press, 2006.

Carnevale, Anthony P., Peter Schmidt, and Jeff Strohl. *The Merit Myth: How Our Colleges Favor the Rich and Divide America.* New York: The New Press, 2020.

Christensen, Clayton M., and Henry J. Eyring. *The Innovative University: Changing the DNA of Higher Education from the Inside Out*. San Francisco: Jossey-Bass, 2011.

Clark, Ian D., Greg Moran, Michael L. Skolnik, and David Trick. *Academic Transformation: The Forces Reshaping Higher Education in Ontario*. Montreal and Kingston: McGill-Queen's University Press, 2009.

Collins, Jim. *Good to Great*. New York: HarperCollins Publishers Inc., 2001.

Craig, Ryan. *A New U: Faster and Cheaper Alternatives to College*. Dallas: BenBella Books Inc., 2018.

Crow, Michael M., and William B. Dabars. *Designing the New American University*. Baltimore, MD: Johns Hopkins University Press, 2015.

Curaj, Adrian, Ligia Deca, and Remus Pricopie. *European Higher Education Area: The Impact of Past and Future Policies*. Cham, Switzerland: Springer Open, 2018.

Deller, Fiona, Jackie Pichette, and Elyse Watkins, eds. *Driving Academic Quality: Lessons from Ontario's Skills Assessment Projects*. Toronto: Queen's Printer for Ontario, 2018.

Duderstadt, James J. *A University for the 21st Century*. Ann Arbor: The University of Michigan Press, 2000.

Fish, Stanley. *Save the World on Your Own Time*. Oxford: Oxford University Press, 2008.

Gallagher, Sean. *The Future of University Credentials: New Developments at the Intersection of Higher Education and Hiring*. Cambridge, MA: Harvard University Press, 2016.

Giamatti, A. Bartlett. *A Free and Ordered Space: The Real World of the University*. New York: W.W. Norton and Company, 1990.

Greenlee, James G. *McMaster University. Vol. 3, 1957–1987*. Montreal: McGill-Queen's University Press, 2015.

Hazelkorn, Ellen, Hamish Coates, and Alexander C. McCormick, eds. *Research Handbook on Quality, Performance and Accountability in Higher Education*. Cheltenham, Glos.: Edward Elgar Publishing, 2018.

Kennedy, Donald. *Academic Duty*. Cambridge, MA: Harvard University Press, 1997.

Kerr, Clark. *The Gold and the Blue: A Personal Memoir of the University of California, 1949–1967. Volume One: Academic Triumphs*. Berkeley: University of California Press, 2001.

Kerr, Clark. *The Uses of the University*. Fifth edition. Cambridge, MA: Harvard University Press, 2001.

Keynes, John M. *The General Theory of Employment, Interest, and Money*. London: Macmillan, 1936.

Kotter, John P. *Leading Change*. Boston: Harvard Business School Press, 1996.

Kotter, John P. *A Sense of Urgency*. Boston: Harvard Business Press, 2008.

Krames, Jeffrey A. *Inside Drucker's Brain*. London: Penguin Books, 2008.

MacKinnon, Peter. *University Leadership and Public Policy in the Twenty-First Century: A President's Perspective*. Toronto: University of Toronto Press, 2014.

McLaughlin, Kenneth. *Out of the Shadow of Orthodoxy: Waterloo @ 50*. Waterloo, ON: University of Waterloo, 2007.

McLaughlin, Kenneth. *Waterloo: The Unconventional Founding of an Unconventional University*. Waterloo, ON: University of Waterloo, 1997.

Merisotis, Jamie. *America Needs Talent*. New York: Rosetta Books, 2015.

Paul, Ross. *Leadership under Fire: The Challenging Role of the University President*. Montreal and Kingston: McGill-Queen's University Press, 2011.

Pocklington, Tom, and Allan Tupper. *No Place to Learn: Why Universities Aren't Working*. Vancouver: University of British Columbia Press, 2002.

Reich, Robert B. *I'll Be Short: Essentials for a Decent Working Society*. Boston: Beacon Press, 2002.

Reich, Robert B. *The Work of Nations*. New York: Vintage Books, 1992.

Rosovsky, Henry. *The University: An Owner's Manual*. New York: W.W. Norton and Company, 1990.

Schulich, Seymour (with Derek DeCloet). *Life and Business Lessons: Getting Smarter*. Toronto: Key Porter Books, 2007.

Servant, Virginie F.C. *Revolutions and Re-iterations: An Intellectual History of Problem-Based Learning*. Riddekerk: Ridderprint BV, 2016.

Weingarten, Harvey P., Martin Hicks, and Amy Kaufman, eds. *Assessing Quality in Postsecondary Education: International Perspectives*. Montreal and Kingston: McGill-Queen's University Press, 2018.

Wildavsky, Ben, Andrew P. Kelly, and Kevin Carey. *Reinventing Higher Education: The Promise of Innovation*. Cambridge, MA: Harvard Education Press, 2011.

Zakaria, Fareed. *In Defense of a Liberal Education*. New York: W.W. Norton and Company, 2015.

Index

Academic Rankings of World
Universities, 148
academic unsustainability, 121–3
access: definition, 30; as public goal,
87; and quality, 175
administrative bloat, 134–6
AHELO, 48
Aoun, Joseph, 73
Arizona State University: inclusion,
152; innovation, 110, 164
assessment entrepreneurial skills, 59
assessment learning outcomes, 53–4,
55–6; Association of American
Colleges and Universities, 57;
Council for Aid to Education,
57; NILOA, 57; Wabash College
Center of Inquiry in the Liberal
Arts, 57

Barber, Michael, 84, 87, 97
barriers to innovation, 110–17
Benjamin, Roger, 56, 59
Blough, Max, 54
Bok, Derek, 44, 55, 156
Bologna Accord, 48
Business–Higher Education
Roundtable, 75

California Master Plan for Higher
Education, 100
Canada 150 Research Chairs
Program, 137
Canada Emergency Student Benefit,
162
Canadian Association of University
Business Officers (CAUBO),
deferred maintenance, 123
Canadian universities in world
rankings, 149–50
Carey, Kevin, 151
Carnegie Classification of Institutions
of Higher Education, 99
Carnevale, Anthony, 20, 28; equity
of access, 42; quality, 157
College scorecards, 28;
recommendation, 171–2
colleges vs. universities, 6
Collegiate Learning Assessment
test, 56, 58
Collins, Jim, 169–70
companies hiring with no
transcripts, 60
competency-based education:
Canada, 79–80, 109; framework,
77–8

Council of Ontario Universities
(COU), 140, 143; consultation,
160; service, 143; teaching
loads, 142
COVID-19: financial challenge,
164; impact on enrolment, 32;
impetus for change, 118, 163;
international students, 131,
164–5; job loss, 27; online
learning, 163; retraining, 162
Craig, Ryan, 162
credentials, 59, 81–2
critical thinking, 51, 58–9; Arum
and Roksa, 58
criticisms of ranking systems, 151–3
Crow, Michael, 110, 175

deliverology, 84–5
Deller, Fiona, 42
department structure, 104–5
differences Canada and US
university systems, 11–12
differentiation: defined, 99; impact
of COVID, 167–8; importance
in performance-based funding,
100–1; recommendation, 167, 173
different uses of term "skills," 51–2
direct vs. indirect costs of research,
127–8
Drucker, Peter, 57, 115
Duderstedt, James, 124, 136

earning premium of university
education, 17–18
Education and Labour Market
Longitudinal Linkage
Platform, 89
Education Policy Research Initiative
(EPRI), 21, 37
employers and skills gap, 69

endowments, 129
enrolment growth demographics,
31; women, 31
Equality of Opportunity Project, 24
equity of access: financial issues,
34–7; Longitudinal and
International Study of Adults
(LISA), 37; nonfinancial issues,
37–40; recommendation, 175
equity of workload policies, 145, 146
ESDC, skills and jobs, 73
Essential Adult Skills Inventory
(EASI) trial, 58; relationship to
jobs, 71–2
essential skills assessment, 62–3
Evans, John, 106, 108, 116
experiential learning, 59, 75

faculty salaries, 136–9
field of study and jobs, 19–23
Finnie, Ross, 21, 37
first-generation students and
intergenerational mobility, 25;
university participation, 37
Fish, Stanley, 44, 135
Ford, Doug, 35, 90
free tuition policy in Ontario, 34–5
Frenette, Marc: earnings, 17, 21, 24;
equity of access, 35–6
Future Skills Canada, 75

Gates, Bill, 16
Georgetown University Center on
Education and the Workforce, 18,
20, 28, 157
Giammati, A. Bartlett, 44, 105
governance, 111–12; impact on
innovation, 113–15
government intrusions on
university autonomy, 83–4,

93–4, 146; recommendation,
173; regulation, 119; steering of
university behaviour, 94–5
graduation rates, 88, 92
growth university system, 30–3

Hagey, Gerald, 106, 108, 110
Harris, Mike, 7, 98, 126
Harrison, Alan: credentials, 81; and
skills, 52
Harvard, 24, 103; innovation, 109
HEQCO Act and mandate, 10–11, 57;
EASI study, 58; learning outcomes,
48–9; teaching loads, 142

Iacobucci, Frank, 10
inability to predict labour
markets, 66
Indigenous access, 38–9
Institute for Fiscal Studies, 20
intergenerational mobility, 23–5
International Organization for
Standards (ISO), 154
international students, 130; COVID
impact, 164–5

job readiness: different views of
employers vs. academics, 69–71;
student views, 71
Jobs, Steve, 16
jobs in regulated professions, 66

Kennedy, Donald, 7
Kerr, Clark, 9, 105; saying "no," 114
Keynes, Maynard, 68

Labour Market Information
Council, 67
lack correlation between fields of
study and jobs, 66–7

last mile training, 76
learning outcomes: classes of, 50–1;
defined, 45; framework, 46–7;
link to quality, 154–5
liberal arts and jobs, 76–7
Lindsay, David, 160
LinkedIn, 76
literacy and numeracy, 51, 58;
economic impact, 74; and jobs,
71–2
Lumina Foundation: competency-
based education, 80; degrees
qualification framework, 49;
learning outcomes, 45

MacKinnon, Peter, 111, 114
Maclean's, classification of
institutions, 100; rankings, 150, 152
mandatory retirement, 137–9
Maple League universities, 100
McGill, 4, 103, 104, 111
McGuinty, Dalton, 10, 125; Reaching
Higher, 32, 124
McLaughlin, Ken, 108
McMaster University, 7–8; health
sciences program, 46; history of
medical school, 106–7

National Center for Education
Statistics, 141
National Study of Instructional
Costs and Productivity
(Delaware Study), 142
net tuition, University of Toronto, 40

Obama, Barack, 28
OECD enrolment, 32–3; learning
outcomes, 47–8; PISA &
PIAAC, 63
Office for Students, 57, 153

Ontario Council of University
Faculty Associations, 140
outcome measures, 88–90; Ontario,
90–1, 97; Canada vs. US, 91–2;
unintended consequences, 92–3

Pathways to Education, 41
People for Education, 40–1
performance measures: move to
outcomes, 90; Ontario, 90–1;
types, 88
performance-based funding:
defined, 95; effective design
principles, 96–9; impact of
COVID, 165–6; recommendation,
173; in US, 95–6
president salaries, 133–6
problem-based learning, 107
promissory note of universities,
15, 23
public goal setting process, 86–8;
list of, 87
purposes of university, 44–5; and
quality, 156–7

Quacquarelli Symonds World
University rankings, 148–9
Quality assurance, defined, 115;
impact on innovation, 115–16
quality measurement approaches,
147–8
Quest University, 109

Rae, Bob, 10
ranking systems, 148–54; Canada
performance, 149–50
rankings, quality and learning
outcomes, 154–6
recommendations for reform, 27, 43,
62, 81, 101, 119, 145, 159, 167

Reich, Robert, 82
relationship field of study to
earnings, 19–22
return on investment from
university, 18–19
Rosovsky, Henry, 93
Royal Bank of Canada, 68, 69

scepticism about universities,
12–13, 16
Schulich, Seymour, 129
sessional instructors, 139–40
skills of PhD students, 61
skills training, private sector, 76
skills vs. credentials for jobs, 68, 73,
80, 82; recommendation, 174
skills vs. disciplinary knowledge,
52; recommendation, 174
social benefits of university, 25–6
social contract higher education, 5
Statistics Canada, 17, 31, 35, 39,
133, 140
STEM, economic return, 19; and
jobs, 67
sustainability solutions: ancillary
operations, 130; compensation,
132–40; higher tuition, 125–7;
international students, 130–2;
more public grants, 123–5;
philanthropy, 128–30; productivity
increases, 140–4; research funding,
127–8
sustainability, defined, 120–1

Teaching Excellence Framework,
153–4
teaching loads, 91, 141–2, 172
teaching vs. research, 7
tenure, 137
Thiel, Peter, 16

Thode, Harry, 106, 108, 110
Times Higher Education World
   University Rankings, 148–9
transferable "soft" skills, 51

U-15 universities, 100, 133
under-represented groups and
   access, 39–43
Universities Canada, 18, 120
University of Calgary, 8, 9;
   health sciences program, 46;
   budgeting, 112
University of Minnesota-Rochester,
   110–11, 119

University of Texas, 144
University of Toronto, 103, 111
University of Waterloo: history, 106;
   Waterloo Plan, 106
urgency and change, 117–18
Usher, Alex: enrolment, 31; financial
   aid, 34, 161–2; online learning, 164

Western Governor's University,
   78, 109
Wilson, Woodrow, 64, 170
Wynne, Kathleen, 34

Zakaria, Fareed, 76

 **UTP** insights

Books in the Series

- Harvey P. Weingarten, *Nothing Less than Great: Reforming Canada's Universities*
- Allan C. Hutchinson, *Democracy and Constitutions: Putting Citizens First*
- Paul Nelson, *Global Development and Human Rights: The Sustainable Development Goals and Beyond*
- Peter H. Russell, *Sovereignty: The Biography of a Claim*
- Alistair Edgar, Rupinder Mangat, and Bessma Momani (eds.), *Strengthening the Canadian Armed Forces through Diversity and Inclusion*
- David B. MacDonald, *The Sleeping Giant Awakens: Genocide, Indian Residential Schools, and the Challenge of Conciliation*
- Paul W. Gooch, *Course Correction: A Map for the Distracted University*
- Paul T. Phillips, *Truth, Morality, and Meaning in History*
- Stanley R. Barrett, *The Lamb and the Tiger: From Peacekeepers to Peacewarriors in Canada*
- Peter MacKinnon, *University Commons Divided: Exploring Debate and Dissent on Campus*
- Raisa B. Deber, *Treating Health Care: How the System Works and How It Could Work Better*
- Jim Freedman, *A Conviction in Question: The First Trial at the International Criminal Court*
- Christina D. Rosan and Hamil Pearsall, *Growing a Sustainable City? The Question of Urban Agriculture*
- John Joe Schlichtman, Jason Patch, and Marc Lamont Hill, *Gentrifier*
- Robert Chernomas and Ian Hudson, *Economics in the Twenty-First Century: A Critical Perspective*
- Stephen M. Saideman, *Adapting in the Dust: Lessons Learned from Canada's War in Afghanistan*
- Michael R. Marrus, *Lessons of the Holocaust*
- Roland Paris and Taylor Owen (eds.), *The World Won't Wait: Why Canada Needs to Rethink its International Policies*

- Bessma Momani, *Arab Dawn: Arab Youth and the Demographic Dividend They Will Bring*
- William Watson, *The Inequality Trap: Fighting Capitalism Instead of Poverty*
- Phil Ryan, *After the New Atheist Debate*
- Paul Evans, *Engaging China: Myth, Aspiration, and Strategy in Canadian Policy from Trudeau to Harper*